*Inside the
New Gilt-edged
Market*

Inside the New Gilt-edged Market

Patrick Phillips

Second Edition

Woodhead-Faulkner

New York   London   Toronto   Sydney   Tokyo

Published by Woodhead-Faulkner Limited
Simon & Schuster International Group
Fitzwilliam House
32 Trumpington Street
Cambridge CB2 1QY
England

First published June 1984
Second impression March 1985
New edition 1987
Second impression 1987
Third impression 1988

British Library Cataloguing in Publication Data

Phillips, Patrick
    Inside the new gilt-edged market.—
    2nd ed.
    1. Government securities—Great Britain
    I. Title
    332.64′2   HG5438

    ISBN 0-85941-346-2

Library of Congress Cataloging-in-Publication Data

Phillips, Patrick.
    Inside the new gilt-edged market.

    Includes index.
    1. Securities — Great Britain. I. Title.
HG5432.P48 1986   332.63′232′0941   86-24692
ISBN 0-85941-346-2

Designed by Ron Jones
Typeset by H Charlesworth & Co Ltd, Huddersfield, England
Printed in Great Britain by St Edmundsbury Press, Bury St Edmunds, Suffolk

Contents

Preface to Second Edition

This second edition of *Inside the Gilt-edged Market* is published just after the advent of 'Big Bang' which introduced major structural changes to the market.

Since Big Bang on 27 October 1986 the old order of single-capacity trading, under which in the United Kingdom there has historically been a separation of the roles of principal (jobber) and agent (broker), has been swept away to be replaced by a dual-capacity system in which the two roles can be combined; and a new gilt-edged market, modelled largely on the United States Treasury bond market, has come into operation.

This change coupled with the opening up of Stock Exchange membership to international and corporate entities alters the face of the gilt-edged market almost beyond recognition. Many new 'players' have entered the 'game', and the focus of the marketplace itself has shifted from The Stock Exchange floor to the telephone and telescreen-driven operations of 'upstairs' dealing rooms.

As if that were not enough, some major alterations in the way gilt-edged investments are taxed have also occurred. From 28 February 1986 onwards the gross accrued interest content in the total price of a gilt-edged stock (and many other fixed-interest stocks) has been treated for tax purposes as an item of income and not as capital as it has been in the past. Additionally, from 2 July 1986, Capital Gains Tax has no longer applied to these issues.

Taken together this combination of structural and taxation change represents little less than a revolution for the gilt-edged market, the long-term repercussions of which are hard to predict. Many time-honoured methods of operation have disappeared as new dealing practices have emerged. In this edition the emphasis will, however, be upon the latter, but not to the extent of losing all historical perspective.

As with the first edition (published in June 1984) this work is basically designed to be a working manual and a book of reference for market participants, rather than a study of economic factors. Whilst economic analysis is at the heart of macro-market assessments, below that level is a welter of technical detail and factors with which market practitioners need to be conversant. It is that area with which this book is primarily concerned.

It is hoped that by bringing together in this volume full consideration of the many facets of the gilt-edged market that exist today – from a description of its new structure through to the calculative intricacies of gilt-edged futures and options – this book will be of value, not only to domestic investors, but also to the international investment community.

F.P.S.P.

June 1987

Acknowledgements

My sincere thanks go to all those people who have helped and encouraged me in the writing of this book. These range from my partners and colleagues at de Zoete & Bevan (and more latterly at BZW), through institutional clients to friends and family at home, who quickly learnt how to humour the strange creature who locked himself away in his study, at times for hours on end.

On the technical side, special thanks are due to Stewart Millman for his work in reading and vetting the proofs, Graham Chadwick and Richard Hurford for their help in producing the computer graphics, and Alan Redstone for contributing so greatly to the chapter on gilt-edged settlement procedures.

Finally a bouquet to my wife, Jolly, for undertaking the daunting job of typing, amending and editing the manuscript – mathematical and actuarial symbols notwithstanding – and for maintaining her sense of humour throughout.

1

The origins of the gilt-edged market

What precisely is meant by the generic term 'the gilt-edged market'? To be specific, it is the market in securities issued by, or guaranteed by, Her Majesty's Government. Many people misuse the term, mostly to include local government issues (corporation stocks) and, in the old days, Colonial and Commonwealth stocks as well. This was never, in fact, correct, since such issues never carried the explicit guarantee of the British Government; and since 1968 the tax treatment of capital gains on these stocks has differed from that on 'pure' gilts, so that it is not only incorrect but also inadvisable to include them in the same category.

Whilst gilt-edged stocks form a large part of the National Debt, they do not by any manner of means constitute the whole of it. Other than gilt-edged, there are National Savings, Treasury bills, short-term borrowings from the Bank of England and overseas borrowings, sometimes in the form of loans raised in other world markets, or other direct loans such as those from the International Monetary Fund.

It is generally accepted that the origin of the National Debt stems from around the year 1694, when the Government of William III found it necessary to raise the sum of just over £1 million to help finance the cost of waging war against the French. Indeed the National Debt and the Bank of England both came into being at the same time, since the *quid pro quo* to the financiers who raised that initial sum for the Government was the granting to them of a charter to form a bank – that bank becoming the Bank of England. Historically, one of the major factors in the inexorable increase in the size of the National Debt has been the incidence of wars and the recourse of successive governments to borrow in order to finance them. In the present century, the National Debt multiplied twelve times as a result of World War I, from £650 million in 1914, to £7,500 million in 1919; and whilst there was a small diminution during the inter-war years, it trebled again as a result of World War II, to stand at approximately £21,000 million by 1945. Since 1945, however, the reasons for the continuing expansion in the National Debt have been completely different. The nationalisation of the coal, steel, gas, electricity and railway industries involved the issuance of government stock in compensation, and whilst these industries theoretically represent assets offsetting this debt, in practice the nationalised industries taken *en bloc* have tended to generate working deficits which in turn have had to be financed by further borrowing. Additionally, the post-war application of Keynesian economic principles – a long way removed from balanced budget philosophies – has caused there to be a budget deficit (as it used to be described) or Public Sector Borrowing Requirement (PSBR in modern parlance) in all but a handful of years since 1945.

Table 1.1   *National Debt relative to Gross Domestic Product, 1946–85*

31st March each year	National Debt (£ million)	GDP (£ million)*	Ratio
1946	23,842	10,060	2.37
1947	25,834	10,765	2.40
1948	25,722	11,823	2.18
1949	25,267	12,492	2.02
1950	25,899	13,056	1.98
1951	26,017	14,571	1.79
1952	25,984	15,814	1.64
1953	26,051	17,046	1.53
1954	26,583	17,979	1.48
1955	26,934	19,352	1.39
1956	27,039	20,909	1.29
1957	27,007	21,110	1.27
1958	27,232	23,057	1.18
1959	27,376	24,301	1.13
1960	27,733	25,751	1.08
1961	28,252	27,488	1.03
1962	28,674	28,807	1.00
1963	29,848	30,632	0.97
1964	30,226	33,382	0.91
1965	30,441	35,856	0.85
1966	31,341	38,258	0.82
1967	31,936	40,459	0.79
1968	34,194	43,918	0.78
1969	33,984	46,920	0.72
1970	33,079	51,465	0.64
1971	33,442	57,793	0.58
1972	35,840	63,997	0.56
1973	37,156	73,761	0.50
1974	40,448	83,923	0.48
1975	46,404	106,014	0.44
1976	56,584	126,436	0.45
1977	67,166	145,565	0.46
1978	79,180	167,844	0.47
1979	86,885	196,378	0.44
1980	95,315	230,011	0.41
1981	113,037	253,688	0.45
1982	118,390	276,013	0.43
1983	127,927	300,490	0.43
1984	142,855	318,339	0.45
1985	158,029	348,950	0.45

Source: *Financial Statistics.*

*Based on expenditure measures at market prices.

Table 1.1 shows the values of the nominal National Debt since 1946, together with nominal Gross Domestic Product (GDP) for the same period. It should be noted, however, that the rate of growth of the National Debt has been markedly less than that of GDP, as the ratio between them indicates. In 1951 the nominal National Debt was just over twice the nominal GDP for that year; by 1980 the National Debt had fallen relative to GDP to be about half the nominal GDP for that year.

Table 1.2   *Debt service costs relative to PSBR, 1946–85*

Calendar year	Debt service costs (£ million)*	PSBR (£ million)*	Excess of debt service above PSBR (£ million)
1946	532	646	−114
1947	562	137	425
1948	551	−270	821
1949	548	−313	861
1950	549	−352	901
1951	591	241	350
1952	652	552	100
1953	683	702	−19
1954	689	435	254
1955	767	394	373
1956	799	547	252
1957	803	532	271
1958	893	448	445
1959	909	560	349
1960	1,021	707	314
1961	1,270	727	543
1962	1,288	511	777
1963	1,294	834	460
1964	1,368	980	388
1965	1,468	1,169	299
1966	1,553	949	604
1967	1,711	1,846	−135
1968	1,907	1,253	654
1969	2,049	−534	2,583
1970	2,145	−51	2,196
1971	2,213	1,320	893
1972	2,403	1,953	450
1973	2,982	4,093	−1,111
1974	4,035	6,452	−2,417
1975	4,776	10,161	−5,385
1976	6,140	8,938	−2,798
1977	7,132	5,463	1,669
1978	8,015	8,436	−421
1979	9,822	12,679	−2,807
1980	12,153	11,822	331
1981	13,701	10,590	3,111
1982	15,072	4,954	10,118
1983	15,190	11,609	3,581
1984	16,938	10,150	6,788
1985	18,537	7,568	10,969

Source: *Economic Trends.*

*Prior to 1961 the figures relate to Central Government Debt interest (as a proxy for Total Debt Service Costs) and the public sector financial deficit (as a proxy for the PSBR).

A very great deal of the pre-World War II debt and early post-war debt was issued at low interest rate levels. As such, the burden on the Exchequer of its debt servicing was fairly small, although, as Table 1.2 shows, debt servicing costs have, since the war, always represented a substantial part of the total Public Sector Borrowing Requirement (PSBR). But whereas debt servicing costs were growing at a modest rate up to about 1970, the advent of higher inflation then caused interest rates to rise, which in turn increased the debt service costs each

Table 1.3   *The PSBR as a percentage of GDP, 1946–85*

Calendar year	PSBR (£ million)*	GDP (£ million)†*	PSBR as % of GDP
1946	646	10,060	6.42
1947	137	10,765	1.27
1948	− 270	11,823	− 2.28
1949	− 313	12,492	− 2.51
1950	− 352	13,056	− 2.70
1951	241	14,571	1.65
1952	552	15,814	3.49
1953	702	17,046	4.12
1954	435	17,979	2.42
1955	394	19,352	2.04
1956	547	20,909	2.62
1957	532	22,110	2.41
1958	448	23,057	1.94
1959	560	24,301	2.30
1960	707	25,751	2.75
1961	727	27,488	2.64
1962	511	28,807	1.77
1963	834	30,632	2.72
1964	980	33,382	2.94
1965	1,169	35,856	3.26
1966	949	38,258	2.48
1967	1,846	40,459	4.56
1968	1,253	43,918	2.85
1969	− 534	46,920	− 1.14
1970	− 51	51,465	− 0.10
1971	1,320	57,793	2.28
1972	1,953	63,997	3.05
1973	4,093	73,761	5.55
1974	6,452	83,923	7.69
1975	10,161	106,014	9.58
1976	8,938	126,436	7.07
1977	5,463	145,565	3.75
1978	8,436	167,844	5.03
1979	12,679	196,378	6.46
1980	11,822	230,011	5.14
1981	10,590	253,688	4.17
1982	4,954	276,013	1.79
1983	11,609	300,490	3.86
1984	10,150	318,339	3.19
1985	7,568	348,950	2.17

Source: *Economic Trends.*

*Prior to 1961 the Central Government Debt Interest is used as a proxy for the PSBR.

†Based on expenditure measures at market prices.

time maturing low-coupon issues had to be replaced with higher-coupon stock. Additionally, the mid 1970s was a period in which British governments of both political persuasions allowed public expenditure to rise very sharply, so that by 1980 debt service costs were over $5\frac{1}{2}$ times what they had been ten years previously.

One great problem associated with prolonged deficit financing, such as that conducted by British governments in recent years, is the compounding effect that occurs when further borrowing is incurred in order to meet interest payments on existing debt.

What may originate as a matter of simply paying interest on a loan, soon becomes one of paying interest on the interest, and before too long becomes one of paying interest on the interest on the interest. Whilst the problem is relatively obscure when interest rates are low, it becomes very significant in periods of double digit rates such as were experienced in the late 1970s and early 1980s; and it has sometimes caused the more cynical among market observers to incline to the view that some British governments have had less than a full comprehension of the power of compound interest!

The political response to such criticism has tended to be that interest payments are simply transfer payments from one sector of the economy to another; that, as they are taxable, the government claws back into its coffers some of this outflow anyway, and that as long as the total deficit (PSBR) does not get out of control in real terms (inflation adjusted) there should be no fundamental cause for concern. In this latter respect, the relationship between the PSBR and GDP is worthy of observation. Table 1.3 is illustrative: column 3 shows the PSBR as a percentage of Gross Domestic Product year by year, and the reader will note the quantum shift in the relationship in 1973 coinciding with the beginning of a period of higher inflation and widely fluctuating exchange-rate movements.

2

Financing the PSBR and its impact on the money supply

In Chapter 1 we have observed the Public Sector Borrowing Requirement (PSBR) in its wider context, and the questions now arise: where does the gilt-edged market fit into all this and what is its precise role in financing the PSBR? To answer these properly, it is first necessary to understand how the PSBR is constituted. Basically, it has three main components (but see also the tailpiece at the end of this chapter):

1. The Central Government Borrowing Requirement (CGBR).
2. The borrowing requirements of local government (LABR).
3. The borrowing requirements of public corporations such as the nationalised industries (PCBR).

It is tempting to suppose that the PSBR would be the simple aggregate of these three items, but this is not so since one of the most important components in the CGBR is loans made by central government to both the other sectors. It is necessary to deduct these from the equation before summation.

The figures in Table 2.1 for the years 1980/81 to 1984/85 show how the various components fit together, and how these items have varied in recent years. It can be seen from this table that some part of both the LABR and PCBR is financed under their own auspices – for example by sales of local authority short-term bonds, or by borrowing from the money markets or directly from the banking system. However, since the central government is the prime name for credit, it is much easier (and cheaper) for it to raise finance, and a significant proportion of local authority and public corporation finance is obtained through 'on-lending' by the central government. It is when one investigates the different ways in which the CGBR is financed that the role of the gilt-edged market becomes clearer.

The main borrowing options open to the Government are as follows:

1. To issue further notes and coin to the public.
2. To borrow from the Bank of England.
3. To sell National Savings instruments.

Table 2.1   *Components of the Public Sector Borrowing Requirement, 1980/81 to 1984/85*

	£ millions				
	1980/81	1981/82	1982/83	1983/84	1984/85
Central Government Borrowing Requirement	12,744	7,614	12,733	12,288	10,092
− Lending to local authorities	1,301	− 1,172	2,757	3,431	3,329
− Lending to public corporations	2,363	2,406	2,733	670	144
= Central government 'own deficit'	9,080	6,380	7,243	8,187	6,619
+ Local Government Borrowing Requirement	2,120	− 225	87	1,206	2,385
+ Public Corporations Borrowing Requirement	1,486	2,477	1,535	335	1,110
= Public Sector Borrowing Requirement	12,686	8,632	8,865	9,728	10,114

4. To sell tax instruments such as tax reserve certificates to people/companies with deferred tax liabilities.
5. To sell Treasury bills – mostly 91-day maturities.
6. To sell gilt-edged securities.

Additionally, it can borrow abroad, and certain of its routine transactions in money markets and the foreign exchange market have direct financing implications, e.g.:

7. Net transactions in public sector debt and commercial bills.
8. Direct borrowing from overseas governments and institutions.
9. Net change in the level of the UK Official Gold and Foreign Currency Reserves.

This last factor is not always appreciated properly, but follows logically because when there is a capital outflow from the country, the Government (through the Exchange Equalisation Account) sells foreign currencies and in exchange obtains sterling. The official overseas currency reserves are therefore depleted, but the sterling thus produced is available to help finance the Borrowing Requirement.

An idea of the relative magnitude of these items can be obtained from Table 2.2 covering the financial years 1980/81 to 1984/85.

Closer scrutiny of these figures reveals some interesting trends about the various components, such as the increasing role played by National Savings over the past few years, and the diminishing size of the Treasury bill contribution, but the salient feature is abundantly clear: it is through the gilt-edged market that the great bulk of government financing is done.

A major reason for wishing to finance through these media, rather than from the banking system, is the need to keep control of the money supply. This is a topic of continuing debate between politicians and economists of the Keynesian and monetarist schools into which it is not intended to enter in this book. Suffice it to say, however, that since the time of the sterling crisis of 1976, when the

7

Table 2.2   *Central Government Borrowing Requirement, 1980/81 to 1984/85*

	1980/81	1981/82	£ million 1982/83	1983/84	1984/85
Increase in notes and coin	552	189	1,206	323	900
Borrowing from Bank of England	50	55	−69	−143	−4,855
Increase in National Savings	2,140	4,321	3,028	3,258	3,117
Sales of tax instruments	490	558	1,035	−235	771
Net sales of Treasury bills	−1,025	−111	195	126	−185
Net sales of gilt-edged stocks	13,107	5,959	5,140	11,677	10,223
Other public sector debt and commercial bills	−1,697	−4,505	658	−2,934	118
Direct borrowing overseas	100	−75	−202	−100	−447
Net change in UK Official Reserves	−153	2,749	2,062	32	921
Miscellaneous others	−820	−1,526	−320	+284	−471
Total	12,744	7,614	12,733	12,288	10,092

Source: *Financial Statistics.*

Labour Government of the day found it necessary to make application to the International Monetary Fund (IMF) for stand-by credit, and in 1979 with the emergence of a Conservative Government of monetarist persuasion, control of the rate of growth of the money supply has been accorded one of the highest priorities in government economic policy.

The key point to comprehend is that if a Government's spending is financed by making sales of securities to the non-bank public, the money supply in aggregate remains unchanged, since the amount placed in the hands of the public by virtue of the Government's spending is exactly counterbalanced by the reduction in the total stock of money caused by the purchases of the securities. In contrast, when the Government finances its spending by borrowing from the banking system its spending increases the amount of money in the system, as before, but there is no counterbalancing reduction in bank deposits, and as a consequence the money supply is expanded. This latter effect also occurs when the banks make loans to the private sector.

Whilst one often speaks of 'money supply' in general terms, it is important to appreciate that there are a number of differently defined money supply aggregates, all of which are monitored closely by the monetary authorities. In the Green Paper entitled *Monetary Control*, published in 1980, it was written:

'No single statistical measure of the money supply can be expected fully to encapsulate monetary conditions, and so provide a uniquely correct basis for controlling the complex relationships between monetary growth and prices and nominal incomes. A degree of substitutability between forms of money or liquidity just inside or outside their respective measures means that it is insufficient to rely on one measure alone.'

The exact importance of any one statistic as a measure of monetary conditions is very much subject to the vagaries of government policy. In the late 1970s and the early 1980s Sterling M_3 was clearly a prime focal point. But in a speech at the Mansion House on Thursday, 20 October 1983, the Chancellor of the Exchequer (Mr Nigel Lawson) seemed to indicate that in future short-term interest rates would be used to control and reflect the progress of M_0, whilst fiscal and funding policy would be influenced more by the fluctuations in the wider aggregates, such as Sterling M_3 and PSL_2.

Two years later, in his Mansion House speech of 17 October 1985, and after a period in which both Sterling M_3 and PSL_2 had persistently overshot their targets, the Chancellor appeared to write '*finis*' to monetary targetry and over-funding (the practice of deliberately selling more government debt than was needed simply to fund the PSBR in order to reduce monetary growth). In future, he said, the Government would restrict sales of gilt-edged stock to the level required to finance the PSBR in each fiscal year.

It is nevertheless important for the gilt-edged analyst to understand the com-position of the various aggregate measures in current usage. These are as follows:

1. Wide Monetary Base (or M_0 as it is now known).
2. M_1.
3. M_2 (transactions balances).
4. Sterling M_3.
5. Total M_3.
6. Private Sector Liquidity: narrower measure – PSL_1.
7. Private Sector Liquidity: wider measure – PSL_2.

Table 2.3 shows the clinically defined components of the monetary and liquidity aggregates used in the United Kingdom, but from the gilt-edged analyst's point of view it is often more useful to view changes in them by looking at the changes in their 'counterparts' – those elements that cause the changes in bank deposits, etc., to occur. The relationships between the various counterparts and Sterling M_3 can be monitored month by month in the *Banking Statistics* published by the Bank of England. (The statistics are also to be found in Table 11.3 of both the *Bank of England Quarterly Bulletin* and the monthly Central Statistical Office publication *Financial Statistics*.)

The chief counterparts are sterling bank lending to the public and private sectors. The former basically equates to the Public Sector Borrowing Require-ment, less sales of public sector debt (mostly central government debt), and tends to be the smaller of the two. Both of these are 'domestic counterparts', and the sum of them and sterling bank lending to the overseas sector constitutes what used to be known as Domestic Credit Expansion (DCE). (One tends to refer to DCE in the past tense here because although it came to prominence as the key IMF monitoring criterion in the late 1970s, it started to disappear from Table 11.3 at the end of 1981, and has latterly no longer been a focal point of monetary analysis.)

To proceed from DCE to changes in Sterling M_3, it is necessary to deduct

Table 2.3   *Components of the various monetary and liquidity aggregates*

Item	M_0	M_1	M_2	$£M_3$	M_3	PSL_1	PSL_2
(1) Notes and coin in public circulation	●	●	●	●	●	●	●
(2) Banks' till money	●						
(3) Bankers' balances with Bank of England	●						
(4) Private sector non-interest-bearing sterling sight bank deposits		●	●	●	●	●	●
(5) Private sector interest-bearing sterling sight bank deposits		●		●	●	●	●
(6) Private sector interest-bearing retail sterling bank deposits				●			
(7) Private sector sterling time bank deposits of original maturity up to two years				●	●	●	●
(8) Private sector holdings of sterling certificates of deposit (CDs)				●	●	●	●
(9) Private sector sterling time bank deposits of original maturity greater than two years				●	●		
(10) Public sector sterling sight and time deposits				●	●		
(11) Foreign currency bank deposits of private and public sectors					●		
(12) Private sector holdings of money market instruments and certificates of tax deposit						●	●
(13) Private sector holdings of building society deposits* and National Savings instruments†							●
(14) MINUS building society holdings of money market instruments and bank deposits, etc.							●

*Excluding term shares and SAYE.
†Excluding certificates, SAYE and other longer-term deposits.

certain components representing the following:

1. The external and foreign currency finance of the public sector.
2. Any increase in overseas sterling deposits.
3. Any increase in banks' net foreign currency deposits.
4. Any increase in banks' non-deposit liabilities, e.g. changes in their capital structures.

The post-1981 (ex-DCE) form of presentation of the statistics incorporates in Table 11.3 (see page 9) the impact of sterling lending to the overseas sector with items (1), (2) and (3) above, under the heading 'External and foreign currency counterparts', and enables the relationships between the PSBR and the change in Sterling M_3 to be summarised as shown in Table 2.4.

Table 2.4 *Counterparts of changes in Sterling M_3*

	£ million				
	1980/81	1981/82	1982/83	1983/84	1984/85
PSBR	12,676	8,632	8,858	9,754	10,182
− Debt sales to non-bank private sector					
Central government instruments	11,453	11,721	8,708	12,861	13,064
Other debt sales	−638	−387	−274	−284	−455
= Bank lending to UK public sector	1,841	−2,702	424	−2,823	−2,427
+ Sterling lending to UK private sector	9,248	14,928	14,354	15,387	18,585
= Total domestic counterparts to money supply growth	11,089	12,226	14,778	12,564	16,158
+ External and foreign currency counterparts (total)	653	−1,062	−3,147	−2,654	−1,687
− Increase in banks' non-deposit liabilities (net)	1,470	1,467	1,852	2,305	2,658
= Increase in Sterling M_3	10,272	9,697	9,779	7,605	11,813
Increase per cent per annum	17.7	14.1	11.4	7.9	11.4

Source: *Financial Statistics.*

Tailpiece

Analysis of the PSBR trends since the early 1980s has been complicated by the UK Government's asset-sales policy. Since 1980, the Government has sold off part or all of its holdings in a number of entities such as British Petroleum, Cable and Wireless, Amersham International, Britoil and British Telecom, whilst the future privatisation of other parts of the nationalised industries, such as British Airways and British Gas is planned. The proceeds of these sales are taken into the public sector accounts as revenue, thus deflating the PSBR. This sort of accounting, which would almost certainly cause an auditor's qualification if applied to a public company, obscures the true trend of the PSBR. It can be argued strongly that asset sales are a means of financing the PSBR, rather than a (negative) component of it, and to observe the true picture the gilt-edged analyst is advised to add back the asset sales to the published PSBR figure.

3

The players in the game and the role of the 'Authorities'

In the last chapter it was shown how the gilt-edged market provides a means by which a large part of the public sector deficit can be funded. It is clear that within the gilt-edged arena the Government itself is thus a major, if not *the* major player in the 'game'. Whilst for all sorts of tactical and strategic reasons the government 'authorities' may at some times be a seller of stock and at other times a buyer, over most periods they can be expected to be net sellers of debt for funding purposes. Only if deficit financing were to become a thing of the past would this situation be likely to change.

On the other side of the coin are the investors, the wide range of individuals, corporations, financial institutions, etc. who need to invest and for whom gilt-edged stock represents one potential investment medium.

Between them is interposed the gilt-edged market itself where business is conducted and where stock and money change hands. It is sometimes difficult to appreciate the enormity of the change in the gilt-edged market brought about by the 1986 deregulation. Apart from the fact that the dealings in the new market are now very largely conducted via telephone and telescreen networks instead of face to face on the market floor, the roles to be played by market participants have been radically altered by the change from single- to dual-capacity trading.

Under the old single-capacity system a Stock Exchange firm was required to opt to act in either a jobbing or a broking role, but was not permitted to perform both functions. This distinct separation of capacity produced a clear demarcation of interests. The jobbers were the 'stallkeepers' of the market. They traded their 'book' for profit and stood in the market quoting two-way (bid and offer) prices in the full range of gilt-edged stocks. Brokers, on the other hand, acted solely as the agents for the investing public. They had a prime responsibility to effect their clients' orders to the client's best advantage, and for carrying out such bargains brokers charged their clients commission.

One of the main criticisms of the old market was that there were not enough jobbing firms with large enough capital resources to provide the market with the level of liquidity it really required. By 1985 there were only eight jobbing firms operating in gilts. Two of these were large: Wedd Durlacher Mordaunt and Akroyd & Smithers PLC. Next in size came Pinchin Denny followed by three smaller firms, Wilson & Watford, Charlesworth, and Giles & Cresswell, and then the small regional firms Moulsdale (Liverpool) and Aitken Campbell (Glasgow). Thus it was hardly surprising that when revolutionary change and the end of single capacity became inevitable the Bank of England should decide to replace the old gilt-edged market with a new system in which there would be a greater number of market-making firms and substantially increased amounts of dedicated capital. Rather than 'redesign the wheel' the Bank chose to model the new gilt-edged market very closely on the United States Treasury bond market.

Gilt-edged Market-makers (GEMMs)

In the new market the old separation between jobber and broker has been done away with and it is now permissible to combine principal and agency functions within the same firm, though not all firms wish to do so. The core of the new market is a number of registered market-making firms with obligations to make – on demand and in any trading conditions – continuous and effective two-way prices at which they stand committed to deal, in appropriate size as discussed in advance with the Bank of England, thereby providing continuous liquidity for the investing public. The sizes of positions that these market-makers can take are constrained by the need for each firm's aggregated position risk to be contained within certain prudential limits which are determined and monitored by the Bank. Each market-maker is required to commit an amount of dedicated capital to his gilt-edged operation and the greater this is the wider are his prudential limits.

In return for the obligations to make prices without favour 'in fair weather and in foul' and submit to the prudential control of the Bank, market-makers are able to avail themselves of certain privileges which are not open to other participants in the market. These are as follows:

1. To have a direct dealing relationship with the Bank in gilt-edged securities.
2. To have, subject to the agreement of the Government, exemption from Section 472(1) of the Income and Corporation Taxes Act 1970, which enables them to claim relief against tax for the full trading loss made by buying stock cum-dividend and selling it ex-dividend in the ordinary course of business, regardless of the time interval between purchase and sale.
3. To be able to offset, for tax purposes, dividends paid by them on stock they have sold against dividends received on stock they have purchased.
4. To be able both to lend and borrow stock through approved Stock Exchange money-brokers.
5. To have borrowing facilities at the Bank of England against approved security up to maximum amounts related to the market-maker's capital and reserves.
6. To have access to the Inter-Dealer Broker (IDB) mechanism (see later in this chapter).

On top of all this there was one further stipulation to the effect that all gilt-edged market-makers would be required to become members of The Stock

Exchange for regulatory purposes and for the maintenance of professional standards.

In the first half of 1985 the Bank of England invited applications from investment houses prepared to operate under these conditions as market-makers. There then followed a period when each prospective market-maker's candidature was thoroughly scrutinised before the Bank issued a list of twenty-nine firms to whom it was prepared to award a 'franchise'. These GEMMs (gilt-edged market-makers) were as follows:

1. Aitken Campbell & Co. (Gilts) – a relatively small Glasgow-based jobbing firm.
2. Akroyd, Rowe & Pitman, Mullens & Co. – part of a powerful all-British financial conglomerate being put together by Mercury Securities, the parent company of S. G. Warburg; a jobber (Akroyd & Smithers) plus two brokers.
3. Alexanders, Laing & Cruickshank – a discount house and broker combination backed by the capital of Mercantile House.
4. Bank of America – which subsequently withdrew in March 1986 before 'coming under starter's orders'.
5. Barclays de Zoete Wedd – another powerful all-British house combining a jobber (Wedd Durlacher) and a broker (de Zoete & Bevan) with the largest UK clearing bank.
6. Barings, Wilson & Watford – merchant bankers Barings plus smallish jobbers Wilson & Watford but without any obvious distributive arm.
7. BT Gilts – the newly set-up gilt-edged operation of Bankers Trust.
8. Cater Allen Holdings – a discount house.
9. Chase, Laurie & Simon – Chase Manhattan Bank plus two UK brokers, Laurie Milbank and Simon & Coates.
10. Citicorp Scrimgeour Vickers – a very powerful American bank in combination with two UK brokers.
11. County Holdings Group – National Westminster Bank's operation involving its merchant banking arm (County Bank) plus jobbers Bisgood Bishop and brokers Fielding Newson-Smith.
12. CSFB (Gilts) – Credit Suisse First Boston, a major Eurobond house with brokers Buckmaster & Moore in the same stable.
13. Gerrard & National – one of the top two discount houses.
14. Goldman Sachs Government Securities (UK) – a major American house.
15. Greenwell Montagu Gilt Edged – brokers W. Greenwell plus merchant bank Samuel Montagu with the power of the Midland Bank behind them.
16. Hill Samuel Wood Mackenzie (Sterling Debt) – merchant bank Hill Samuel combining with brokers Wood Mackenzie.
17. Hoare Govett Sterling Bonds – UK brokers Hoare Govett owned by the American bank Security Pacific.
18. James Capel Gilts – UK broker owned by Hongkong and Shanghai Bank.
19. Kleinwort, Grieveson and Charlesworth – major merchant bank Kleinwort Benson linked with the broking house of Grieveson, Grant and the relatively small jobbing firm of Charlesworth.

20. Lloyds Merchant Bank – a *de novo* operation under the wing of this UK clearing bank.
21. Merrill Lynch, Giles & Cresswell – major US securities house Merrill Lynch using the smallest of the UK gilt jobbers as an accelerated way into the market.
22. Messel/Shearson Lehman – US financial conglomerate Shearson Lehman together with UK broker L. Messel.
23. Morgan Grenfell Government Securities – merchant bank Morgan Grenfell plus brokers Pember & Boyle and jobbers Pinchin Denny.
24. Morgan Guaranty Sterling Securities Ltd.
25. Orion Royal Bank/Kitcat & Aitken – a Canadian bank best known for its involvement in the Eurobond market combined with UK broker Kitcat & Aitken.
26. Phillips & Drew Moulsdale – Liverpool-based jobbers Moulsdale moved their operation to London in order to combine with powerful London brokers Phillips & Drew. Both are owned by Union Bank Suisse.
27. Prudential Bache (of the USA) in a joint venture with Clive Discount.
28. Salomon Brothers UK – the major US bond house's UK operation.
29. Union Discount Securities – the other of the top two UK discount houses, but which withdrew in July 1986.

Although many well-known names from the old gilt-edged market are to be found in the above list, the salient feature is the emergence of new alliances of capital (in the form of the banks) and the market skills of both jobbers and brokers, made possible by the change in The Stock Exchange's rules to permit 100% ownership after 1 March 1986. One other aspect should be made clear here. Despite being described as 'Gilt-edged Market-makers' – a generic title chosen for them by the Bank of England in preference to the American term 'primary dealers' – these firms do not necessarily limit their operations to market-making and transacting other firms' orders. Most of them have trained sales teams backed up by economic and technical research, each working to bring high-quality order flow to its own market-makers. It can be seen that there is a very high level of inter-dependence between the three essential elements of such firms. The salesmen need their market-makers' prices to be competitive in width and size, the market-makers need the salesmen to understand and, if possible, anticipate investor demands, and the whole operation needs a strong capital base and fine credit lines in order to maximise its profitability.

Inter-dealer Brokers

The change to a US-style market also brings into existence here a new type of intermediary: the inter-dealer broker (IDB). IDBs exist to provide a means by which market-making firms can trade with each other whilst maintaining anonymity. They form an inner ring to the market, matching one market-maker's bid with another's offer and vice versa. They only deal with registered gilt-edged market-makers. They do not deal with the public.

Just in the same way that the Bank of England vetted the applications of prospective market-makers for the new market, so they did also with firms wishing to set up as IDBs. In this case, however, the Bank required applicants to demonstrate that there was a demand for their individual services from the twenty-nine GEMMs. This caused a certain amount of difficulty because the general consensus of opinion amongst the GEMMs was that the optimum number of IDBs to combine choice without undue fragmentation of the inner market was either three or four, whilst there were six very similar candidates all planning to do very much the same thing. In the end the Bank decided to authorise all six to operate, namely:

1. Charles Fulton (IDB).
2. Garban Gilts.
3. Mabon Nugent International.
4. Fundamental & Marshall Brokers.
5. Tullett & Tokyo (Gilts).
6. Williams Cooke Lott and Kissack.

Stock Exchange Money Brokers

There is another rather less well-known activity on the edge of the gilt-edged market, without which it would be unable to function efficiently, and this is the business of borrowing and lending stock. Whilst most people can easily identify with the concept of borrowing or lending money, the idea of doing so with stock is often found to be confusing. Why, the question goes, should anybody need or want to borrow stock? The answer to this is quite simple: dealers borrow stock in order to be able to deliver it to somebody to whom they have sold it, in order to obtain cash payment. The most usual case is that of a market-maker who has a bear book in a certain stock, but still makes a two-way market in the stock. If he then satisfies further buying orders in that stock, he will be unable to demand payment unless he can deliver stock to the buyer. This will mean that he will be out of the cash which could be earning interest for him. If, however, he borrows the stock and delivers it, he will receive payment, and at some later time when his book in that stock turns round he can unwind his borrowed position. The ability of market-makers to lend and borrow stock easily is thus an essential ingredient in the general fluidity of the day-to-day market. Since the cost of borrowing stock is small (about $\frac{3}{4}$% per annum), compared with usual money-market interest rates, it will nearly always pay a market-maker to borrow rather than be out of the money. Stock-lending is a specialised activity and is operated through nine Stock Exchange Money Brokers (SEMBs). In the old gilt-edged market there were only six such entities, all of whom were specialist departments of broking firms, namely Cazenove, Sheppards & Chase, Laurie Millbank, Rowe & Pitman, James Capel & Co., and Hoare, Govett. In making arrangements for the new market the Bank of England was concerned wherever possible to increase the supply of borrowable stock and with this aim in mind invited applications for further moneybroking firms. The result of this was that the merchant bank of Lazard Brothers, the discount house of King & Shaxson, and the joint venture of Prudential Bache and Clive Discount were added to the list of SEMBs. It is, of course, a total necessity of the system that these firms' moneybroking departments are hermetically separated from their other commercial activities, and that complete confidentiality of market-makers' and lenders' (normally the major institutions) stock position is observed.

Broker/Dealers

In the foregoing section of this chapter the focus has been directed very much on the activities of market-making firms and those closely related to them. Whilst it is through these firms that the bulk of institutional and international business passes, it is important not to lose sight of the independent broker/dealers. They act as agents for the public to achieve best execution for their bargains. They carry out very much the same function in the new market as did the brokers in the old, but in one specific regard their role has changed. Whereas previously they were not allowed to take principal positions they are now permitted to transact their clients' business with their own book, provided that by so doing they are dealing on better terms (not just equal terms) than if they were dealing with a registered market-maker. There is also the question of commission. Since most bargains transacted between clients and market-makers direct are of a principal nature, commissions are very rarely charged when dealing in this way. But when dealing through a broker/dealer one can expect a commission to be charged to remunerate them for establishing the most advantageous place in which to deal and processing the necessary paperwork.

The Role of the 'Authorities'

In the old market there was one broker that was different from all the others and that was the Government Broker (or the GB, as he was colloquially known in the market). By tradition the Government Broker was the senior partner of the firm of Mullens & Co. and was responsible for carrying out the day-to-day market activities of the 'authorities' acting through the Bank of England. This function was a long way removed from ordinary stockbroking and the operations of the Government Broker were strictly separated from Mullens's non-government business. The GB had his own team usually consisting of himself, his deputy (another partner in Mullens) plus market-dealing staff. His team had no dealings with any other brokers (including the other part of Mullens), but dealt solely with the jobbing system. This particular system was well suited to the needs and requirements of the old jobbing system but was obviously inappropriate for the new market with its far greater number of market-makers. So tradition gave way to practical reality and the Government Broker and his team gave up their lives as stockbrokers and moved inside the Bank of England to become members of its gilt-edged division. From there a team of about a dozen staff keep in daily communication (between 9.00 a.m. and 5.00 p.m.) with the gilt-edged market-makers dealing with them over the telephone rather than on the floor of the 'house'.

To understand how they operate it is important to comprehend the way in which government stocks are sold in the United Kingdom. Unlike other countries where stock is sold directly to the banks or underwriting groups, or directly auctioned as in the United States, the prime form of sale of gilt-edged stock is an offer for sale to the general public. Traditionally announcements of new issues were made in The Stock Exchange at 3.30 p.m. on the relevant Friday for applications on the next Thursday, but in recent years announcements have been made at other times, and issue dates have been Wednesdays as well as Thursdays. However, there is a basic timetable which normally allows at least three business days to elapse between announcement and date of issue. In the old days the issue price would be fixed at the time of announcement, and if the market moved down substantially in these three days this could jeopardise the success of an issue. If prices rose, however, this could leave the stock to be issued looking cheap in comparison with the rest of the market and create excess demand for it. This fixed-price offer for sale method had its most (in)famous day when in February 1979, Treasury $13\frac{3}{4}$% 2000/03 was issued. Between the Friday evening announcement and the following Thursday morning the long end of the gilt-edged market rose by about four points. The resulting demand for the new stock was so large that in the half-hour between 9.30 a.m. and 10.00 a.m. when the application list closed in Watling Street, the Bank of England's new issue department was swamped with brokers' and bankers' messengers, all trying to lodge applications for their clients, and 'disorderly scenes' took place. The affair subsequently became known as 'The Battle of Watling Street', and since that occasion the Bank has normally used a tender-price method instead. Under this system, investors tender the price which they are prepared to pay for stock. Sometimes the Bank of England stipulates a minimum tender price, below which applications will not be considered; at other times there is no formal minimum tender price. Basically stock is allotted to those applicants tendering the highest prices, though the actual issue price is fixed as the lowest price at which any stock is allotted, and is the same for all successful applicants.

The following example may clarify this point.

Imagine an issue of £1,000 million stock with a minimum tender price of 96. When the applications are collected and analysed it is found that

£5 million stock has been applied for at $97\frac{1}{4}$
£25 million stock has been applied for at 97
£670 million stock has been applied for at $96\frac{3}{4}$
£1,200 million stock has been applied for at $96\frac{1}{2}$
£1,000 million stock has been applied for at $96\frac{1}{4}$
£1,000 million stock has been applied for at 96

The stock applied for at $97\frac{1}{4}$, 97 and $96\frac{3}{4}$ totals £700 million and will be allotted in full. This leaves £300 million further stock to be allowed to applicants for £1,200 million at $96\frac{1}{2}$. These are proportionately scaled down, each applicant at this price receiving 25% of his requirement. The issue price, however, is the lowest price at which applications are successful even in part – in this case $96\frac{1}{2}$ – and all stock is allotted at this price.

Not all issues are as successful as this. In some cases insufficient applications occur at or above the minimum tender price, and the issue is undersubscribed.

Sometimes, in cases where no minimum tender price is specified, the tenders are so low that the Bank of England decides to accept only those above a certain level, and does not allot all the stock to the public. In both cases, the Bank of England is left with the rump of the issue, which is allotted temporarily to the Government 'departments'. This is where the 'authorities'' task begins. Their function will be to operate a 'tap' feeding this stock into the secondary market subsequently, as and when demand for it comes about. Tap operations require a degree of finesse to be successful. Immediate cutting of the tap price after a not-fully-subscribed issue produces instant losses for those who actually applied for stock, and is the sort of action that ensures that any such applicants will think twice before applying for future issues. On the other hand, unless the whole market moves upwards, the 'authorities' will have some difficulty in selling stock at prices above that at which the issue failed. They do, however, have one strong psychological card to play. If it is perceived that they are not going to sell stock cheaply through their tap, but are going slowly and steadily to increase their tap price, the very fear that the price may be higher tomorrow than it is today can often drive investors to hasten their purchases. Occasionally they may play hard to get and not respond to the first bids for their stock, in the hope of obtaining a higher level. If this tactic should fail, or the market fall badly in general, leaving the tap price stranded high and dry, then they will probably withdraw temporarily and wait for the market to stabilise at some lower level before responding to further bids from market-makers and re-opening their tap.

No book on the gilt-edged market would be complete on this subject without some reference to the 'Grand Old Duke of York', whose activities were involved in a number of funding initiatives, particularly in the five years between 1976 and 1981. Contrary to the assumption of one overseas investor, the 'Grand Old Duke of York' was not the name of the Government Broker, nor that of the Governor of the Bank of England, nor that of the Chancellor of the Exchequer, but was the name given to the tactic of the authorities, at times of funding crises, of forcing up interest rates, so that gilt-edged prices would collapse, thereby allowing tap prices to be re-established at a much lower level. If successfully operated, this tactic would bring buyers flocking back to the market at the new higher yield level, the tap stock would be sold out, and (with luck) prices would start to rise once more. The yo-yo progress of the market's yield structure in all this was considered by market participants to be similar to that of

> 'The Grand Old Duke of York
> He had ten thousand men.
> He marched them up to the top of the hill
> And he marched them down again.'

Not much has been seen of the 'Duke' since 1981. There are those who think he is dead and buried, but more likely he is in quiet retirement, ready to be called upon if future circumstances demand his return.

It was stated above that the offer for sale, whether by fixed price or tender, is the primary issue method. It is not, however, the only way new gilt-edged stock is created and brought to the market. In recent years the practice has become established whereby the authorities create small additional tranches of existing stocks (referred to in the market as 'taplets' or 'tranchettes') and sell these directly to the Bank of England, which in turn 'taps' them out to the market as demand dictates. This is a convenient and very quick method, and particularly well suited for bringing out relatively small amounts of stock (tranchettes are typically between £100 million and £250 million) when a full-blooded new issue of, say, £1,000 million might be less than easily digested.

In all the foregoing, the emphasis has been placed on the 'authorities'' part in selling debt. But they operate on the buying tack also. One of their functions is to smooth out the redemption of maturing issues by gradually buying in stock over the last few months of their lives. This action helps spread the period of cash outflow caused by redemption, and also improves the liquidity of the very short end of the market as it is known that any such stock offered for sale will be readily bought in by the Bank of England. Apart from this, there are a number of government or Bank of England funds whose investments may include gilts, of which the National Insurance fund is a good example, and the Bank will deal for them, either as a buyer or seller according to their needs.

There can be other times when, for tactical reasons, the 'authorities' may be buyers of stock. They may act to stabilise a falling market by coming in and buying stock, even to the extent of creating a bear squeeze. They may also facilitate switch business by being prepared to buy in shorter issues in exchange for longer 'tap' stocks. Such stock as they do take in in this way then becomes available for subsequent sale back to the market should it be wanted. It can thus be seen that, other than official 'taps' and 'tranchettes', there is a third category of stock: these 'unofficial taps' that the 'authorities' may have in their portfolio ready for sale at any given time.

The Financial Institutions

Reference has been made above to the financial institutions as investors in gilts. These institutions fall broadly into two main categories: those with deposit liabilities, and those with longer-term liabilities, such as life assurance funds and pension funds. There are, however, other classes of investor which do not readily fit into these convenient compartments, of which unit trusts, investment trusts, the trustee departments of the banks, and the private investor in general, are particular examples.

All of these have differing investment requirements, some of which may be met by the gilt-edged market. In order to understand the market, it is thus necessary to understand the needs of those whose actions will tend to have the greatest impact on the supply and demand for stock. As we have already seen, the Bank of England, acting for the authorities, is (usually) the largest player on the supply side. It is now necessary to look at the institutions, and examine their impact on the demand side.

Commercial Banks

The prime function of the commercial banks is to take in deposits and make loans to all sections of the general public. Although in the United Kingdom the London clearing banks and the Scottish clearing banks – both having extensive branch banking systems – dominate the scene, they are only a part of a much wider banking system, all of which comes under the regulation of the Bank of England for the purposes of monetary control. The monetary sector includes both banks and a second category of licensed deposit takers (LDTs), all of whom (except for the very smallest) are subject to certain liquidity requirements. Broadly speaking, these are to maintain at the Bank of England a non-operational, non-interest-bearing, cash balance of $\frac{1}{2}$% of such an institution's eligible liabilities (ELs – see below). It used to be that all eligible banks undertook to maintain secured money with members of the London Discount Market Association (LDMA), and/or secured call money with either the six recognised Stock Exchange money brokers or the gilt-edged jobbers – all interest earning – to the extent of 5% of their ELs on average, and not less than $2\frac{1}{2}$% of ELs with the LDMA on any particular day. But in making arrangements for the new gilt-edged market the Bank signalled its proposal to withdraw such arrangements. However, money lent by the banking system to GEMMs is accorded the prime liquidity rating (equal to that left with Discount Houses) and it is not expected that GEMMs will experience difficulties in financing their positions.

An explanatory note is due here. One cannot proceed very far in any description of the banking system before coming up against the words 'eligible' or 'eligibility', and it is important to understand their meanings. To do so, it is necessary to have an idea of how the bill market operates. A bill is basically an IOU issued by a person or company in respect of a deferred payment. The owner of a bill, should he wish to receive more immediate payment, will seek to sell his bill to a third party on a discounted basis. This third party may wish for some assurance as to the credit standing of the originator of the bill, and the practice arose long ago of having the bill 'accepted' by a bank, which would place its stamp upon it. Once 'accepted', the bill is effectively treated as being underwritten by the bank, and the credit standing of the bill becomes as good as that of the bank accepting it. Only the highest-quality bank bills are 'eligible' for discount at the Bank of England. Recognised banks can apply for 'eligibility' at any time, and the Bank of England judges their applications on the following criteria:

1. Whether the applicant has and maintains a broadly-based and substantial acceptance business in the United Kingdom.
2. Whether its acceptances command the finest rates in the market for ineligible bills.
3. Whether, in the case of foreign-owned banks, British banks enjoy reciprocal opportunities in the foreign owners' domestic market.

Eligible liabilities are basically sterling deposits (not including those whose maturity was longer than two years at the time of deposit) plus sterling resources obtained from switching foreign currencies into sterling.

Over and above these formal liquidity requirements, the banks are also subject to a degree of prudential control as to their lending and investment policy. The attitude of the Bank of England is generally to leave these matters to individual banks' best judgements, but it does monitor their books and it will in certain circumstances 'suggest' that a bank changes its portfolio posture. As regards taxation on their investment portfolios, all interest payments and realised capital gains or losses are treated as being a part of a bank's general trade and business, and are aggregated with their other profit for taxation purposes. There is thus no tax discrimination in favour of or against capital relative to income, and for stock selection purposes most banks use redemption yields net of corporation tax (see note at the end of the chapter) on both income and capital gains as a basic criterion. These produce stock selection preferences not greatly unlike those produced using gross redemption yields, but differing to the extent that whilst income tax is paid as interest payments occur, tax on capital gains can be deferred until the time of sale or redemption, or in practice some time even later.

Trustee Savings Banks

The trustee savings banks have very much the same prudential limitations acting upon them as the clearing banks, but since historically they were precluded from making loan advances, a much higher proportion of their assets needed to be invested in securities. They obtained their name because their activities were controlled by local groups of trustees to protect the savings of the poor. In recent years, however, they have developed into commercial banks, and since 1979 have offered cheque books, loan facilities and even a credit card facility (Trustcard) to their customers. Their investments, which used to be handled locally by the individual TSBs, are now grouped under the Central Trustee Savings Bank (CTSB) in London, and the TSB Scotland in Edinburgh, whilst the Trustee Savings Bank of Northern Ireland retains its autonomy. Their taxation basis which used to be 52% on income and 30% on capital gains, is now similar to that of the commercial banks, i.e. corporation tax on both income and capital gains.

Discount Houses

There are seven discount houses – Union Discount, Gerrard & National, Alexanders Discount (incorporating Jessel Toynbee), Cater Allen, Clive Discount, King & Shaxson (incorporating Smith St Aubyn), and Seccombe Marshall – which, together with a discount broker, Gerald Quin Cope, form the London Discount Market Association. Pre-1985 these institutions were all British and completely independent. Nowhere else in the world were similar entities to be found. Their strength and importance sprang from the pivotal position they occupied in the UK banking system, and the fact that it is through the discount market that the Bank of England conducts its operations in the money market. But the wind of change that blew through the City in the wake of The Stock Exchange's 'revolution' caused alliances of money market and gilt-edged market operations to be forged so as to be able to offer clients dealing capability right down the maturity spectrum, from the shortest dates to the irredeemables. Furthermore, as shown earlier, many of these alliances involved overseas (especially American) interests. Seccombe Marshall was bought by Citicorp, and Clive Discount started joint ventures with Prudential Bache. Alexanders Discount and Jessel Toynbee were both acquired by Mercantile House and their gilt-edged skills combined with those of broker Laing & Cruickshank, whilst Banque Belge took up a stake in Gerald Quin Cope.

Basically, the discount houses borrow the day-to-day surpluses of the commercial banks and invest this money, together with their own capital, in other short-term instruments, such as Treasury bills, commercial bills, gilt-edged stocks, local authority bills, bonds and stocks, certificates of deposit, etc. By the reverse token, they also undertake to repay the banks their funds when required. Such demands from the banks can often leave the discount market short, and these situations are alleviated by the access the market has to the Bank of England. Under this arrangement a discount house has two opportunities (one in the morning and the other before 2.30 in the afternoon) to offer parts of its bill portfolio within four prescribed maturity bands, for the Bank of England to purchase. The rate at which the Bank of England is prepared to buy such bills are one of the crucial money market interest rates, and the Bank can, through its activity in this field, exert great influence over the whole range of short-term interest rates, especially when it is realised that if the Bank of England is not satisfied with the rate at which bills are offered, it can decline to take them, and force the discount house to borrow directly at a rate of the Bank's choosing at 2.30 p.m.

Another vital feature of the discount market is its agreement to underwrite the weekly Treasury bill issue by submitting tenders that collectively total not less than the amount of bills to be issued. In earlier years this commitment, *inter alia*, caused a preponderance of Treasury bills in the portfolios of the houses, but the size of the Treasury bill issue has become much reduced since the early 1980s, and their commercial bill book is now many times larger than that of their Treasury bills.

Before August 1981 the discount houses' investment policy was to a very great degree regulated by what was called the 'undefined assets' multiple. Each house's holding of 'undefined assets' was limited to a maximum of twenty times its capital and reserves. 'Undefined assets' were classed as all assets other than balances at the Bank of England, UK and Northern Ireland Treasury bills, government stock with not more than five years to final maturity (i.e. short-dated gilts), short-dated local authority stocks, local authority and other public boards' bills eligible at the Bank of England, local authority negotiable bonds, and bank bills drawn by a nationalised industry under specific government guarantee.

In practice, that meant that the bulk of 'undefined assets' were commercial bills, certificates of deposit, gilts and local authority stocks longer than five years to final maturity, and miscellaneous loans to other parties. In August 1981, however, this system of control was abandoned by the Bank of England and replaced by a more flexible system of prudential control. Under the new system various classes of assets suitable for discount house investment are accorded risk coefficients on a scale in which the risk factor (broadly speaking) increases as maturities increase. The size of a discount house's book is thus not only related to that of its capital and reserves, but also to the type of assets it chooses to hold.

Thus, if a discount house wishes to take an aggressive stance in a relatively high-risk area this will have a restrictive effect on the size of their permissible operations in other areas.

However, as a result of the City changes, there is an unusual differentiation in the way different discount houses can 'play' the gilt-edged market. Those with GEMMs will be governed by their set of prudential rules and those without by the traditional (post-1981) discount market rules.

Building Societies

As their name suggests, the main *raison d'être* of the building societies has been the provision of mortgage finance for house purchase. The societies have not been companies but non-profit-making friendly societies, and as such their activities have been regulated by the Chief Registrar of Friendly Societies. Despite a considerable incidence of mergers in recent years, there are still a large number of individual building societies, ranging in size from multi-branch societies with assets of over £10,000 million to single-office societies with assets not much greater than £1 million. Whilst at the lower end of the scale not much is likely to change, the effects of the Building Societies Act 1986 on the larger societies will be substantial. This Act permits them to undertake a whole new range of commercial activities such as owning and developing land, lending on an unsecured basis and for non-housing purposes, and opens the door to incorporation and the public flotation of building societies.

However, these new freedoms are unlikely to interfere with their traditional business. Basically the societies take in deposits from the general public (some of them also obtain wholesale funds from the negotiable bond market, by issuing certificates of deposit, and, more recently, through the Euronote market), and lend on house mortgages. Since their borrowing is potentially short term, and their lending essentially long term, they require to have some considerable protection against adverse events. One protection they have is that their mortgage lending rate is not fixed permanently, but can be moved upwards and downwards in line with interest rates in general and their own deposit rates in particular. Furthermore, building societies are required to hold a minimum of $7\frac{1}{2}\%$ of their liabilities in certain forms of liquid assets. In practice, most of them prefer to have markedly higher liquid ratios for prudential reasons, e.g 15%–20%. Such investments are governed by the Building Societies Authorised Investment order, which sets out in precise detail the categories of instruments in which they may invest, which include gilt-edged stocks and certain other types of fixed-interest stocks. Building society investments are subdivided also by maturity bands. Part I stocks mature within five years, Part II stocks mature between five years and fifteen years from the relevant date, and Part III stocks have maturities in the fifteen- to twenty-five-year range. No investment may be made in Part II stocks unless at least $7\frac{1}{2}\%$ of liabilities are already invested in Part I, and no investments may be made in Part III stocks unless 15% minimum are already invested in Parts I and II together (of which $7\frac{1}{2}\%$ minimum must be in Part I). From this it can be seen that building society gilt-edged portfolios can be expected to be heavily weighted towards the short end of the market, and that holdings of stocks longer than fifteen years are relatively rare.

There is the possibility that these arrangements may be changed in future. On 28 August 1986 the Chief Registrar of Friendly Societies issued a consultative document in which proposals for Building Societies capital adequacy of a different sort were suggested. If implemented these would require Building Societies to hold capital and reserves sufficient to protect their investments from the adverse effect of a 3% upward movement in interest rates or gross yield. This is substantially more discriminatory against medium- and longer-dated maturities than the existing legislation and has important implications for the future operation of the gilt-edged market.

The other major influence on building society investment policy is their taxation basis. Prior to 24 February 1984 building societies were subject to corporation tax at a special rate of 40% on investment income, whilst capital gains were taxed under the then existing capital gains tax rules at a rate of 30% for gilt-edged gains realised within a year of purchase, or at a nil rate for gilts held for more than a year. Since that date their capital gains have been treated as part of their trading 'profit' and subject to corporation tax at either their special rate of 40% or the standard rate of corporation tax for the year in question, whichever is the lower.

Corporate Funds

Although their presence is dwarfed by the size of the financial institutions, a significant number of industrial and commercial companies make use of the gilt-edged market as a place in which to deploy some part of their surplus funds. The main attractions to corporate funds are the higher net-of-tax returns that can often be found in the gilt-edged market compared to the money market. These come about largely because the rate of tax applicable to capital gains on gilt-edged stock is lower than the rate of tax on income receivable from money market instruments. Most companies, other than those for whom dealing in securities is part of their basic trade or business, will tend to be taxed at corporation tax on investment income, and since 2 July 1986 at nil on capital gains from their gilt-edged holdings. The grossed-up net yields on gilt-edged stocks in the last two years of their lives often comfortably exceed period money market rates, and offer significant investment opportunities to corporate bodies with excess medium-term funds.

General Insurance Companies

The term 'general' is used to distinguish those companies whose trade and business is to write insurance against general risks – motor insurance, fire, marine, property, etc. – from those which deal with life insurance business. In the course of business, general insurance companies receive premiums, which are investable. The nature of the business is such that investments require to be reasonably liquid, and the short and medium sectors of the gilt-edged market provide these companies with a suitable form of investment. Their tax position is that both income and capital gains are subject to corporation tax at the same rate, and on these considerations alone there would normally be no preference between them, but in recent years their physical underwriting operations have tended to produce losses, and many companies have preferred to have a higher guaranteed income flow to offset these losses, rather than an eventual capital gain. As a result, some have shown a preference for higher-coupon stocks rather than lower-coupon stocks in the gilt-edged portfolios.

Life Assurance Companies

Nowadays, life companies do more than simply write life assurance business, they have annuity funds, they write pension business, and have a plethora of marketing devices that have taken them into unit-linked savings schemes also. However, in the main their liabilities are essentially long term, and in many cases their major investment concern is to produce real rates of return (i.e. after allowing for the ravages of inflation) on the various contracts and policies they write. Life funds will thus be invested in equities, property and overseas securities, as well as gilt-edged stocks. Within the gilt-edged market their natural habitat is at the longer end of the market, thus roughly matching the nature of their liabilities, though their investments often include short- and medium-dated stocks for tactical purposes. Tax can play a very important part in the fund management of a life office. Under a long-standing arrangement with the Inland Revenue the rate of tax on income of a pure life office has been established as the ruling corporation tax rate or $37\frac{1}{2}\%$, whichever is the lesser. In addition, life offices are considered to be investors rather than traders and as such qualify for freedom from capital gains tax on gilts.

However, the situation is complicated by the fact that few life assurance companies are *pure* life funds. The expansion of their activities over the years has taken them heavily into the pensions and annuity businesses, and in most cases they are a composite pot-pourri of all three forms. Since pensions business is free of tax on income and capital, and annuity business subject to corporation tax on both, the overall composite tax position of a life office is far from straightforward, and even varies from year to year as the relative weightings change. It is even not unusual for the investment managers of life funds to have to operate using estimates of the funds' tax position, as the actual basis is often not known until the tax year in question has passed. With regard to gilt-edged investment, the situation is further complicated by the fact that most life offices offset their management expenses against their gilt-edged investment income. If these expenses exceed their gilt dividends then, to all intents and purposes, their marginal effective tax rate on gilt-edged income is zero.

Pension Funds

These are perhaps the institutions which can have the longest-term liabilities. A pension fund accepting a new entrant aged 20 now may still be paying benefits in sixty years' time; and even a closed fund with no new entrants can still face the prospect of having outflows for some years forward. Since in most schemes benefits are linked to final (or final-average) salaries, and salaries are in turn influenced by inflation, it can be appreciated how inflation is the major long-term concern of the pension fund managers. Accordingly, pension funds have been much larger investors in real assets such as equities and property, which (it is hoped) offer longer-term protection against inflation, rather than in fixed-interest stocks. Some funds have gone so far as to have zero gilt-edged or fixed-interest exposure, but a figure of 20% to 25% of assets is a more usual proportion.

Most funded schemes need to produce real rates of return (i.e. in excess of inflation) of between 2% and 3% per annum to meet their actuarial requirements, and this has not always been easy to achieve, especially during the 1970s, when inflationary pressures were at their height. Their task has been made somewhat easier by the advent of index-linked gilts with long-dated maturities and benefits linked to the Retail Price Index, and significant amounts of these stocks have found their way into pension fund portfolios, often at the expense of 'conventional' gilts.

The majority of pension funds are 'approved' schemes, by which is meant that they have been given exemption from tax on their investment activities by the Inland Revenue. This applies to both investment income and capital gains tax, and as such they are known as 'gross' funds.

Merchant Banks and Fund Management Companies

A great deal of pension fund investment is carried out by external fund managers, especially when the funds in question are insufficiently large to warrant the expense of setting up an independent fund management operation. This business has very largely been captured by the merchant banks, fund management groups such as the investment and unit trust managers, and the investment departments of the life offices. It is a fiercely competitive business, where investment performance is closely monitored, and league tables abound. Because these funds are that much smaller, it is that much easier for managers to effect investment policy changes with substantial proportions of their funds, and investment postures are frequently aggressive.

Another activity of the fund management groups that grew rapidly in the early 1980s was the gilt-edged unit trust. Before the 1980 Finance Act, the taxation climate was impropitious for unit trusts investing in gilts. Legislative changes introduced at that date made these trusts liable only to basic rate income tax on dividends, and exempted them from all capital gains tax. These funds are therefore theoretically free to pursue a highly active investment policy (should they so wish), without a tax penalty, but the Inland Revenue has warned them that too high a level of activity could result in them being deemed to be 'trading' rather than 'investing' and cause them to be taxed at corporation tax rate on both dividends and capital gains. As a result, most trusts' investment policy can be expected to be reasonably conservative.

From an investor's point of view the important thing to remember is that despite having gilt-edged stocks as its underlying investments, a gilt-edged unit trust is treated in exactly the same way as equity unit trusts for tax purposes. This means that capital gains arising from the change in the value of the units are not exempt from capital gains tax, though this impost is greatly reduced by the first £6,300 (for 1986/87) of gains in the year being exempted, and by a provision allowing inflation indexation of book costs to be taken into account when calculating the chargeable gain.

Higher Rate Taxpayers

Although it is an obvious misnomer to describe these people as an institution, collectively they have a dominant effect upon the low-coupon, short-dated sector of the gilt-edged market. Because the top rate of tax on investment income is as high as 60% (and has been as high as 83%), the needs of the high-rate taxpayer are/have been for minimum income and maximum capital gain. Low-coupon stocks standing at substantial discounts to par offer an obvious solution to their problem. The shorter-dated of these stocks are particularly suitable where the investor needs a degree of protection against capital depreciation, such as members of underwriting syndicates at Lloyds, and stockbroking partnerships.

Overseas Funds

With international bond markets increasingly becoming intertwined the gilt-edged market is frequently the focus of attention of the overseas investor, especially when the outlook for sterling is strong, offering the prospect of currency gains as well as gilt-edged appreciation. At such times the money flows into gilts from abroad can be very substantial. Overseas investors broadly break down into three categories: central monetary institutions such as central banks; international organisations such as the World Bank, the EEC and the United Nations agencies; and 'others', a blanket expression covering investors of many varieties from Japanese insurance companies to Swiss banks. Because of the diverse nature of overseas investors it is difficult to be specific about their coupon and maturity preferences, but taken as a whole they tend to prefer short- and medium-dated stocks and relatively high-coupon rates. In one way, however, the structural changes that have taken place in the market have enhanced the attractiveness of gilts for the foreign investor. The change to a US-style market here means that

Table 3.1 *Market impact matrix*

Type of investor	Income tax rate (%)	CG tax rate (%)	Shorts (0–5 years)	Mediums (5–15 years)	Longs (over 15 years)
Pension funds	nil	nil	small	moderate	large
Life offices	10–20 on average	small (see text)	small	moderate	large
Gilt-edged unit trusts	30	nil	small	small	small
Building societies	35	35	large	large	small
Corporate funds	35	nil	moderate	small	negligible
Banks and discount houses	35	35	large	large	small
General insurance companies	35	35	large	large	small
Higher-rate taxpayers	up to 60	nil	large (low coupons)	small	negligible

Note: The rates of corporation tax for the next few years were set in the 1984 Finance Act as 45% for the year to 31 March 1985, 40% for the year to 31 March 1986, and 35% for the year to 31 March 1987.

they are now more at home with market practice than they were previously in the old gilt-edged market with its 'quaint' jobber/broker demarcation and (what they perceived as) lack of liquidity.

Summary

Table 3.1 summarises the preferred maturity habitats and incidences of taxation upon the major classes of investor, and illustrates where the impact of their activities has most effect on the market.

4

Basic factors affecting general market values

There are a multitude of different factors which affect levels of prices and yields in the gilt-edged market. Some are economic, some are political, some are psychological, some are technical. A number of these are more or less permanent features of the gilt-edged scene whilst others are more transient. It is not practically possible in a book such as this to list and analyse all of them, but there are a number of key factors about which the gilt-edged analyst should be conversant. Certain of these have a direct effect on the market, whilst others impact it only indirectly. Many, however, are interrelated and the schematic diagram in Fig. 4.1 illustrates their main linkages. It can be seen that two of the chief determinants of market levels are interest rates at the short end and inflation (or, more correctly, inflationary expectations) at the long end.

The reasons for this are not hard to find. An investor such as a pension fund whose liabilities are essentially defined in 'real' terms must, of necessity, seek to invest in instruments whose prospective return will exceed (by whatever margin he deems necessary) the rise in his liabilities brought about by inflation. Since this sort of investor dominates the long end of the gilt-edged market, it follows that yields there will be affected by the broad consensus of opinion as to prospective inflation rates in the long-run future. The fact that it is *prospective* inflation that needs to be assessed cannot be stressed too strongly. All sorts of words get written in newspaper articles, journals, and so on, about the current relationship between gilt-edged yields and 'inflation', which are potentially devalued by virtue of the fact that the 'inflation' to which reference is made is most usually 'current' rather than prospective. In fact, the situation is probably even worse, since in the United Kingdom the most usual definition of 'current' inflation is the percentage increase of the most recently issued Retail Price Index over the comparable month a year earlier. As the RPI is issued a month after the date to which it pertains, 'current' inflation so defined relates to the period thirteen months to one month in retrospect. The best that can be said about this simplistic sort of inflation analysis is that it gives the investor a historical backdrop against which he must make his own ideas about prospective inflation. In this regard, the level of long-

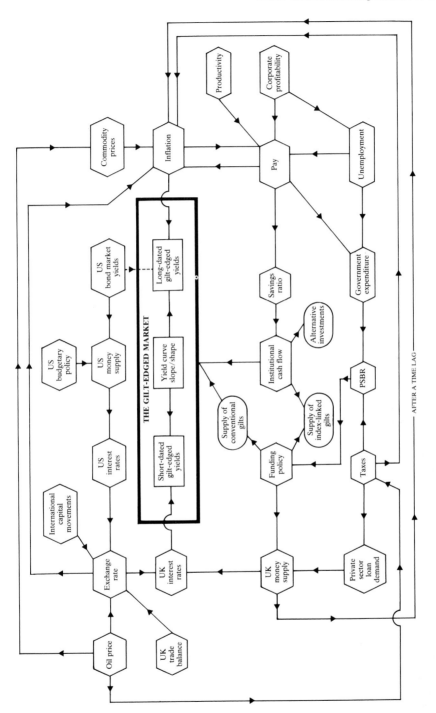

Fig. 4.1 *The main determinants of values in the gilt-edged market and their interrelationship*

term gilt-edged yields can be considered as an amalgam of two key elements: (a) expectations of future inflation trends and (b) the required level of 'real' yields. Changes in either of these components will affect the level at which investors are happy to buy or hold long-dated gilts against their real liabilities.

The impact of inflation is very much less on deposit-taking investors who predominate at the short end of the market. With such investors inflation applies more or less equally on both sides of their equation, i.e. on the real value of their deposit liabilities, and also on that of their invested assets. To these funds what really matters is the difference between the outward payments of deposit interest, and the realised rate of total return on their investments. It should be stressed that one is *not* stating that inflation has *no* impact whatsoever on short-term rates – this is patently untrue, and the 'real' level of short-term interest rates is a vital parameter in the management of the economy – but that it is *less* of a market factor for investors at the short end than at the long end of the market.

Interest rates are affected by both external and domestic factors. On the external front, high interest rates are sometimes needed to buttress the exchange rate, and in this regard the level of comparable interest rates in other world financial centres, especially the United States, is often critical.

Taking domestic considerations alone, interest rates are basically the price of money, and are theoretically determined by the demand for finance and the supply of savings. In this respect a flow-of-funds analysis is a useful tool for observing the variations of the net demand for funds for various sectors of the economy. The four basic sectors of the economy used in flow-of-funds analysis are as follows:

1. The UK personal sector.
2. The UK company sector.
3. The UK public sector.
4. The overseas sector.

Detailed figures for these sectors are published quarterly by the Bank of England but, because of their complexity, the most recent figures only relate to a period two quarters in arrears.

The sum of the net balances of the sectors should by definition equate to zero, since if one sector is a net provider of funds, and another a net taker, the two balances cancel each other out. However, in practice, life is not that easy, and despite the valiant efforts of the statisticians it is not always possible to track down every item, so that even the Bank of England's flow-of-funds matrix table requires there to be a column for 'Residual error' before it will balance. Table 4.1, showing figures for the fourth quarter of 1984, illustrates.

The characteristics of each sector vary. The personal sector is more or less always in a state of financial surplus (1984 IV = £1,571 million), as its savings generally exceed its physical investments. On the other hand, it is normal for the public sector to be in deficit (1984 IV = £2,677 million), though the size of this deficit is normally smaller than the personal sector's surplus. The company sector and the overseas sector move in a more random way and do not have distinct

Table 4.1   *Bank of England flow-of-funds matrix, 1984 IV*

	Flow-of-funds (£ million)				
	Personal sector	Public sector	Company sector	Overseas sector	Residual error
Savings	+ 5,537	+ 950	+ 11,101	− 1,296	—
+ Taxes on capital and capital transfers	+ 318	− 358	+ 40	—	—
− Physical investment (including stock-building)	− 4,284	− 3,269	− 8,217	—	—
= Financial surplus (+)/deficit (−)	+ 1,571	− 2,677	+ 2,924	− 1,296	− 522

Note: The public sector financial deficit should not be confused with the Public Sector Borrowing Requirement, which also includes lending to other sectors and asset sales.

normality patterns, though in recent years the company sector has more often than not been in deficit (though not 1984!).

Since it is the public and corporate sectors that are most usually in deficit, it is possible to use their combined requirements as a proxy for the net demand for credit, and thus as a pointer to interest rates. Sadly, the publication of data lags well behind events, and for this approach to be effective requires good economic forecasting of these two entities. Suffice it to say, however, that a period in which it is expected that both the public sector and the corporate sector will both be in deficit will also be one in which upward pressure on interest rates can be expected to occur.

It must, however, be stressed that this sort of analysis only gives a broad background to the interest rate scene, and provides little if any guide to interest rate changes over the very short term. In particular, it does not go to the root of the problem and consider the factors which actually determine the net flow of funds, nor does it make allowance for interest rates being a specific target of the Government's official policy.

In this regard, political considerations impinge upon the economic, and essential questions of governmental priorities emerge. Very often these centre on the triangular relationship between three interdependent entities – foreign exchange rates, interest rates, and inflation. Much as governments might like to be able to control all three variables independently, the choice open to them is most often between that of running an exchange-rate policy or an interest-rate policy; so that a key question for the gilt-edged analyst is to decide upon which of these two is prevalent at any particular time.

Whilst the activities of the Bank of England in the foreign exchange market cannot normally be overtly observed (although the net cost often shows in the monthly Currency Reserve figures), the Bank's day-by-day interest rate interventions are publicly declared and are often used as signals to the banking sector as to the direction the Bank feels interest rates should move. Normally this happens by the Bank altering the rate of interest at which it is prepared to deal with the discount market in order to relieve the day-to-day money market shortage.

There are three ways in which the Bank can do this. Firstly, it can buy Treasury bills, local authority bills and eligible bank bills offered by the discount houses. Secondly, the Bank can enter into a sale and re-purchase agreement with the discount houses, such that the Bank buys Treasury bills, local authority bills and eligible bank bills on the understanding that the houses will re-purchase them on a specified future date. In the last resort, the discount houses can be invited to borrow directly from the Bank, normally on an overnight basis or for seven days.

The rates at which the Bank of England conducts these open market operations with the discount market are published through the media daily, and can and should be monitored by the gilt-edged analyst. There are various maturity bands used by the Bank, namely:

Up to 14 days to maturity	Band I
15–33 days to maturity	Band II
34–63 days to maturity	Band III
64–91 days to maturity	Band IV

Of these, the most important to watch are normally Bands I and II, which roughly equate in maturity to one week and one month, and are comparable with inter-bank rates for these periods. These rates, together with the clearing banks' base rates, form the key short-term interest rate structure which acts as an anchor for yields at the short end of the gilt-edged market.

Whilst interest rates and inflation are undoubtedly key fundamental influences on the market's yield structure, there are other factors of a more technical nature that also have a direct market impact. First and foremost of these is the supply and demand for gilt-edged stock.

On the supply side of this equation are factors such as size of the PSBR, the proportion of it to be financed by gilt sales, and policy decisions as to the type of stock to be offered: shorts, mediums, longs, or index-linked.

The PSBR is itself very largely a function of the difference between the levels of government expenditure on the one hand and revenue from taxation, etc., on the other. It is thus tempting to assume that from a gilt-edged point of view all spending cutbacks or tax increases are positive. However, if the additional revenue is produced by raising *indirect* taxes such as VAT or excise duties, this will have an adverse effect on prices and will be negative for the market through its impact on inflation.

The question of how much stock the Government will issue and of what kind is part of the daily bread-and-butter of the gilt-edged analyst's life. Between 1976 and 1985 the state of the money supply at any given time was one of the prime factors influencing the level of sales, but longer-term strategic decisions perhaps reflecting political stances have often determined the type of stock to be offered. For example, from the time the Thatcher Government came to power in 1979 until early 1985 the whole emphasis was on funding in the short or medium areas of the market, eschewing issuing conventional gilts at the long end and issuing index-linked in their place whenever possible. This policy probably had its roots in the disinclination of the Prime Minister and her Cabinet colleagues (whose first priority was to de-escalate inflation and thereby reduce long yields) to burden future generations with (what they considered to be) unnecessarily high-coupon payments a long way into the future. It has also had the effect of leaving the long end of the market free for corporate fixed-interest issues which, if they were to take the pressure of financing companies off the banks, would also assist in moderating monetary growth. Sadly, and despite the capital gains tax concessions in the 1984 and 1985 Finance Acts, very few British companies have yet availed themselves of this opportunity and the gap has been largely filled by overseas borrowers who have created the so-called 'Bulldog' market.

On the demand side, three critical factors are the size of institutional investable cash flows, the natural investment habitats of those institutions with the greatest inflows and the relative attractions to investors of alternative forms of investment, such as money market instruments, equities, property, and overseas securities. Of these, the last mentioned is inextricably bound up with currency considerations as well as the prospects for overseas stock markets, and property investment is essentially long-term in nature. Many institutional investors have upper limits on the proportion of their assets that they are prepared to hold in such categories – and because of the nature of their liabilities most long-term funds tend also to restrict their holdings of cash or money market assets. This leaves what may be termed the 'equity–gilt relationship' in an important position in the determination of the strength of demand for gilts, and this is a factor which should not be underestimated in making medium-term market assessments.

By contrast, there has been to date only an indirect relationship between the US Treasury bond market and gilt-edged yields. This is because up to now only a very few investors have been prepared to treat them as interchangeable alternatives and switch between them in the longer sectors of the two markets. However, this may now start to change since the entry of American houses on to the gilt-edged scene has brought with it a significant amount of professional cross-market arbitraging often allied to currency swaps. A classic example of this occurred in the spring of 1985 when the levels and shapes of the gilt-edged and US Treasury yield curves greatly favoured medium-dated gilts at a time when sterling was recovering fast against the dollar. Even when dealing opportunities like this do not exist there are often sympathetic price movements in the gilt-edged market with those in the New York bond market. These are most prevalent when key economic statistics such as the quarterly GDP figures are released in the United States. All in all, however, the really important relationship between the two markets is the linkage through relative interest rates and the exchange rate at the short end of the market.

5

The fundamental characteristics of gilt-edged stocks

If asked to give a simple description of what represented a gilt-edged stock, the average investor might easily reply by saying that it was a redeemable fixed-interest security issued by or guaranteed by Her Majesty's Government, on which interest would be paid every half-year. Whilst this description covers most of them, it by no means covers all of the stocks that comprise the gilt-edged market.

General Features of Conventional Stocks

In its simplest form the standard gilt-edged stock has a name, a nominal interest rate (known as the 'coupon' rate), and a redemption date.

Name

To all intents and purposes, the name of the stock is of no special significance, except as a matter of identification. There is no difference in the market standing of stocks with different names, such as Treasury, Exchequer, Funding, Conversion, Transport, Electricity, Gas, Redemption and so forth, on account of their name. It may be that certain issues with a given name may be less marketable than others, but this will be for other reasons, such as perhaps the size of the issues outstanding, rather than simply because of their name.

Nominal Rate of Interest (or 'Coupon' Rate)

For the standard gilt-edged stock, this represents the annual amount of interest paid per £100 of nominal stock. In most cases this is paid semi-annually, on fixed days six months apart, e.g. 15th January and 15th July, or 10th March and 10th September, etc. One stock only breaks this rule: Consolidated $2\frac{1}{2}$% stock, which for historical reasons pays four coupons of $\frac{5}{8}$% each year, on the 5th of January, April, July and October. For those who worry about jargon, the word 'coupon' derives from the days of bearer bonds, where, in order to claim one's dividend when it fell due, it was necessary to clip the requisite coupon from one's bond, and present this coupon to a paying agent, usually a bank, in order to obtain one's interest. Since the great majority of gilts nowadays are securities registered at the Bank of England, whence dividends are paid directly to stockholders, coupon clipping has become mostly a thing of the past. However, the words 'coupon' or 'coupon rate' persist in this context, for which one is abundantly thankful – since the phrase 'nominal rate of interest per cent per annum' is, to say the least, unwieldy.

Most gross coupon payments amount to half the stock's coupon rate, but there are exceptions to this rule, notably in cases where the coupon to be paid reflects interest for a period other than a simple half-year. This happens frequently with new issues when the date of issue does not happen to be precisely six months before the first interest payment date, and/or when the new issue is partly paid. In such cases, an adjusted interest payment is made that takes into account both these factors.

The other non-standard interest payments are those related to variable-rate stock and index-linked stock, both of which are specialist subjects dealt with in detail later on in this book, but are distinguished from normal gilts by the simple fact that their half-yearly interest payments are tied to Treasury bill rates in the case of the variable stocks, and to the progress of the Retail Price Index in the case of the index-linked stocks.

Redemption Date

The standard gilt-edged stock will have a specified date on which it is due to be redeemed (repaid) by the Government. A good many have two dates between which they must be redeemed. The Government has the option of redeeming such stock at any time after the first redemption date, and must redeem it at the very latest on the last redemption date. For most stocks, redemption is at par, i.e. £100 per £100 nominal stock, but this is not so in the case of index-linked stocks, where not only are interest payments linked to the Retail Price Index, but redemption values also. Two older stocks, Redemption 3% 1986/96 and Conversion $3\frac{1}{2}$% 1961/after, have sinking funds which accelerate redemption. In the case of the former, the sinking fund has the option of buying in outstanding stock or investing in similar issues (e.g. Gas 3% 1990/95), but with the latter a sum of not less than 1% of the amount outstanding at the end of any half-year in which the daily average price is below 90 is applied in the next half-year to purchasing stock for cancellation.

Size of Issue

Although not part of a stock's name or identification, an important item is the size of any particular issue. At the time of writing, the normal size for an issue of stock is of the order of £1,000 million. There is, however, no such thing as a standard size of issue; the amount of stock being brought into existence at the time of each new issue is obviously tailored to meet the circumstances, but stocks where the issue size is below £500 million or £600 million tend to have restricted marketability in comparison with the larger issues.

The size of issue of any particular stock is one item which can change during its lifetime. When the Government wishes to fund, it has become increasingly commonplace for additional tranches of existing stocks to be issued to the market, rather than continually create completely new entities, which would have the effect of expanding the gilt-edged list and making it unwieldy. By virtue of this tactic, some of the issues which started life as £800 million issues, or £1,000 million issues, have during the course of a few years become over £2,000 million in size. At the end of March 1986 the daddy of them all was Treasury 11¾% 2003/2007, of which there is £3,100 million of stock in existence.

'Tax Free to Non-resident' Status

There are also a significant number of gilt-edged stocks which are exempt from all UK taxation to non-residents of the United Kingdom, on application to the Inland Revenue. A major advantage of these stocks is the payment gross of dividends which would otherwise have tax at basic income tax rate deducted at source. One of the stocks is War 3½% 1952/after, the (in)famous War Loan, which differs from every other stock in the gilt-edged list in that its dividends are automatically paid gross (without tax deduction) to *all* holders, wherever they are resident. This is not to say that dividends from War Loan are not subject to tax in the hands of a UK investor – they are. It is simply that, for historical reasons, the Bank of England does not deduct tax at source, but leaves that pleasure to the subsequent actions of the Inland Revenue.

Gross Accrued Interest, Taxation of Income and Price Conventions

The date 28 February 1986 was a watershed for the gilt-edged market, for on that day the whole basis of taxation of income derived from gilt-edged stocks (and most other fixed-interest stocks) changed radically. Until then the whole of the consideration of any gilt-edged bargain was considered to be a capital item, and only actual dividends received were treated as income for tax purposes. But since that date income has been assessed as accruing on a day-to-day basis, and only the 'clean price' element of a bargain's total value has been considered to be capital. Under the new system income tax is now levied on the sum of the dividends received plus the gross accrued interest at the time of sale less the gross accrued interest at the time of purchase. The effect of this is to ensure that the taxable amount is proportional to the period of time a stock is held; and to remove the ability to convert income into capital by selling stocks full of accrued interest shortly before their ex-dividend dates. It also opened up the way for the abolition of capital gains tax on gilts (and most other fixed-interest stocks) on 2 July 1986. A major repercussion of all this was to cause a change in the way prices of gilt-edged stocks are quoted separating the capital and income components, so that since 28 February 1986 *all* gilts have been quoted as a basic price plus or minus so many days' gross accrued interest.

However, since the whole area of price conventions in gilts has tended to be one of some confusion to many people, and because it is important to understand both the old and the new systems we shall now, at the risk of being pedantic, set out some formal definitions and detail certain mathematical relationships.

Firstly, let us define certain entities:

Market price (MP). This is the market price quoted by the market-makers, published in the press, etc., and at which bargains are struck. This is the price which will be shown as the bargain price on any contract note.

Gross accrued interest (GAI). This is an amount per £100 nominal stock that represents the interest that has accrued on the stock in question in respect of the time period between the most recently paid interest payment date and the current settlement date. In cases where a stock is quoted ex-dividend (XD) in respect of a coupon payment still to be received, the accrued interest relates to the number of days from the settlement date to the date of this forthcoming dividend, *and is a negative quantity*. Where the stock in question is a new issue which has not yet paid its first interest payment, accrued interest is counted from the day of issue, i.e. the day on which cash payments are made in return for the issue of stock. If, as is often the case, such stock is issued partly paid, accrued interest is computed on a proportionate basis (see later examples).

Total price (TP). This is a stock's total cash value per £100 nominal stock. It is the total amount of money (excluding dealing expenses) that would change hands between buyer and seller, should a bargain be struck at a given market price.

Settlement date. Unless specific arrangements have been made for special settlement, gilt-edged bargains are settled on the first business day following the bargain date.

Having defined these items let us now examine the relationships between them.

Under the post-28 February 1986 regime the following relationship applies to *all* gilt-edged stocks:

Total price (TP) = Market price (MP) + Gross accrued interest (GAI).

Before 28 February 1986 gilt-edged prices were quoted in different ways depending on whether the stock had a life to final maturity of five years or less. Stocks of this sort were (and still are) called 'short-dated stocks' or 'shorts', and were quoted in the same way as all stocks are now. But for longer-dated stocks the gross accrued interest was included in the market price, i.e. the total price equalled the quoted price.

Clean price (CP). This is the total price (TP) minus accrued interest. In normal usage, 'clean price' is deemed to mean total price less *gross* accrued interest, but where funds are subject to tax on income, the phraseology 'net clean price' is often encountered. In such cases the net clean price is simply the total price minus the *net* accrued interest after deduction of tax on the accrued interest at the relevant rate.

It is thus clear that post-28 February 1986 (gross) clean prices are identical with market prices, i.e.

$$CP = MP$$

whilst before that date we had the following price relationships:

For short-dated stocks:

Total price (TP) = Market price (MP) + Gross accrued interest (GAI)
Clean price (CP) = Total price (TP) − Gross accrued interest (GAI)
$$= (MP + GAI) - (GAI)$$
$$= \text{Market price (MP)}.$$

For stocks with lives to *final* maturity longer than five years:

Total price (TP) = Market price (MP)
Clean price (CP) = Total price (TP) − Gross accrued interest (GAI)
$$= MP - GAI$$
i.e. = Market price − Gross accrued interest.

Consider now some examples relating to certain stocks as they stood in the market on Wednesday, 26 March 1986 (settlement day: Thursday, 27 March 1986):

1. Treasury 12% 3.11.1987 with a quoted price 101 cum-dividend.

To find the gross accrued interest (GAI), adopt the following procedure:

(a) Establish the date of the most recently-paid interest payment = 3.11.1985.
(b) Calculate the number of days between this date and the settlement date (27.3.1986) = 144 days.
(c) GAI = 12 × 144/365 = 4.734.

Thus the total price (TP) = MP + GAI
$$= 101 + 4.734$$
$$= 105.734.$$

The clean price is found by subtracting the accrued interest from the total price. For a gross fund (i.e. a fund not taxed on income), the (gross) clean price will thus equate to the market price, but for a fund subject to tax at, say, 30%, the net (@ 30% tax) clean price (NCP) is found as:

NCP (@ 30%) = (TP) − (1 − 0.3) × (GAI) = 105.734 − (0.7 × 4.734)
$$= 102.421.$$

Next, let us have a look at a second stock on the same day, 26 March 1986:

2. Exchequer 15% 27.10.1997 with a market price 125 ex-dividend.

The first thing to realise here is the stock is quoted in an ex-dividend form. This means that a buyer of the stock would be acquiring it without the rights to the forthcoming interest payment, i.e. $7\frac{1}{2}$% on 27.4.1986. The gross accrued interest inherent in the stock on this date reflects the time period between this date and the settlement date (27.3.1986) and, since these dates are in reverse order, the accrued interest is negative, viz. number of days between 'last' interest date and settlement date = − 31 days.

Thus, gross accrued interest (GAI) = 15 × (− 31)/365
$$- 1.274.$$

Thus once again the total price (TP) = MP + GAI, but in this case the accrued interest is negative, so that

$$TP = 125 + (-1.274)$$
$$= 123.726.$$

Dividends and Accrued Interest on Partly Paid Stocks

In recent years, it has become increasingly common for new stocks to be issued in a partly-paid form, whereby the issue price is paid in instalments spread over, say, one or two months.

Exchequer $13\frac{1}{4}\%$ 1987 'A' stock is such an example. This was issued on 8 February 1982, at an issue price of $93\frac{1}{4}$ spread as follows:

$$20 \quad \text{on 8 February 1982}$$
$$35 \quad \text{on 8 March 1982}$$
$$38\frac{1}{4} \text{ on 5 April 1982}$$
$$\overline{93\frac{1}{4}}$$

Problem: Calculate the relevant gross accrued interest for bargains done on 26 March 1982 (for settlement 29 March 1982).

For the twenty-eight days between 8 February and 8 March 1982, the stock 'earns' accrued interest at 20/93.25 of the full rate, i.e.

$$13\frac{1}{4} \times 28 \times (20/93.25)/365 = 0.21800.$$

Between 8 March and settlement day 29 March, it 'earns' accrued interest at 55/93.25 of the full rate for the twenty-one days involved, i.e.

$$13\frac{1}{4} \times 21 \times (55/93.25)/365 = 0.450.$$

making the total gross accrued interest for that day 0.668.

Many people make the mistake of thinking that because a stock is, say, £20 paid, for, say, twenty-eight days, it would earn $28 \times 20/100$ days' accrued interest. *This is incorrect.* It is the proportion of the amount paid up to the full issue price that provides the correct scaling factor. This is also the basis under which the Bank of England determines the first coupon payment on such issues.

Ex-dividend Status

The great proportion of gilt-edged debt is in the form of stock registered at the Bank of England, and dividends are paid by the Bank directly to the beneficial owners. The administrative logistics of this requires a certain amount of time to prepare the dividend warrants and arrange for their despatch to the correct owners of stock. To enable this to be done, gilt-edged stocks are made 'ex-dividend' about thirty-seven days before the interest payment is due, and dividend warrants are sent to the holders on the Bank of England's register at the date. After a stock has become 'ex-dividend' or 'XD', a buyer of stock purchases it without the right to receive the next (pending) interest payment, and the market, allowing for this factor, will adjust the *total* price down accordingly. The amount by which the ex-dividend *total* price is lower than the cum-dividend *total* price is approximately equal to the discounted value of the pending dividend and thus varies according to market conditions and short-term interest rates. The effect of this on *market* (quoted) prices is normally to make the ex-dividend *market* price about $\frac{1}{16}$ or $\frac{1}{8}$ higher than the previous day's cum-dividend *market* price, but this can vary a bit depending on the quirks of the calendar (since not all half-years contain the same number of days).

The precise formula for ascertaining ex-dividend dates has never (to the author's knowledge) been formally published, but from practical experience over many years the following rules appear to apply.

1. The basic rule is that the ex-dividend date is five weeks and two days (thirty-seven days) before the relevant interest payment date. If this date is a weekend date or public holiday, then the ex-dividend is the first business day following it.
2. The basic rule above does not apply to Consol 2$\frac{1}{2}$% stock, which pays interest four times a year on the 5th of January, April, July and October. For historic reasons this stock goes ex-dividend on the first day of the previous month, i.e. 1st December, 1st March, 1st June, 1st September, or the next business day if this is a holiday or weekend date. This rule also extends to any other stock, which has dividend payments on any of these days, e.g. Funding 5$\frac{3}{4}$% 87/91, Treasury 8% 02/06, and Treasury 3% 1966 or after, and any others which have 5th January, 5th April, or 5th July, 5th October dividend dates.
3. These two rules used (it was thought) to cover all possible eventualities, until the authorities in their great wisdom issued Exchequer 10$\frac{1}{2}$% 1987 with dividend dates 6th April, 6th October. This created the anomaly that applying Rule (1) above would normally give this stock ex-dividend dates 28th February (29th in leap years) and 30th August, both of which pre-date the ex-dividend dates of Consol 2$\frac{1}{2}$%, etc., despite the fact that the dividends are to be paid a day later. To avoid this juxta-positioning, the Bank of England decided to make the stock go ex-dividend on the same basis as Consol 2$\frac{1}{2}$% stock, and have indicated that this principle would be extended to any other stock where a similar problem may occur, i.e. any stocks with interest dates 6th, 7th or 8th January and July, or 6th, 7th or 8th April and October. It is the author's considered opinion that the Bank of England will probably manage to avoid giving new stocks such awkward dividend dates in the future!

Special Ex-dividend Status

In addition to the ex-dividend period defined above, for gilt-edged stocks other than 'shorts' (of less than five years' life to final maturity) and War 3$\frac{1}{2}$% 1952/ after, there is a three-week period immediately prior to the ex-dividend date in which stocks can be traded either cum-dividend in the ordinary way, or specially ex-dividend (Sp. XD). The effect of this facility is to create an overlap between the market in a stock cum-dividend and ex-dividend, thus allowing market makers to match buyers and sellers in either mode over a three-week period, rather than experience unnecessary congestion in business over the official ex-dividend date.

Non-standard Gilt-edged Stocks

At the beginning of this chapter we outlined the basic features of conventional gilt-edged stocks. The use of the word 'conventional' in this context implies that there are also other gilts with differing characteristics, and these fall into three categories:

1. Convertible stocks.
2. Variable-rate stocks.
3. Index-linked stocks.

Convertible Stocks

These are similar in most regards to the standard conventional gilt, expect that they carry the option for the owner to convert his or her holding into predefined amounts of a different gilt-edged stock at some time or times in the future. Normally, they take the form of a short or short-medium stock that can be converted into a longer issue. The conversion terms are normally arranged so as to make this a more expensive way of acquiring the longer stock than purchasing it in the market at the outset – the difference in price being the value to the investor of having the option to convert or not.

The first of these stocks was issued in 1973, and was Treasury 9% Convertible 1980; each £100 nominal was convertible into £110 nominal of Treasury 9% 2000 as an alternative to redemption on 3 March 1980. As things turned out, market values on that day were such that a holding of this new stock would have been worth rather less than the straightforward redemption value of the Treasury 9% 1980, and as a result the conversion opportunity was exercised only by a handful of people (presumably) in the search for some form of esoteric wallpaper! Of the £1,000 million Treasury 9% Convertible Stock 1980, only £577,364.59 was converted into Treasury 9% 2000, making this stock at that time one of the smallest-ever gilt-edged issues, and one which only rarely traded in the gilt-edged market. Needless to say, the administrative inconvenience of having a tiny issue such as this in existence did not appeal to the Bank of England, and for its next sally into the field of convertibles it changed its *modus operandi*.

Subsequent convertible issues have worked rather differently, and the second convertible issue, Exchequer 12% Convertible 1985, is a good example of how the latter-day system operates.

The conversion terms of this second stock, Exchequer 12% Convertible 1985, permit the holder to convert into Exchequer $13\frac{1}{2}$% 1992 (an existing issue) on various terms during the life of the stock, not simply at redemption. These were as follows:

On 22 September 1981	£99	nominal of Exchequer $13\frac{1}{2}$% 1992 for each £100 nominal Exchequer 12% Convertible 1985
On 22 March 1982	£98	,,
On 22 September 1982	£97	,,
On 22 March 1983	£95	,,
On 22 September 1983	£92	,,

Variable-rate Stocks

It is a matter of history that, during the mid 1970s, the UK authorities started to place an increasing amount of importance in the month-by-month management of the monetary aggregates – in particular, DCE, M_3 and Sterling M_3. In order to neutralise the excess money supply in the system, they sought to make sales of gilt-edged stock to the non-bank public. This seemingly simple plan often proved rather less easy to implement in practice, as a result of an essential 'Catch 22' element involved. UK domestic investors, especially the financial institutions (who were then pretty well awash with gilts anyway), felt that they needed to have the prospect of falling interest rates, and some confidence that the money supply was in control, if they were to invest further in the gilt-edged market; and, whilst exactly the reverse conditions pertained, these potential buyers tended to be extremely conspicuous by their absence. Thus, when the authorities badly needed to sell stock, the buyers were unwilling, and vice versa.

How, then, could the authorities get over this impasse? The search was joined for some form of capital protective instrument that would be saleable at times when interest rates were already high but not necessarily expected to fall. The preferred solution to this problem was the issuance of a number of variable-rate stocks, whose characteristics are very similar to those floating-rate stocks now well known in international markets. There was, however, one very distinct difference between the variable-rate gilt-edged stocks and other 'floaters'. Whereas it is customary on most floating rate stocks to have each coupon determined before the beginning of the period for which interest is to be paid, the UK authorities in their wisdom decreed that the variable coupon should be linked to the average Treasury bill rate over the period involved. Apart from anything else, this made calculations of such key items as accrued interest extremely cumbersome, and the fact that the stocks were issued with lives of less than five years to maturity (i.e. they were shorts), meant that they were much more suitable to the banking system than to the non-bank public, at which they were primarily aimed.

The precise details of the method used to determine both the coupon payments and the day-to-day accrued interest of variable-rate stocks are shown in the appendix at the back of this book. At this juncture, it is probably sufficient to state that for those variable-rate stocks dated 1981, 1982 and 1983 (i.e. all those issued up to the time of writing), the coupon rate was set as the average Treasury bill tender rate over the relevant period, plus $\frac{1}{2}$%.

Index-linked Stocks

Of the three categories of non-standard gilts, these are the most recent to arrive on the investment scene. They first saw the light of day following the 1981 Budget speech on 10 March 1981, when the Chancellor of the Exchequer, the Rt Hon. Sir Geoffrey Howe, announced the issue of £1,000 million in 2% Index-linked Stock 1996. The issue was made by tender on 27 March 1981, and was restricted to pension funds, or similar institutions writing pension business. Between then and the Budget of 1982 there were further issues of similar long-dated stocks, namely:

£1,000 million 2% Index-linked Stock 2006.

£750 million 2½% Index-linked Stock 2011.

Whilst there were certainly some sound reasons for restricting ownership of these stocks to pension funds and the like, this did not enhance their marketability. This factor requires the existence of a body of willing buyers and willing sellers at any given price and time, which one-class ownership tends to preclude. Since it seemed to be the Government's intention to do a fair part of its funding by selling index-linked debt, this was unfortunate. Finally, after (it is suspected) much agonising in the Treasury and the Bank of England, it was announced in the 1982 Budget speech that henceforth ownership restrictions were to be removed, and index-linked gilt-edged stocks were to be made available to all and sundry, non-residents included, and at the same time a medium-dated issue, £750 million in 2% Index-linked Stock 1988, was created.

The form of indexation used by HM Government gets over the sort of problems experienced with variable-rate stock. Each index-linked payment, either of interest or capital, is related to the General Index of Retail Prices (RPI) for the month eight months prior to that in which it is received. Values are adjusted by the ratio of this RPI to a 'base RPI' which is that pertaining to the month eight months before the month of issue.

The following example illustrates the *modus operandi*:

> 2% Index-linked Stock 1988 was issued in March 1982. Counting back eight months from this date brings one to July 1981 as the base month for this stock. The Retail Price Index for July 1981 was 297.1, and this is established as the base RPI for this stock.
>
> The stock is due to be redeemed on 30 March 1988. Again, counting back eight months, one arrives at July 1987. The capital repayment to be made on redemption will be 100 × (RPI for July 1987)/(RPI for July 1981).
>
> Coupon payments are computed in an identical fashion. The nominal coupon rate is here 2% per annum, i.e. 1% per half-year, index-linked. The coupon payment to be made on, say, 30 September 1985, will be 1 × (RPI for January 1985)/(RPI for July 1981), and so on.

One main reason for choosing this form of eight-month-lagged indexation was to ensure that the next receivable coupon could be determined well in advance of the time period to which it related. Since gilt-edged stocks normally become quoted 'ex-dividend' about thirty-seven days before the due interest payment date, and since the RPI for each month is announced in the middle of the following month, it is clear that eight months is the minimum practical lag period.

It does, however, have the somewhat unusual effect of making the redemption value adjusted for inflation up to the date of issue other than 100 (normally higher than 100), and by the reverse token offers no protection against inflation over the last eight months of its life.

Two simple examples illustrate these points:

1. As shown above, the base RPI for Index-linked 2% 1988 was 297.1. The RPI for the month of March 1982 in which it was issued was 313.4 (although this was not known until mid April). Thus, even if there were

to be no inflation after the date of issue, and the RPI were to remain constant at 313.4 for ever more, the stock would still be redeemed at $(100 \times 313.4/297.1) = 105.486$.

2. Now, if we vary the inflation scenario a little, and let there be zero inflation until July 1987, followed by a sudden burst of hyper-inflation between July 1987 and March 1988, in which prices double so that the RPI becomes 626.8 by that date, the redemption value will still only be

$$100 \times \text{RPI of July 1987/RPI July 1981}$$
$$= 100 \times 313.4/297.1$$
$$= 105.486$$

just as before, with no compensation for the July 1987–March 1988 hyper-inflationary period.

For many index-linked stocks with long periods to maturity this feature is not over-important, but it is a vital factor for stocks where the last eight months to maturity is a significant proportion of their total life, and once an index-linked stock moves into its last eight months' life, it becomes a fixed-interest stock pure and simple.

6

The mathematics of the gilt-edged market: redemption yields, compound interest, and all that

Most people who invest money normally have two main considerations to take into account when choosing where it should be placed: security and rate of return. The security aspect of gilt-edged stocks has been treated elsewhere in this book; this chapter deals with rates of return and yield.

Flat Yield and Redemption Yield

To the layman, the concept of yield is a simple one, normally being thought of as the dividend, rental or interest rate, divided by price. Whilst this definition may suffice for equities and property, it is far from satisfactory for gauging the returns from redeemable securities where allowance has to be made for capital gains or losses to redemption, as well as income flow. It is thus timely at this point to describe and define 'flat yield' and 'redemption yield'.

Flat yield (alternatively called 'interest yield', or 'income yield') is the gross coupon rate divided by the *clean* price of a given stock:

$$f = \frac{g}{(P - a)} \tag{6.1}$$

where g represents the stock's coupon rate
P represents the stock's total price
a represents the stock's accrued interest.

As an example, consider a stock with a 12% coupon, priced at $92\frac{1}{8}$, with forty-three days' accrued interest included in the price.

In this case the flat yield is

$$f = \frac{12}{92.125 - (12 \times 43/365)} \tag{6.2}$$

$$= 0.1323$$

i.e. 13.23% gross.

Whilst flat yields are most frequently considered in gross terms, it is perfectly acceptable to use the equation (6.1) to calculate *net flat yields*, where both the coupon rate and the accrued interest have been subjected to income tax.

Using the same example as above, but applying tax at a rate of 30% on income, produces a net flat yield

$$= \frac{12(1 - 0.30)}{92.125 - [12(1 - 0.30) \times 43/365]}$$

$$= 0.0922$$

i.e. 9.22% net of tax at 30% on income.

It is important to note that, because the accrued interest quantity is 'netted' as well as the coupon rate, the net flat yield is *not* equal to the net of the gross flat yield (except when the accrued interest is zero).

Redemption yield is a measure of value which combines the benefits to the investor of both the income flow and the eventual capital profit (or loss) to its redemption value (not always necessarily at par) in a single figure, expressed as a rate of return per cent per annum.

There is a convention concerning yields which it is important to understand properly. Because (most) gilt-edged and (most) other fixed-interest stocks in the United Kingdom make interest payments every half-year, redemption yields are computed as rates of return per half-year, and then doubled. Thus, when one speaks of a redemption yield of, say, 11.56% per annum, the true rate being used is actually 5.78% per half-year.

For those people who may not at first sight appreciate the significance of this, it is worth considering the difference between the compounded values of:

(a) 11.56% compounded over ten years, and
(b) 5.78% compounded over twenty half-years.

(a) $= 1.1156^{10} = 2.986$
(b) $= 1.0578^{20} = 3.077$, a difference of some 3%.

The foregoing introduces the reader to an elementary facet of compound interest theory, on which all redemption yield analysis is based. Because it is fundamental to the whole of this subject, the following section is included at this juncture, before going on to a formal definition of a redemption yield.

Compound Interest Theory

Imagine that it is possible to invest only in an investment that gives a constant return of y% per annum paid half-yearly.

An initial investment of 1 would, after the first half-year, produce interest of $y/200$. (For the sake of convenience and also because it concurs with actuarial notation, this value of $y/200$ is denoted by the symbol i.) After being credited with interest of i, the total value of the investment has thus grown to $(1 + i)$. If this amount is left invested for a further six months, it will produce a second interest payment – this time equal to $i(1 + i)$.

Adding in this, the total value of investment now becomes

$$1 + i + i(1 + i)$$
$$= 1 + 2i + i^2$$
$$= (1 + i)^2.$$

This procedure can be repeated *ad nauseam*, but the essential feature of compound interest theory now becomes patently clear – that the future compounded value of 1 invested for n half-years at a rate of $y\%$ per annum

$$= (1 + i)^n, \quad \text{where} \quad i = y/200.$$

Obversely, the present (discounted) value of 1 receivable in n half-years' time

$$= \frac{1}{(1 + i)^n}.$$

Again, following actuarial notation, this value is written v^n

$$\text{where} \quad v = \frac{1}{1 + i}.$$

We have now established the basis for calculating the present value (PV) of any future payment of either capital or dividend given a particular interest rate at which to discount them.

For instance, the PV of a series of payments of 6, 8, 10, 15, 20, 25, at the end of 1, 2, 3, 4, 5, 6 half-years respectively, is the expression

$$PV = 6v + 8v^2 + 10v^3 + 15v^4 + 20v^5 + 25v^6.$$

If the rate of interest to be used in this discounting process is, say, $y = 10\%$ per annum,

$$\text{then} \quad v = \frac{1}{(1 + y/200)} = \frac{1}{1.05}$$

$$\text{and} \quad PV = \frac{6}{1.05} + \frac{8}{1.05^2} + \frac{10}{1.05^3} + \frac{15}{1.05^4} + \frac{20}{1.05^5} + \frac{25}{1.05^6}$$

$$= 5.714 + 7.256 + 8.638 + 12.341 + 15.671 + 18.655$$

$$= 68.275.$$

Taking another example, where the benefits to be received are half-yearly interest payments of 6 over the next three years, followed by capital repayment of 100 at the end of that time, the present value can be written as

$$PV = 6v + 6v^2 + 6v^3 + 6v^4 + 6v^5 + 6v^6 + 100v^6$$

$$\text{where} \quad v = \frac{1}{(1 + i)} \quad \text{and} \quad i = y/200.$$

We have thus established from first principles the formula for calculating the present value or price of the investment producing such a series of benefits – i.e. a 12% coupon rate three-year fixed-interest stock, redeemable at 100.

Table 6.1 shows the relationship between price (present value) and yield in this example, using three different yield bases, 10%, 12% and 14%.

Table 6.1   *Relationship between present value and yield (using yield bases of 10%, 12% and 14%)*

Yield % p.a. $= y$	10%	12%	14%
$i = y/200$	0.05	0.06	0.07
$1 + i$	1.05	1.06	1.07
$v = 1/(1 + i)$	0.95238	0.94340	0.93458
$6v$	5.714	5.660	5.607
$6v^2$	5.442	5.340	5.241
$6v^3$	5.183	5.038	4.898
$6v^4$	4.936	4.752	4.577
$6v^5$	4.701	4.484	4.278
$6v^6$	4.477	4.230	3.998
Present value of income flow	30.453	29.504	28.599
PV of capital repayment $= 100v^6$	74.622	70.496	66.634
Total present value $=$ price	105.075	100.000	95.233

Redemption Yield: Definition and Equations

DISCOUNTED CASH FLOW

Once an understanding of the method of constructing a stock's value has been grasped, it is now possible to make the following formal definition:

A redemption yield is that rate of interest at which the total discounted values of future payments of income and capital equate to the current total price.

It has to be realised that, whereas given a particular yield it is possible to compute the corresponding price of a stock, there is no explicit formula for the reverse operation – i.e. given price, compute yield. Instead it is necessary to use some form of iterative process to solve the problem, and computer programs used for this purpose do just that, albeit at a very fast speed. But for those people who ask the perennial question 'What is the formula for yield?', the answer is that there isn't one – there is only a formula for price.

In the simple case where a stock is standing at a dividend payment date (and is quoted without the right to receive that dividend, i.e. ex-dividend), the following formula applies:

$$P = \frac{g}{2}v + \frac{g}{2}v^2 + \frac{g}{2}v^3 + \ldots + \frac{g}{2}v^n + 100v^n \tag{6.3}$$

where g denotes the coupon rate
        n denotes the period to maturity in half-years
        v $= 1/(1 + \text{yield}/200)$
and P represents the *total price* of the stock inclusive of accrued interest.

This can be rewritten as

$$P = \frac{g}{2}(v + v^2 + v^3 + \ldots + v^n) + 100v^n \tag{6.4}$$

The expression with brackets is known actuarially as an 'annuity certain', and is denoted by the symbol $a_{\overline{n}|}$.

The components of $a_{\overline{n}|}$, i.e. v, v^2, $v^3 \ldots v^n$ form a geometric series, whose sum can be found by this (neat) method:

$$a_{\overline{n}|} = v + v^2 + v^3 + \ldots + v^n$$

$$\text{Therefore} \quad va_{\overline{n}|} = \qquad v^2 + v^3 + \ldots + v^n + v^{n+1}$$

$$\text{Thus} \quad (1 - v)a_{\overline{n}|} = v + 0 + 0 + \ldots + 0 - v^{n+1}$$

$$\text{leading to} \quad a_{\overline{n}|} = \frac{(v - v^{n+1})}{(1 - v)} = \frac{(1 - v^n)}{i},$$

a formula frequently found in actuarial work.

Equations (6.3) and (6.4), however, are specific to the case of a stock being valued on a dividend payment date; in the more general case the basic equation of value is

$$P = \frac{g}{2}(v^q + v^{q+1} + \ldots + v^{q+n}) + Rv^{q+n} \tag{6.5}$$

where g denotes the annual coupon rate

      R denotes the redemption value

      q denotes the time (measured in half-years) between the current settlement date and the next receivable interest or dividend payment date

and n denotes the time (in half-years) from the next receivable interest date to redemption.

For convenience again, this can be written as:

$$P = \frac{g}{2}[v^q(1 + v + v^2 + \ldots + v^n)] + Rv^{q+n}$$

$$= v^q\left[\frac{g}{2}(1 + a_{\overline{n}|}) + Rv^n\right] \tag{6.6}$$

Given the *total price P*, solving this equation for v and using the relationship $y = 200[(1/v) - 1]$ enables yields to be determined.

Several variations of this basic equation exist to take into account the incidence of tax on either income of capital gains, and also to deal with the complications caused by partly-paid stocks.

Net redemption yields. Prior to 28 February 1986 net redemption yields after allowing for income tax on dividend payments only were established from the equation (assuming tax to be deducted at source)

$$P = \frac{g}{2}(1 - t)(v^q + v^{q+1} + \ldots + v^{q+n}) + Rv^{q+n} \tag{6.7}$$

where t = the rate of tax on income/100, e.g. when income tax rate = 30%,
$t = 0.3$, $(1 - t) = 0.7$.

Under the accrued interest scheme which came into operation on 28 February 1986 an investor is additionally liable to income tax on the gross accrued interest at the time of sale, with a similar offsetting tax credit relating to the gross accrued interest at the time of purchase. According to the terms of the 1985 Finance Act these tax payments are deemed to be payable (or receivable) on the next actual dividend date following disposal or acquisition. Thus in order to compute net redemption yields under these arrangements it is necessary to know that the size of these items, let us say, $= a$ at purchase and $= b$ at sale; and the time periods between acquisition and the next following dividend date, say, $= s$, and between sale and its next following dividend date, say, $= z$. Given all these quantities the general equation of value for net redemption yields becomes

$$P - tav^s = \frac{g}{2}(1 - t)(v^q + v^{q+1} + \ldots + v^{q+n}) + Rv^{q+n} - tbv^{q+n+z}.$$

The final term in this equation is usually redundant since in most cases redemption takes place on a scheduled dividend date. In such cases $b = 0$ and the relationship simplifies to

$$P = tav^s + \frac{g}{2}(1 - t)(v^q + v^{q+1} + \ldots + v^{q+n}) + Rv^{q+n} \tag{6.8}$$

One cannot emphasise too strongly that the item P used throughout this analysis is the *total price* of the stock and (since February 1986) is composed of its quoted price, Q, plus gross accrued interest, a. If one chooses to write $P = Q + a$ the above equation transforms to

$$Q = \frac{g}{2}(1 - t)(v^q + v^{q+1} + \ldots + v^{q+n}) + Rv^{q+n} - a[1 - tv^s] \tag{6.9}$$

which is the generally accepted net redemption yield equation under the accrued interest taxation scheme.

No mention has been made so far of capital gains tax, mainly because since 2 July 1986 this tax has no longer been applicable to disposals of gilt-edged (and 'qualifying' corporate bonds) by investors. However as mentioned in Chapter 3 there are many other market participants for whom gilt-edged transactions form part of their trade or business (as opposed to being considered investments), and in such cases both dividends and capital gains are treated as components of their overall profits and subjected to corporation tax accordingly. It is important to realise that the accrued interest scheme does not apply to such traders so that for them their general net redemption yield equation takes the form,

$$P = Q + a = \frac{g}{2}(1-c)(v^q + v^{q+1} + \ldots + v^{q+n}) + [R - c(R-P)]v^{q+n} \quad (6.10)$$

where c = the rate of corporation tax$/100$ (e.g. when corporation tax = 35%, $c = 0.35$).

Where stocks are partly paid the outstanding calls due form part of the 'price side' of the equation, e.g.

$$P + C_1 v^{m_1} + C_2 v^{m_2} + \ldots$$

where P denotes the total partly paid price
and C_1, C_2 denote the calls dues
and m_1, m_2 denote the time periods (in half-years) between the current settlement date and the dates of payment of those calls.

With partly paid stocks there is also liable to be a further complication: because the stock is partly paid, the first interest payment will most often be non-standard, i.e. not equal to half the coupon rate. If this first (non-standard) coupon payment is represented by g^*, then the following equations apply:

For investors under the accrued scheme,

$$Q + a + (C_1 v^{m_1} + C_2 v^{m_2} + \ldots) - tav^s$$

$$= (1-t)\left[g^* v^q + \frac{g}{2}(v^{q+1} + \ldots + v^{q+n}) \right] + R v^{q+n} \quad (6.11)$$

whilst for traders in securities subject to corporation tax,

$$Q + a + (C_1 v^{m_1} + C_2 v^{m_2} + \ldots)$$

$$= (1-c)\left[g^* v^q + \frac{g}{2}(v^{q+1} + \ldots + v^{q+n}) \right]$$

$$+ R v^{q+n} - c(R - Q - a - C_1 - C_2 - \ldots)v^{q+n} \quad (6.12)$$

Net Cash Flow Yields

The problem with all the above approaches to net yields is that in every case there is an implicit assumption that the rate of tax in question will remain constant during the life of the investment. In practice this is not always the case. For example, the progressive reduction in corporation tax between 1982/83 and 1986/87 gave rise to five different rates ranging from 52% down to 35% during this period. The hard facts of the matter are that in order to make truly meaningful net present value assessments of a specific stock's benefits to a taxed investor or trader it is really necessary to build a detailed model of every item of net cash flow and discount them individually rather than use generalised formulae. When such a method is used the rates of return so obtained are termed 'net cash flow yields'.

Redemption Yield and Total Return

It will not have escaped notice that in the foregoing section there has been a welter of mathematical formulae, and whilst these are essential in a book such as this, they may have tended to obscure the scene for the less than mathematical of readers who may wish to have a more qualitative answer to the question 'What exactly is a redemption yield?'

To help in this respect Table 6.2 details the prices of three different stocks, with coupon rates of 3%, 9% and 15% respectively, valued on a constant gross redemption yield basis of 12%, using the formulae established earlier. To get an idea of how a redemption yield combines both the income and capital components of total return, it is instructive to look at the return produced from holding any of these stocks over some sample six-month periods.

Table 6.2   *Yield 12% per annum compounded semi-annually*

Term (years)	3% coupon	9% coupon	15% coupon
0.5	95.7547	98.5849	101.4151
1.0	91.7497	97.2499	102.7501
1.5	87.9714	95.9904	104.0095
2.0	84.4070	94.8023	105.1977
2.5	81.0443	93.6814	106.3185
3.0	77.8720	92.6240	107.3760
3.5	74.8793	91.6264	108.3736
4.0	72.0559	90.6853	109.3147
4.5	69.3924	89.7974	110.2025
5.0	66.8796	88.9598	111.0401
5.5	64.5090	88.1696	111.8303
6.0	62.2727	87.4242	112.5758
6.5	60.1629	86.7209	113.2790
7.0	58.1725	86.0575	113.9425
7.5	56.2949	85.4316	114.5684
8.0	54.5235	84.8411	115.1588
8.5	52.8523	84.2841	115.7159
9.0	51.2758	83.7586	116.2414
9.5	49.7885	83.2628	116.7372
10.0	48.3853	82.7951	117.2049

Firstly, consider the total return brought about by holding the 9% coupon stock over the time when its maturity reduces from ten years to nine-and-a-half years. At the end of this time a gross coupon of $4\frac{1}{2}$ will be received. From the table above it can be seen that, *whilst the stock stays on a 12% gross redemption yield basis*, its price will move over this period from 82.7951 to 83.2628 – a capital gain of 0.4677. Combining these two elements produces a total return of 4.9677 on an initial value of 82.7951. The percentage return after the six months is therefore $100 \times 4.9677/82.79513 = 6.00\%$, equivalent to 12% per annum.

It can be shown that the same result will be obtained from any other pair of adjacent values in the above table, even when a stock is above par and the capital element is negative.

This approach can now be expanded further by the following logical approach. Since the total return over each separate six-monthly period, using this price progression, is equal to 6%, then the total compound interest rate of return over the whole period will be 6% per half-year – i.e. 12% per annum using the standard convention.

However, the important words in the last paragraph are '*using this price progression*', for the above result will not occur in any other circumstances, except perhaps by chance. Once this is fully appreciated it becomes easier to understand what a redemption yield is, and equally importantly what it is not. A redemption yield is, as stated earlier, the rate of interest at which the sum of all discounted future benefits to be obtained from an investment equate to current price. *It is not a guaranteed compound rate of return to be earned from making an investment at that price.* For that to happen would require all further coupon payments to be investable on precisely that same yield basis also, which in practice is highly unlikely.

This brings us to the next important concept – that of the 'roll-up' rate. The roll-up rate of interest is the rate at which (it is considered that) forthcoming coupon or interest payments can be invested – or 'rolled-up' – in future. If the roll-up rate is greater than the initial redemption yield then the realised rate of return will exceed the redemption yield, and vice versa.

The importance of roll-up rate considerations are greatest when dealing with higher-coupon stocks and long maturities, but the fixed interest analyst should remember the existence of this factor at all times, especially when making comparisons between stocks of widely differing coupon rates.

As an example of this factor, it is worth looking at Tables 6.3 and 6.4 which show the results of investing £100,000 by purchasing a holding of our 9% ten-year stock (neither a particularly high coupon nor long-dated maturity), on a 12% gross redemption yield, and compounding the dividend flows by reinvesting in the same stock on one of the two following bases:

1. Using a roll-up rate of 12%, by assuming the price stays on a constant 12% gross redemption yield.
2. Using a roll-up rate of 9%, by assuming the stock moves immediately to par and remains there.

Using a 12% roll-up rate, £100,000 becomes £320,713 and the realised compound rate of return is (surprise, surprise!) 12% per annum. With a 9% roll-up rate the accumulated value is some £29,427 less, at £291,286, and the realised return just over 1% less at 10.98%.

Whilst the two schedules shown in Tables 6.3 and 6.4 are instructive in showing how the compounding effect can work, they are – to say the least – cumbersome, and the figures quoted above can be derived more elegantly thus:

Let us take a general example of a stock with coupon rate = g per annum, term to maturity = n 1/2 years and current price = P. If it is only possible to reinvest coupons as they occur at $Z\%$, i.e. using a roll-up rate of $Z\%$, then for every £100 nominal stock the accumulated value at maturity will consist of the sum of the following:

(i) Capital repayment at redemption = 100

Table 6.3   *Compound accumulation of a 9% ten-year stock on a constant 12% reinvestment basis*

Cash for investment (£)	Term to maturity (years)	Price (GRY = 12%)	Nominal stock purchased (£)	Total nominal stock (£)	Coupon payment at end half-year (£)
100,000.00	10.0	82.79513	120,780.05	120,780.05	5,435.10
5,435.10	9.5	83.26283	6,527.65	127,307.70	5,728.85
5,728.85	9.0	83.75861	6,839.71	134,147.41	6,036.63
6,036.63	8.5	84.28412	7,162.24	141,309.65	6,358.93
6,358.93	8.0	84.84116	7,495.10	148,804.75	6,696.21
6,696.21	7.5	85.43163	7,838.10	156,642.85	7,048.93
7,048.93	7.0	86.05753	8,190.95	164,833.80	7,417.52
7,417.52	6.5	86.72098	8.553.32	173,387.12	7,802,42
7,802.42	6.0	87.42424	8,924.78	182,311.90	8,204.04
8,204.04	5.5	88.16969	9,304.82	191,616.72	8,622.75
8,622.75	5.0	88.95988	9,692.86	201,309.58	9,058.93
9,058.93	4.5	89.79747	10,088.18	211,397.76	9,512.90
9,512.90	4.0	90.68532	10,490.01	221,887.77	9,984.95
9,984.95	3.5	91.62643	10,897.46	232,785.22	10,475.34
10,475.34	3.0	92.62402	11,309.52	244,094.75	10,984.26
10,984.26	2.5	93.68146	11,725.12	255,819.87	11,511.89
11,511.89	2.0	94.80234	12,143.04	267,962.91	12,058.33
12,058.33	1.5	95.99048	12,562.01	280,524.92	12,623.62
12,623.62	1.0	97.24991	12,980.60	293,505.52	13,207.75
13,207.75	0.5	98.58491	13,397.33	306,902.85	13,810.63

Redemption capital value $\qquad$ 306,902.85

Final coupon payment $\qquad$ 13,810.63

Total accumulated value (reinvesting at a constant 12% GRY) = £320,713.48

Since $(320{,}713.48/100{,}000)^{1/20} = 1.06$, the realised semi-annually compounded rate of return = 12% p.a.

(ii) The final coupon payment $\qquad = g/2$

(iii) The compounded value of the coupon 6 months from maturity
$$= (g/2)(1 + Z/200)$$

(iv) The compounded value of the coupon 1 year from maturity
$$= (g/2)(1 + Z/200)^2$$

. . . .

and so on, until

. . . .

(xxi) The compounded value of the coupon $(n-1)$ 1/2 years from maturity
$$= (g/2)(1 + Z/200)^{n-1}.$$

Summing these items produces a total accumulated value of

$$100 + (g/2)[1 + (1 + Z/200) + (1 + Z/200)^2 + \ldots + (1 + Z/200)^n]$$

$$= 100 + \frac{(g/2)[(1 + j)^n - 1]}{j} \quad \text{where } j \text{ represents } Z/200.$$

The item $\dfrac{(1 + j)^n - 1}{j}$ is another actuarial function and is often written as $s\frac{i}{\overline{n}}$.

Table 6.4   *Compound accumulation of a 9% ten-year stock initially priced on a 12% gross redemption yield basis but accumulating dividends at a 9% reinvestment rate*

Cash for investment (£)	Term to maturity (years)	Gross redemption yield	Price	Nominal stock purchased (£)	Total nominal stock (£)	Coupon payment at end half-year (£)
100,000.00	10.0	12%	82.79513	120,780.05	120,780.05	5,435.10
5,435.10	9.5	9%	100	5,435.10	126,215.15	5,679.68
5,679.68	9.0	9%	100	5,679.68	131,894.83	5,935.27
5,935.27	8.5	9%	100	5,935.27	137,830.10	6,202.35
6,202.35	8.0	9%	100	6,202.35	144,032.45	6,481.46
6,481.46	7.5	9%	100	6,481.46	160,513.91	6,773.13
6,773.13	7.0	9%	100	6,773.13	157,287.04	7,077.92
7,077.92	6.5	9%	100	7,077.92	164,364.96	7,396.42
7,396.42	6.0	9%	100	7,396.42	171,761.38	7,729.26
7,729.26	5.5	9%	100	7,729.26	179,490.64	8,077.08
8,077.08	5.0	9%	100	8,077.08	187,567.72	8,440.55
8,440.55	4.5	9%	100	8,440.55	196,008.27	8,820.37
8,820.37	4.0	9%	100	8,820.37	204,828.64	9,217.29
9,217.29	3.5	9%	100	9,217.29	214,045.93	9,632.07
9,632.07	3.0	9%	100	9,632.07	223,678.00	10,065.10
10,065.10	2.5	9%	100	10,065.10	233,743.50	10,518.46
10,518.46	2.0	9%	100	10,518.46	244,261.97	10,991.79
10,991.79	1.5	9%	100	10,991.79	255,253.75	11,486.42
11,486.42	1.0	9%	100	11,486.42	266,740.17	12,003.31
12,003.31	0.5	9%	100	12,003.31	278,743.48	12,543.46

Redemption capital value   278,743.48

Final coupon payment   12,543.46

Total accumulated value on this reinvestment basis = £291,286.94

Which represents a compound realised rate of return of 10.98% p.a. (compounded semi-annually)

In the second of our previous examples the term to maturity was ten years, so that $n = 20$. The coupon rate was 9%, so $g = 9$, $g/2 = 4.5$ and the reinvestment rate for dividends was 9%, i.e. $Z = 9$, $j = 0.045$. Applying this formula gives the following results:

For every £100 nominal stock the accumulated value at maturity

$$= 100 + 4.5(1.045^{20} - 1)/0.045$$
$$= 100 + 141.1714$$
$$= 241.1714.$$

At the outset the price of £100 nominal stock (on a 12% gross yield basis) was 82.7951. To find the compound rate of return over the ten years represented by these values it is necessary to solve the simple equation

$$82.7951(1 + r)^{20} = 241.1714$$
$$(1 + r)^{20} = 241.1714/82.7951$$
$$= 2.912869.$$
Thus $(1 + r) = 1.0549$
and $r = 0.0549,$

equivalent to a compound rate of $0.0549 \times 200 = 10.98\%$, as previously calculated.

The use of the functions $a_{\overline{n}|}$, v^n, $s_{\overline{n}|}$, are basic to a whole range of compound interest calculations, and any aspiring gilt-edged analyst should aim to be totally proficient in their application.

Accumulated Returns

There is no widely accepted name used to describe the compound rates of return found by assuming varying 'roll-up' rates for dividend accumulation, but the expression 'accumulated returns' is broadly descriptive, and this nomenclature will be used in the book for that purpose.

Whilst it has already been demonstrated that if the roll-up rate is lower than the redemption yield, the accumulated return will also be lower, and vice versa, what has not yet been shown is how great the differential effect can prove to be between stocks of widely differing coupons.

Let us now compare the prospective accumulated returns yields of two twenty-year stocks, priced on a 12% gross redemption yield basis, the first having a coupon rate of 3%, and the second a coupon rate of 15%, if, say, a 7% roll-up rate is assumed.

Stock A 3% 20-year	GRY = 12%	Price = 32.2917
Stock B 15% 20-year	GRY = 12%	Price = 122.5695

Using a 7% roll-up rate the accumulated values of £100,000 invested in the two stocks can be found thus:

An initial investment of £100,000 produces

a holding of £309,677 nominal of Stock A or
a holding of £81,586 nominal of Stock B.

The accumulated values of these holdings over twenty years to maturity using a roll-up rate of 7% are

$$\text{Stock A:} \ (1.5s_{\overline{40}|} + 100) \times 309677/100$$

$$= \left(1.5 \times \frac{1.035^{40} - 1}{0.035} + 100 \right) \times 3096.77$$

$$= £702,426.$$

$$\text{Stock B:} \ (7.5s_{\overline{40}|} + 100) \times 81586/100$$

$$= \left(7.5 \times \frac{1.035^{40} - 1}{0.035} + 100 \right) \times 815.86$$

$$= £598,944.$$

If $A_{7\%}$ and $B_{7\%}$ are used to denote the respective accumulated returns using a 7% roll-up rate, then

(i) $$(1 + A_{7\%}/200)^{40} = 702426/100000$$

(ii) $$(1 + B_{7\%}/200)^{40} = 598944/100000$$

from which it can be found that

$$A_{7\%} = 9.99\%$$
$$B_{7\%} = 9.15\%.$$

The magnitude of the difference between these two accumulated returns is elegant testimony to the importance of making correct assessments as to the likely course of future (roll-up) interest rates when choosing fixed interest investments. Simply picking the highest redemption yield (on an equal-risk basis) is no guarantee of best accumulation performance if that involves buying the very high-coupon stock at a time when interest rates are set to fall.

Volatility

All of the foregoing has looked at fixed-interest investment from the longer-term standpoint, e.g. to redemption. In practice, very few investments run to maturity, the vast majority being for intermediate periods ranging from a number of years to a few days, hours or even minutes. Since the gilt-edged market is a very liquid one, and is also a place where dealing expenses are small, it attracts its fair share of short-term activity, some of which may emanate from private investors, but the majority of which is professional in nature. To the short-term operator the long-term yield (redemption or accumulation) attractions of gilt-edged stocks are largely academic. To them a redemption yield represents more a convenient form of rating, by which they can make price relativity judgements, rather than a measure of intrinsic value. What matters more to the short-term trader is not so much the redemption yield itself, but the prospective short-term change in the yield structure that will produce (hopefully) a beneficial price action for him. However, because stocks have differing physical characteristics (coupon rate, term to maturity, etc.) there is a wide difference in the potential price movement of gilt-edged stocks that would be brought about by applying the same change in yield to all of them.

For example, a 10% stock with six months to run to maturity would be priced at 100 to yield 10% gross, and at 100.478 to yield 9%, whereas $3\frac{1}{2}\%$ undated stock would be priced at 35 and 38.889 on a similar basis.

The percentage price movement brought about by an instantaneous (i.e. for the same settlement date) 1% reduction in yield from 10% to 9% would therefore be 0.478 on the former and 11.111 on the latter. This gearing factor which relates instantaneous price movement to yield movement is known as 'volatility', and is defined formally by the differential calculus relationship,

$$\text{Volatility} = -\frac{1}{P}\frac{dP}{dy}$$

where P and y represent Price and yield respectively.

Volatility is a function of three variables: (i) term to maturity; (ii) the coupon rate; and (iii) the level of yields.

1. *Term to maturity.* Normally volatility rises as maturity lengthens, but there are some instances of very low-coupon long-dated stocks having volatilities greater than that of the undateds.
2. *The coupon rate.* Normally lower-coupon stocks have higher volatilities than higher-coupon stocks of the same maturity.
3. *The level of yields.* If all other variables remain constant, volatility rises as the yield level falls. This is easily seen in the case of undated stocks, since the percentage change in price for a 1% change in yield from, say, 6% to 5% is obviously much greater than one from 16% to 15%. In the first case prices rise by 20%, and in the second by $6\frac{1}{4}$%.

It should be noted that in (3) above the price changes have been related to finite differences in the yield basis, in this case -1%, whereas the formal definition is couched in notation of differential calculus where such changes are infinitesimal. Certain investors prefer to define volatility in terms of finite yield changes, but this presents problems as the absolute size of a percentage change in price of a stock can be different for a rise in yield of x from that produced by a fall in yield of the same amount. Whilst this may seem unusual a further example using undated stocks is instructive.

Consider a $3\frac{1}{2}$% undated stock:

Gross yield	Clean price	% change in price from 8% gross yield	
		in absolute	as a % of price to yield 8%
7%	50.000		
		6.250	14.29%
8%	43.750		
		4.861	11.11%
9%	38.889		

This shows that the 'volatility' produced by a 1% finite difference in yield would either be 14.29% or 11.11%, depending on which of the two alternative definitions was chosen. By contrast, the 'calculus' volatility figure on an 8% yield basis turns out to be 12.50% as demonstrated here:

$$\text{Volatility} = w = -\frac{1}{P}\frac{dP}{dy}.$$

In the case of an undated stock (and using clean prices),

$$P = 100\frac{g}{y}$$

where g denotes the coupon rate.

Differentiating with respect to y,

$$\frac{dP}{dy} = -100\frac{g}{y^2}$$

so that $\quad w = \dfrac{-y}{100g} \times \dfrac{-100g}{y^2} = \dfrac{1}{y}$

i.e. that the volatility of undated stock is the reciprocal of its yield.

Clean and Dirty Volatility

The volatility figure for a given stock provides the gilt-edged analyst with a useful approximate ready reckoner for translating instantaneous yield changes into price variation. The word 'approximate' is used because the volatility figure itself varies with the yield level and is not a constant, but for most practical purposes *where the change in yield is not too great*, the percentage price variation (approximately) equals the stock's volatility multiplied by the change in yield.

This follows from the definition of volatility (w)

$$w = -\frac{1}{P}\frac{dP}{dy}, \quad \text{so that} \quad \frac{\Delta P}{P} \simeq -w\Delta y$$

where ΔP and Δy represent finite changes in price and yield respectively.

The left-hand side of this equation is the proportionate change in value relating to an absolute change in price of ΔP. This expression can take differing values depending on the value of the denominator P.

If for any reason an investor bases his investment calculations on 'clean prices', then by using a 'Clean Price', P, as denominator he will obtain a 'clean volatility'.

Conversely, if total market prices (sometimes referred to as 'dirty prices') are used, the ensuing figure will be that of 'dirty volatility'.

When the term of the stock is an integral number of half-years, the mathematical formula for volatility can be derived as follows:

$$P = \frac{g}{2}[v + v^2 + v^3 + \ldots + v^n] + 100v^n$$

Since $\quad \dfrac{dP}{dy} = \dfrac{dP}{dv}\cdot\dfrac{dv}{dy} \quad$ it follows that $\quad \text{volatility} = -\dfrac{1}{P}\dfrac{dP}{dv}\cdot\dfrac{dv}{dy}$

and $\quad v = [1 + y/200]^{-1}.$

Therefore $\quad \dfrac{dv}{dy} = -\dfrac{v^2}{200}$

and $\quad \dfrac{dP}{dv} = \dfrac{g}{2}[1 + 2v + 3v^2 + \ldots + nv^{n-1}] + 100nv^{n-1}.$

The expression within the brackets can be summed thus:

$$S = 1 + 2v + 3v^2 + \ldots\ldots + nv^{n-1}$$

Therefore $vS = v + 2v^2 + \ldots + (n-1)v^{n-1} + nv^n$

Thus $(1-v)S = 1 + v + v^2 + \ldots\ldots + v^{n-1} - nv^n$

so that $S = \dfrac{1-v^n}{(1-v)^2} - \dfrac{nv^n}{1-v}$

and volatility (w) is thus defined by the expression

$$w = \frac{1}{P}\left(\frac{g}{2} \cdot S + 100nv^{n-1}\right)\frac{v^2}{200}$$

As an example, consider an 11% stock, with a term of fifteen years, standing on a gross redemption yield of 12%, i.e. $g = 11$, $n = 30$, $y = 12$:

From this $\qquad v = \dfrac{1}{1.06} = 0.943396$

$$v^{30} = 0.174110$$
$$(1-v) = 0.056604$$
$$(1-v)^2 = 0.003204$$
$$30v^{29} = 5.536702$$
$$30v^{30} = 5.223304$$

$$\frac{dP}{dy} = \left[\frac{11}{2}\left(\frac{0.8258899}{0.003204} - \frac{5.223304}{0.506604}\right) + 553.672\right] \times (-0.00444998)$$

$$= -6.514$$

and since $P = 93.118$,

$$\text{volatility} = -\frac{1}{P}\frac{dP}{dy} = \frac{6.514}{93.118} = 7.00\%.$$

Duration

Another concept somewhat similar to that of volatility is 'duration'.

Duration is the weighted average length of time between purchase of a stock and receipt of its benefits (interest payments, capital repayments, etc.) where the weightings applied are the present values of the benefits involved. It produces a figure that is something like an average life of a stock and (as the following analysis will show) is mathematically related to volatility. It is much more widely known and used in the US bond markets than in the United Kingdom, where the emphasis has historically always been on volatility – but this may well be the result of ignorance rather than preference!

Applying the notations previously used in this chapter, and assuming again the term is an integral number of half-years, the weighted average time period to receipt of benefit is

$$\frac{v\frac{g}{2} + 2v^2\frac{g}{2} + 3v^3\frac{g}{2} + \ldots + nv^n\frac{g}{2} + nv^n 100}{v\frac{g}{2} + v^2\frac{g}{2} + v^3\frac{g}{2} + \ldots v^n\frac{g}{2} + v^n 100} \text{ half-years.}$$

The denominator of this expression is quite simply the stock's price, P, and the numerator can be recognised from an earlier equation as being equal to

$$v \times \frac{dP}{dv}$$

Duration (measured in whole years) can thus be expressed as

$$h = \frac{1}{2}\frac{v}{P}\frac{dP}{dv}$$

Now, since volatility $w = -\frac{1}{P}\frac{dP}{dy}$ and $\frac{dv}{dy} = -\frac{v^2}{200}$

it is possible to relate duration (h) to volatility (w) thus:

$$h = \frac{1}{2}\frac{v}{P}\frac{dP}{dv}$$

$$= \frac{1}{2}\frac{v}{P}\frac{dP}{dy}\frac{dy}{dv}$$

$$= \frac{1}{2}\frac{v}{P}\frac{dP}{dy}\left(-\frac{200}{v^2}\right)$$

$$= \frac{1}{2}v(-w)\left[-\frac{200}{v^2}\right]$$

$$= 100\frac{w}{v}$$

$$h = 100w(1 + i)$$

i.e. Duration (in years) $= 100 \times$ Volatility $\times [1 + (\text{Yield}/200)]$.

Applying this formula to the previous example of an 11% fifteen-year stock yielding 12%, whose volatility was 7%, we obtain a duration equal to

$$100 \times \frac{7}{100} \times [1 + (12/200)]$$

$$= 7.42 \text{ years.}$$

Performance Yields

So far, consideration has been given to two main sets of circumstances: holding stock to redemption or looking at instantaneous price and yield changes. The vast majority of investments fall into neither of these categories, but are of an intermediate nature.

Again, there is no *totally* accepted terminology to describe the total return, or return per cent, from a fixed-interest stock held over such a period, but the words 'performance' and 'performance yield' have been used by many people in this context for some years and are acceptable for this purpose.

Performance yields can be computed on exactly the same principle as redemption yields, with the simple variation that the redemption value is replaced by the sale proceeds value, and the time period is that between purchase and sale.

Imagine an 11%, fifteen-year stock, bought at $93\frac{1}{8}$ (to give a gross redemption yield of 11.99%) and subsequently sold three years later at a price of $98\frac{3}{4}$. The performance yield for this stock over the three years is found by solving the following equation of value:

$$93.125 = 5.5a_{\overline{6}|} + 98.75v^6$$

to give an answer of 13.51%.

Performance yields can either be retrospective, such as above, or prospective. In the latter case, a postulated value has to be put on the stock at the forward point in time, and this forecasting process introduces a further variable into the game, one which did not exist with redemption yields, where the forward value is fixed and known. In such instances, analysts will most likely arrive at their idea of forward price by 'guesstimating' a future (gross redemption) yield basis for the stock, and then translate that yield into price terms.

If the assumed future gross yield basis is lower than the current one, then they will be basically taking a bullish view of the market; if it is higher they will be bearish. The neutral view is to assume (however rightly or wrongly this turns out to be) that the future yield basis is identical with that pertaining at the outset.

Gross performance yields resulting from a *neutral* view turn out to be exactly equal to the gross redemption yield involved. This is hardly surprising when one remembers, say, the progression of stock prices in the tables shown earlier in this chapter, and how, when stock stays on a given yield 'contour', its returns over successive periods each equate to that particular yield. This often unappreciated truism is best summed up as 'If you buy a stock to yield $y\%$, and sell it when it still yields $y\%$, your rate of return will be $y\%$.

The Significance of Duration and its Place in Immunisation Theory

A considerable amount of work has been done (admittedly more in the United States than in the United Kingdom) developing portfolio immunisation techniques to deal with the problem of the uncertainty of realised rates of return caused by roll-up rates almost always (in practice) being different from the redemption yield on which the stock was purchased.

It has been shown earlier in this chapter (Table 6.4) that if one purchases a 9%

ten-year stock on a 12% gross redemption yield but can only reinvest its dividend payments subsequently at 9%, the realised compound rate of return to redemption turns out to be 10.98% – rather *lower* than the purchase yield. If, however, the stock were to be sold on a 9% yield, at the end of the first year the sale proceeds plus dividends rolled-up at 9% would total £131,894.83, representing a 29.69% per annum return – far *higher* than the purchase yield. Obviously if roll-up rates were to be greater than the purchase yield the converse would apply. An investor wishing to be immune from this uncertainty and to obtain a 'guaranteed' rate of return equal to his purchase yield can do so (on the basis of the price action assumed in Table 6.4) by holding the stock for a time period chosen so that the effects of the change in capital value caused by a move to a new yield basis is equally and oppositely balanced by the effect of rolling up income at the new rate. In the analysis that follows it will be shown that this critical holding period happens to equate to the stock's duration.

Consider a stock purchased at a price of P_0 to give a redemption yield of y_0. Next let us assume it moves immediately to a price of P_1 and a corresponding yield of y_1, and that it subsequently remains on that redemption yield basis as time progresses. Let the critical holding period be n half-years.

To meet the investor's demand for a rate of return equal to the purchase redemption yield requires there to be a gross performance over this period of $(1 + y_0/200)^n$.

The actual performance produced by this hypothesis can be considered as the product of P_1/P_0 (caused by the initial change in the yield basis) and $(1 + y_1/200)^n$, the subsequent accumulation for n half-years at the roll-up rate of y_1.

Equating these two entities one obtains

$$(1 + y_0/200)^n = (P_1/P_0) \times (1 + y_1/200)^n.$$

If one now takes logarithms,

$$n = \frac{\log P_1 - \log P_0}{\log (1 + y_0/200) - \log (1 + y_1/200)}$$

$$= -\frac{d(\log P)}{d[\log (1 + y/200)]}$$

$$= -200 \frac{(1 + y/200)}{P} \frac{dP}{dy} \text{ half-years}$$

$$= 100 \times \text{volatility} \times [1 + (\text{yield}/200)] \text{ in whole years},$$

which is the identical formula for duration as that established earlier.

7

Analytical methods

Successful gilt-edged investing is essentially a combination of good timing and good stock selection. Of these two factors, good timing is undoubtedly the more difficult to achieve, but, by the same token, it is probably the factor from which the greatest profitability emanates. In the gilt-edged market, even a cheap stock bought just before a major market decline can hardly be expected to perform positively – whilst a dear stock bought at the onset of a bull market can hardly fail to do well in absolute terms. This is because the margins of inter-stock price fluctuations in the gilt-edged market are generally much smaller than the amplitudes of the market's overall price movements. This is in sharp contrast to the situation pertaining in the equity market, where the benefits from inspired stock selection can very often easily outweigh those of an adverse market movement.

Accordingly, the gilt-edged investor should ask himself questions in the following order, before committing himself to an investment strategy in the gilt-edged market:

1. What is the overall market outlook?
2. What are the relative merits of the differing broad sectors: shorts, mediums, longs?
3. Within the chosen sector, which stocks are cheap and which stocks are dear?

The first question is essentially about general interest rates and yield levels, and relates particularly to timing. It will almost certainly require the investor to make some form of economic assessment before arriving at a conclusion, and perhaps also the use of some of the various forms of technical analysis (charts) that abound today.

The second question will also involve the investor in making judgements on potential changes in both the level and shape of the yield curve over some medium-term time horizon – typically a six-month or one-year view. Again technical analysis can be useful, even if only in allowing past inter-sector movements to be seen in perspective.

A general note about the use of technical analysis of the gilt-edged market may be in place here. There are many learned and distinguished people in and around the investment community who range from being sceptical to downright dismissive of the use of charts, moving averages and the like in the investment area. At the other end of the range there are those who claim that the only information they are prepared to accept is what is 'written' in the observed price actions in the market. Where one wishes to place oneself in the spectrum between these two extreme viewpoints is essentially a matter of individual choice, based upon one's own experience. In the view of the author, technical analysis has a role to play in complementing fundamental judgements, not because the charts can necessarily 'tell' one anything, but because, used intelligently, they can often 'ask' the investor whether his existing prognosis of the market is still valid, or whether the 'game' is undergoing some sort of fundamental change. Many books have been written on the subject of technical analysis and it is not intended to go into detail here. Suffice it to say that the author would recommend any gilt-edged analyst to have as an essential part of his armoury, charts (of one form or another) of the following:

1. An indicator of short-term interest rates.
2. Prices or yields representative of the short-dated sector of the market.
3. Prices or yields representative of the medium-dated sector of the market.
4. Prices or yields representative of the long-dated sector of the market.
5. Comparisons between the three sectors.

To these can be added charts of currency values, prices, yields and interest rates in other international markets, in particular those in the United States.

The charts in Figs. 7.1 and 7.2 are provided as examples. Figure 7.1 shows a

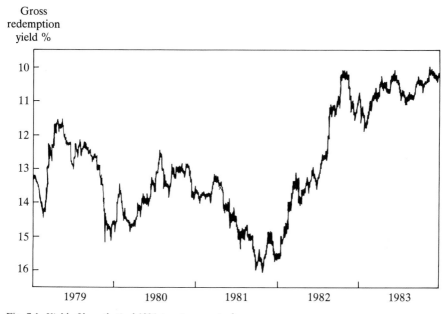

Fig. 7.1 *Yield of hypothetical 12% twenty-year stock*

Price
ratio %

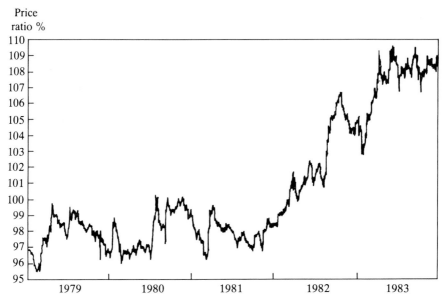

Fig. 7.2 *Ratio of prices of hypothetical 12% twenty-year and ten-year stocks*

chart of long yields and Fig. 7.2 gives a price-orientated comparison between the medium- and long-dated sectors of the market.

The third of the three basic questions is essentially to do with individual stock selection, and a myriad of complex and sophisticated forms of analysis have evolved over the years for answering it. This is the part of gilt-edged analysis where the mathematical approach is at its strongest, and the following section of this book will deal in detail with the techniques in general usage.

In this particular area there are basically two forms of comparative analysis, which comprise a variety of techniques:

1. Methods comparing one stock against another stock:

   (a) Price differences.
   (b) Price ratios.
   (c) Yield differences and ratios.
   (d) Switch profit projections.
   (e) Performance indices.
   (f) Balance-of-term yields.

2. Methods comparing one stock against a market 'average':

   (a) Yield curve analysis.
   (b) Price model analysis.

For reasons of historical precedence, we shall begin by looking at comparisons of one stock against another.

Price Differences

This was probably the very first method of making inter-stock comparisons and is very simple and totally unsophisticated. In this system the difference between two stocks' prices are calculated and recorded regularly (e.g. daily). This 'price difference' history would then be used as a yardstick against which to judge whether the current price difference was 'normal', by lying somewhere in the middle of the historical range, or was 'anomalous' by being at one extremity or the other of that range. If the latter, a price 'anomaly' was considered to exist which could be turned to advantage by the eagle-eyed investor, by selling the dearer stock and switching into the cheaper of the pair. Switching of this sort between stocks of broadly similar coupon and maturity characteristics became known as 'anomaly switching' – terminology that has persisted through to the present day.

The use of price differences has several shortcomings, but, before being derogatory about them, it should be stressed that price differences were mainly in use at a time well before mechanical hand calculators existed, to say nothing of electronic calculators and computers. In those days, calculating a ratio involved long division or using logarithmic tables, both of which were cumbersome and time-consuming, especially when it is appreciated that statistics were also recorded manually.

Nevertheless, the fact that price differences could not reflect the true proportionate changes in valuations between the two stocks (unless their prices were roughly equal), and that discontinuities would come about every time one of the stocks went ex-dividend, made them fundamentally unsuitable as a tool for use in serious gilt-edged analysis, and they were superseded by 'price ratios'.

Price Ratios

This method gets over the above-mentioned problems by forming the ratio of the two stocks' clean prices – i.e. their total prices minus accrued interest net of tax at the relevant rate; and the fact that the method can be tailored to suit gross and net funds alike gives it wide appeal. Furthermore, by operating on clean prices, the price discontinuities at ex-dividend dates are removed, and the fact that one is dealing with a ratio rather than a difference means that proportionate changes in the price of one stock relative to the other are accurately reflected in the relevant statistic.

Table 7.1 illustrates how the method is used to make a comparison for a gross fund between two stocks of broadly similar characteristics.

The current gross price ratio statistic of 96.27 is then compared with its recent history on the chart in Fig. 7.3, from which it can be surmised that, since there have been few occasions when the price ratio has been more advantageous than this, there are at least prima-facie grounds for selling Treasury 13% 2000 and reinvesting in Treasury 14% 98/01.

The reader will notice that this example dates from before the advent of the accrued interest scheme and that the prices quoted were inclusive of accrued interest which then had to be deducted to form the clean price. Since February

Table 7.1   *Comparisons between stocks of broadly similar characteristics*

Date: 28.8.1983

Using gross price ratios, compare the relative attractions of Treasury 13% 2000 to Treasury 14% 1998/2001

Stock	Total market price	Gross accrued interest	Gross clean price
Treasury 13% 2000	113⅞	1.460	112.415
Treasury 14% 1998/2001	120⅜	3.605	116.770

Gross price ratio % = 112.415/116.770 × 100

= 96.27

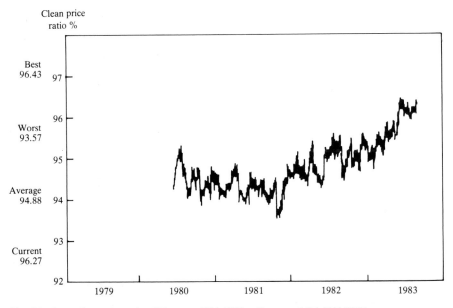

Fig. 7.3 *Gross clean price ratio of Treasury 13% 2000 v. Treasury 14% 1998/2001*

1986 prices of all gilt-edged stocks have been quoted in the clean form plus or minus gross accrued interest so that in order to form a *gross* price ratio it is only necessary to divide one quoted price by the other. However, this short-cut only applies to gross ratios, and whenever one is dealing with net price ratios it is safest first to construct the total price by adding the gross accrued to the quoted price, and then deduct the *net* accrued interest to form the relevant net clean prices.

Price ratios are a very widely used analytical tool in the gilt-edged market, but certain caveats about their use need to be made.

Firstly, a general caveat, applicable to all forms of what may be termed 'retrospective analysis'. By making judgements about *current* valuations in this way, one is essentially using past history as a guide to prospective normality. Before so doing the investor should ask himself whether such an assumption is justifiable, whether there have been, or are in the pipeline, any fundamental changes in, say, taxation, market structure, etc., which might make past relationships a bad guide as to the future.

The second caveat concerning the use of price ratios is that they do not take into account differences in the income flows from the two stocks. A simple example makes this clear:

Let us consider two stocks, A and B, both with lives of exactly five years.

Let A be a 12% stock priced at 100 and
let B be a 3% stock priced at 80.

The gross price ratio (clean price A divided by clean price B) × 100 is thus $(100/80) \times 100 = 125.00$.

Let us further assume that over the course of the next six months stock A moves to a price of 105, whilst stock B moves up to 84. The price ratio will thus be $(105/84) \times 100 = 125.00$, the same as before, but the *total* performances of the two stocks will be far from equal, for stock A will have had a half-yearly dividend payment of 6, whilst stock B will have had one of only $1\frac{1}{2}$.

The total performance of A is equal to the change in price over the period $(105 - 100)$, plus dividends received (6), divided by the initial total price $(100) = 11\%$. Likewise, the total performance of $B = [(84 - 80) + 1.50]/80 = 6.875\%$.

Thus, whilst the price ratio has remained constant, stock A has outperformed stock B by 4.125%.

It will therefore be seen that, when using price ratios as an analytical tool, great care must be taken to compensate for dividend flow differences.

The following formula provides a way of computing the necessary adjustments.

In symbolic terms the price ratio R can be expressed as

$$R = \frac{(P_a - g_a \cdot t_a)}{(P_b - g_b \cdot t_b)}$$

where P_a and P_b represent the total prices of stocks A and B, g_a and g_b the coupons of stocks A and B respectively, and where t_a and t_b denote the time elapsed since the last coupon payments.

At this point, the reader conversant with differential calculus comes into his own (whilst those not well versed in the niceties of this subject will of necessity have to take the validity of the following analysis on trust).

The above equation can be rewritten by taking logarithms of both sides:

$$\log R = \log(P_a - g_a \cdot t_a) - \log(P_b - g_b \cdot t_b).$$

Now differentiate both sides with respect to time:

$$\frac{1}{R}\frac{dR}{dt} = \frac{-g_a}{(P_a - g_a \cdot t_a)} - \frac{-g_b}{(P_b - g_b \cdot t_b)}$$

Since g_a represents coupon and $(P_a - g_a \cdot t_a)$ represents clean price, etc.,

$$\frac{g_a}{(P_a - g_a \cdot t_a)} = \text{flat (income only) yield of stock A, etc., and can be denoted by } f_a,$$
etc.

Thus

$$\frac{1}{R}\frac{dR}{dt} = f_b - f_a$$

leading to the approximation $\Delta R \simeq (f_b - f_a) \cdot R\Delta t$.

Put in words, this states that the simple passage of time will bring about a change in the price ratio (ΔR) equal to (minus), the difference in the two flat yields multiplied by the ratio itself, multiplied by the extent of the time period in years.

Let us now see how this applies to our earlier example.

Here the initial flat yield of stock A, $f_a = 12.00\%$,
the initial flat yield of stock B, $f_b = 3.75\%$.

Thus, $f_b - f_a = 3.75 - 12.00 = -8.25\%$.
The initial ratio = 125.00.
The time period was a half-year.

Using the approximation above, the requisite adjustment to the 125 price ratio figure can be established as

$$= \frac{-8.25}{100} \times 125 \times \frac{1}{2} = -5.15625.$$

It will (one hopes) not surprise the reader to find that this adjustment expressed as a percentage of the price ratio of 125 is 4.125%, the same as the difference in total performance between the two stocks.

Thus, whenever using price ratio charts as a basis of comparison between two stocks, the investor/analyst should first calculate the size of the underlying natural trend in the ratio figure and, where charts are being used, should superimpose the trend upon the graph before making his judgements.

Figures 7.4 and 7.5 show examples of price ratio analysis of the relationship between Treasury 12% 1987 and Transport 3% 78/88. Examination of the chart in Fig. 7.5 with the natural trend superimposed shows that the best terms for performing the switch were those in late July 1983, and not those of September 1982 as might otherwise have been concluded.

Yield Differences and Ratios

It is probably fair to say that yield differences ('spreads') are the most widely used analytical device for making switch assessments in the gilt-edged market (and, for that matter, in most other fixed-interest markets). For a start, the concept of a

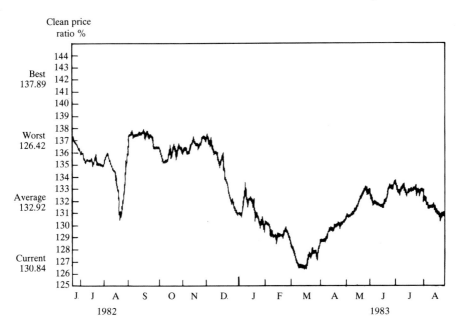

Fig. 7.4 *Gross clean price ratio of Treasury 12% 1987 v. Transport 3% 1978/88 without natural income flow trend shown*

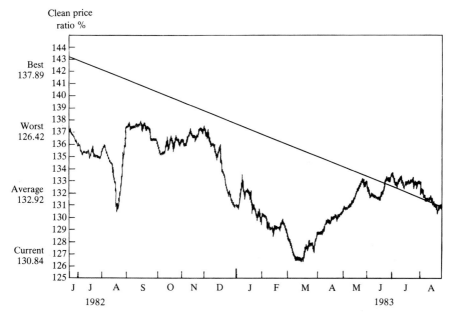

Fig. 7.5 *Gross clean price ratio of Treasury 12% 1987 v. Transport 3% 1978/88 with natural income flow trend superimposed*

gain in yield being obtained by selling a low-yielding stock and buying a higher-yielding one is easily grasped by even the least sophisticated of investors, as is the fact that switching terms of a gain of, say, 0.75% in redemption yield are better than those of a gain of only 0.65%. Furthermore, yield differences do not suffer from the problems associated with price ratios, since the values of both the income flows and capital repayments are taken into account in calculating each individual redemption yield. Yield ratios, which some purists might expect to see used in preference to yield differences, are seldom encountered, although it is the view of the author that they may on occasions give better indications of anomalies, especially when the absolute level of yields changes substantially over the time period under review. Most of the content that follows is as equally applicable to yield ratios as to yield differences, but we shall concentrate on the latter.

A typical yield difference chart looks like the one in Fig. 7.6. From this chart it can be observed that the average (gross redemption) yield difference was 0.065 and the daily recorded figure has tended to fluctuate quite frequently between + 0.175 and − 0.025.

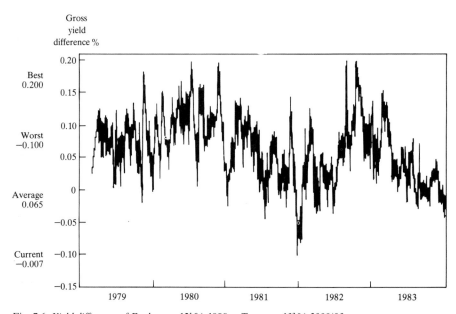

Fig. 7.6 *Yield difference of Exchequer 12¼% 1999 v. Treasury 13¾% 2000/03*

There would therefore appear to be a reasonably good case for preferring to invest in Treasury 13¾% 00/03 when the yield difference is greater than 0.065, and Exchequer 12¼% 1999 when it is below this figure. There would also appear to be a prima facie case for switching out of Exchequer 12¼% 1999 into Treasury 13¾% 00/03 if and when the yield margin exceeds 0.175, or the reverse if the yield difference drops below − 0.25. So, if such a golden opportunity arises, why should not the investor grasp it in both hands? What could go wrong?

Firstly, it is possible that some new factor may appear on the scene which would mean that the yield difference between these two stocks was just about to move into a different range. Secondly, the investor would do well to examine the amplitude of the yield difference to ensure that even if he opened his switch on the very best terms, and subsequently closed the operation towards the lower end of the range, there would be sufficient profit for him after allowing for dealing expenses. Very often apparently attractive switches between similar stocks turn out, on further inspection of this sort, to leave only a minuscule potential profit for the investor.

However, by far and away the greatest caveat that must be applied to the use of yield differences is that they cannot take into account differences of the two stocks' volatilities, i.e. that a given change in the yield of one stock may well produce a change in its value that is markedly different to that produced in the other by precisely the same change in yield. If the two stocks have very similar volatilities, then yield differences are a very satisfactory and simple analytical device for measuring relative values between them. The further apart their volatilities are, the greater the danger becomes that the difference in their total performances may diverge from the corresponding path of their yield difference. Where large differences in volatility exist, and when the market's general yield levels change substantially, it is quite possible to open a switch for a gain in yield, and close it at a later time for a further gain in yield, but end up making a switch loss as a result – as the following, deliberately exaggerated, example demonstrates. This in itself should be warning enough not to use yield differences indiscriminately.

15th Jan.	Sell 12%	25-year stock A:	Price = 76 . .	GRY = 15.90
	Buy 12%	5-year stock B:	Price = 85 . .	GRY = 16.52
	Opening gain in gross redemption yield . .			= 0.62

15th July	Sell 12%	4½-year stock B:	Price 100 . .	GRY = 12.00
	Repurchase 12%	24½-year stock A:	Price 95	GRY = 12.67
	Closing gain in gross redemption yield . . .			= 0.67

Switch accounting

	Stock A	£	Stock B	£	Net cash flow
15th Jan.	− £1,000,000 Stock A @ 76	760,000	+ £894,118 Stock B @ 85	760,000	nil
15th July	Dividend forgone 6.0	60,000	Dividend received 6.0	53,647	− 6,353
15th July	+ £1,000,000 Stock A @ 95	950,000	− £894,118 Stock B @ 100	894,118	− 55,882
			Gross switch profit/loss		− 62,235

Summary of the operation: a gain in yield of over $\frac{5}{8}$% on both opening and closing terms produces a loss of over 8% in relative performance!

Thus, just as the inability to make allowance for differing income flow is the Achilles' heel for price ratios, so the volatility factor is the drawback associated with yield differences, and the investor is entitled to ask what other ways there are of making inter-stock comparisons that do not suffer from these defects.

Switch Profit Projections

One useful method which gets over this problem to a certain extent is to make a series of forward switch projections at different overall market levels based on a common assumption as to the future yield difference, and observe how the potential profits or losses are affected accordingly. Such a method requires the user to make a realistic 'guesstimate' of the future 'normal' yield difference, and this is usually done after consulting the charts of this relationship's recent history. The projection shown in Table 7.2 is a good example of this approach.

Here the investor has already examined the yield difference history of Treasury $13\frac{1}{2}$% 04/08 against Exchequer $10\frac{1}{2}$% 1997 and observed that between the autumn of 1982 and December 1983 this figure has swung from -0.26% to

Table 7.2 *Examples of switch profit projections*

| Switch | Current at 20.12.1983 | | Projected yields at 17.12.1984 | | | | |
	Total price	GRY	Y − 2	Y − 1	Y	Y + 1	Y + 2
Sell Treasury $13\frac{1}{2}$ 04/08	127.50	10.546	8.658	9.658	10.658	11.658	12.658
Buy Exchequer $10\frac{1}{2}$ 1997	101.00	10.830	8.718	9.718	10.718	11.718	12.718
		0.285	0.060	0.060	0.060	0.060	0.060

| Switch | Current at 20.12.1983 | | Projected total prices at 17.12.1984 | | | | |
	Total price	GRY	Y − 2	Y − 1	Y	Y + 1	Y + 2
Sell Treasury $13\frac{1}{2}$ 04/08	127.50	10.546	148.09	136.40	126.14	117.10	109.10
Buy Exchequer $10\frac{1}{2}$ 1997	101.00	10.830	116.56	108.86	101.89	95.55	89.79

| Switch | Current at 20.12.1983 | | Projected returns to 17.12.1984 | | | | |
	Total price	GRY	Y − 2	Y − 1	Y	Y + 1	Y + 2
Sell Treasury $13\frac{1}{2}$ 04/08	127.50	10.546	26.13	17.54	9.70	2.52	− 4.06
Buy Exchequer $10\frac{1}{2}$ 1977	101.00	10.830	25.56	18.84	11.56	5.21	− 0.75
Difference		0.285	− 0.57	0.79	1.86	2.69	3.31

Source: Barclays de Zoete Wedd.

+ 0.29% and has averaged 0.06%. Let us assume that he was considering making the switch from Treasury 13½% 04/08 into Exchequer 10½% 1997 on total prices of 127½:101, terms which represented a gain in gross redemption yield of 0.285%, and was looking to reverse it on a yield difference of 0.06% (the recent average) a year later. Table 7.2 shows how the profitability of such a switch varies with the future market level. The central projection is based on the neutral view that the average of the two stocks' yields will be the same then as it was at the outset, whilst the two on either side assume that the average yield will be 1% and 2% higher and lower respectively. It can be seen that the projected profits range from + 3.31% (if yields rise 2%) to − 0.57% (if yields fall 2%) and the switch breaks even if yields fall about 1.60%.

The investor can now see the essential nature of the trade-off between the yield anomaly and the effect of an overall market movement and can decide whether to make the switch or not, fully knowing the risk–reward relationship involved.

Now let us take a look at an alternative to price ratios.

Performance Indices

These are indices which are reasonably simple to construct and which are designed to measure the total performance – capital movements plus income receipts of each stock. The concept behind the system is to envisage how the value of a fund would fluctuate if it were only invested in a single stock and reinvested the dividends received from that stock by buying more stock at the market price on the first day ex-dividend. Thus the performance index is a product of two items: the stock's net total price (after allowing for the exigencies of the accrued interest scheme) and a nominal amount of stock which rises in relation to the net dividends received each time the stock goes ex-dividend.

As an example, take the case of a 10% stock which at the outset of this analysis (chosen for convenience to be a dividend date for this stock) is priced at, say, 95.

An investment of £100 at this time in this stock would therefore have produced an initial holding of £105.263 stock. The total net value (after allowing for tax on the accrued interest) that this holding would produce if sold becomes the net performance index for this stock. Table 7.3 shows the progress of such an index for a fund taxed at 37½% on income.

Table 7.3 *Example of the use of Performance Indices*

Day	Nominal holding (N)	Quoted price (Q)	Gross accrued interest (A)	Tax on GAI @ 37½% (T)	Total net value (V) = (Q) + (A) − (T)	Net performance index = (N) × (V)
0	105.263	95	0.000	0.000	95.000	100.00
1	105.263	95¼	0.027	0.010	95.267	100.28
2	105.263	96½	0.054	0.020	96.534	101.61
144	105.263	94 cd	3.945	1.479	96.466	101.54
145	108.777	94¼ xd	− 1.014	− 0.380	93.616	101.83
146	108.777	94 xd	− 0.986	− 0.370	93.384	101.58

The compounding of income is demonstrated by the action of this index when the stock goes ex-dividend on day 145 (about thirty-seven days before the first gross coupon payment of 5% is due). After tax at $37\frac{1}{2}$% this dividend becomes 3.125% net and this amount is then 'used' to purchase (notionally) further stock at the first day ex-dividend net value of 93.616. The additional stock thus purchased is $105.263 \times (3.125/100)/(0.93616) = £3.514$ nominal, which when added to the initial holding increases it to £108,777. After this time the system continues as before but using this larger nominal holding until the next ex-dividend when the process is repeated in like fashion.

Two points need to be made clear at this juncture. Firstly, the amount of additional stock purchased is related to the value of the net dividend in the hands of the recipient. In this example the dividend was taxed at $37\frac{1}{2}$%, but if one was making gross fund analyses the incremental amount of stock bought as a result of reinvesting the coupon would be £5.645.

The second point is that since the dividend would not actually be received by a holder until some thirty-seven days or so later, the correct amount of money to be reinvested should actually be the relevant coupon payment net of tax (if any) discounted at the then current money rate for thirty-seven days. It is important not to ignore this factor, but one can sometimes make a meal out of over-precision in this business, and for most practical purposes a standard discounting factor of 0.99 (equivalent to a 9.67% per annum rate of interest for that period) is normally acceptable and is certainly convenient. Applying this factor reduces the additional nominal stock 'purchased' to £5.589 gross and £3.479 net at $37\frac{1}{2}$%.

Making price and performance comparisons (gross or net of any required rate of tax) then becomes a simple matter of forming the ratio of the two relevant performance indices, and comparing the current figure with its historic series.

This type of system is valuable not only because it gets over the main drawback associated with price ratios – namely the problem of accounting for dividend income flow – but also because it allows for the compounding effect of income reinvestment. It is also highly useful in that the method can be easily adapted to form composite indices of performance for groups of stocks and even whole portfolios, rather than being confined simply to single stocks – an invaluable facility when large-scale portfolio reconstructions are being considered. But, like a number of other selective methods, it is a wholly retrospective analytical device.

Balance-of-term Yields

In contrast to performance indices, balance-of-term yields (often referred to as 'reinvestment rates') are a method which produces a critical statistic which can be viewed in a prospective scenario (as well as retrospectively). To understand what balance-of-term yields are, and how they can be applied to make inter-stock selection judgements, consider the following train of thought.

Take first the shorter-dated of the two stocks and make a prospective assessment of its performance to redemption. This will depend on the rate of tax applicable (if any) to dividend income and/or capital gains, and, just as importantly, the 'roll-up' rate (see Chapter 6) at which dividends can be expected to be reinvested as they occur. But because one is making a projection to a redemption date the forward capital value of the stock is known. The next stage is to calculate, using the same assumptions as to tax and roll-up rates, the price that the longer-dated of the two stocks would need to stand on at the date of redemption of the shorter, so as to make the two stocks' performances over that period identical. From this price can be calculated the corresponding redemption yield for the 'balance of the term' of the longer stock. In essence, the analyst is looking at two ways of investing for the full term of the longer stock:

1. To invest outright by buying the longer stock.
2. To buy the shorter stock and on redemption to reinvest in the longer stock for the balance of the term.

The choice of which of these will be most profitable can be gauged by the value of the implied balance-of-term yield. If this is abnormally high, then there will be a prima-facie case for buying the longer-dated stock outright, whilst if it is very low this would indicate that an investor should prefer to invest initially in the shorter of the two stocks and switch longer later. The following example illustrates:

Let stock A be a 12% ten-year stock priced at $98\frac{1}{2}$ and giving a gross redemption yield of 12.27%. Let stock B be a 10% twenty-five-year stock, with a price of $91\frac{1}{2}$ and a gross redemption yield of 11.01%. For the purpose of simplicity, let us assume that there is no question of tax on either income or capital gains, and that in the investor's judgement 10% is a suitable roll-up rate for compounding dividend payments.

On these assumptions, the performance to redemption of the shorter stock A is calculated as the accumulated value of a holding of this stock, divided by its current price, i.e.

$$\frac{\left(\dfrac{g}{2}\, s_{\overline{n}|} + 100\right)}{P_a}$$

$$= \frac{\left(6.0 \times \dfrac{(1.05^{20} - 1)}{0.05} + 100\right)}{98.5}$$

$$= 3.0293982.$$

It is now necessary to calculate the price of stock B (P_b) on the same date to give the same performance.

This is done by solving the equation

$$\frac{\left(5.0 \times \dfrac{1.05^{20} - 1}{0.05} + P_b\right)}{91.5}$$

$$= 3.0293982.$$

$$P_b = 111.86.$$

To judge whether this price is likely to be within the bounds of possibility, it is necessary to calculate the gross redemption yield that it represents at this future date, when stock B will have a remaining life of fifteen years. This is the 'balance-of-term yield', and in this particular case turns out to be 8.58%.

It is interesting to see how much the balance-of-term yield is affected by changes in either the assumed roll-up rate, or the rates of tax applicable to the investor. Taking variations in the roll-up rate first, the balance-of-term yields relating to a range of roll-up rates are shown in Table 7.4.

As balance-of-term yields are so highly dependent upon the choice of roll-up rate assumed, it is important to choose roll-up rates carefully. Frequently-used assumptions include the following:

1. The redemption yield of the shorter stock.
2. The redemption yield of the longer stock.
3. The average of (1) and (2).
4. A constant mid-range figure, say 10%.
5. A rate so chosen that the balance-of-term yield it produces and the roll-up rate equate.

None of these is ideal, but the use of a constant figure (4) has the advantage that a daily balance-of-term yield series computed on this basis will produce a sophisticated form of dividend-adjusted price comparator augmented with prospective aspects. Such an analytical method has much to recommend it.

Turning now to the effect of tax on balance-of-term yields, let us observe what variations in the method are required to allow for income tax and capital gains tax. (In spite of the fact that gilt-edged stocks are free from capital gains tax, this full example is introduced here for educational purposes.)

In our previous example we first chose a suitable roll-up rate of 10% gross. If now the income tax rate applicable is, say, $37\frac{1}{2}$%, and capital gains tax rate 30%, a net roll-up rate of, say, $6\frac{1}{4}$% may be more appropriate. Furthermore, the net dividends to be accumulated will now be $3\frac{3}{4}$% and $3\frac{1}{8}$% per half-year for the 12% and 10% stock respectively. Under these conditions the net performance of the shorter stock A will be:

$$\frac{\left\{ 3.75 \times \dfrac{(1.03125^{20} - 1)}{0.03125} + [100 - 0.3(100 - 98.50)] \right\}}{98.50}$$

$$= 2.0467509.$$

P_b, the projected price of stock B to give level performance with this is found by solving the equation:

$$\frac{\left\{ 3.125 \times \dfrac{(1.03125^{20} - 1)}{0.03125} + [P_b - 0.3(P_b - 91.50)] \right\}}{91.50}$$

$$= 2.0467509.$$

Table 7.4 *Balance-of-term yields relative to a range of roll-up rates*

Roll-up rate (% p.a.)	Break-even price	Balance of term yield (%)
6	108.81	8.98
8	109.99	8.79
10	111.86	8.58
12	113.99	8.35
14	116.41	8.09

giving rise to a price $P_b = 106.83$, which, when translated into a *gross* redemption yield, produces a *net* balance-of-term yield of 9.15%.

This is a very much higher figure than that produced earlier for a gross fund, which indicates that the switch longer from stock A (12%; ten-year term) to stock B (10%; twenty-five-year term) is more advantageous to the net fund than to a gross one.

There is often some confusion associated with the practice of quoting *net* of tax balance-of-term break-even levels by reference to *gross* redemption yields, as in the example above. Why is this done? The reason is that in essence the balance-of-term analysis is used to find the break-even *price* of the longer stock, and is subsequently translated into gross redemption yield terms because it is in yield terms that general market levels are most usually gauged.

Some people, especially those new to this form of analysis, often find difficulty in making the correct interpretation of the figures once they have been calculated. The rule of thumb that can be safely applied is simple: the higher the balance-of-term yield is, the better are the terms for switching longer.

Calculating balance-of-term yields by this classic method is often onerous and time-consuming. An alternative and quicker method exists.

If (and it is a big 'if') one is prepared to assume that during the course of their lives the two stocks under consideration remain on the current gross redemption yields, then the returns they produce can be considered as semi-annual annuities of an amount equal to half their respective yields.

Let us assume that we are trying to ascertain the balance-of-term yield, y_{mn}, between two stocks, the longer-yielding y_n for a term of n half-years, and the shorter-yielding y_m for m half-years. For level performance over the full term of n half-years the present values of the two alternative streams of 'annuity payments' must equate so that

$$y_n a_{\overline{n}} = y_m a_{\overline{m}} + y_{mn}(a_{\overline{n}} - a_{\overline{m}})$$

and thus
$$y_{mn} = \frac{y_n a_{\overline{n}} - y_m a_{\overline{m}}}{a_{\overline{n}} - a_{\overline{m}}}$$

where the functions $a_{\overline{n}}$ and $a_{\overline{m}}$ are calculated at a suitable rate of interest which requires to be chosen very much in the same way as the roll-up rate mentioned earlier.

From this it can be seen that the balance-of-term yield (or reinvestment yield) is the gradient of a line joining the two stocks on a chart where their respective coordinates are $(a_{\overline{n}|},\ y_n a_{\overline{n}|})$ and $(a_{\overline{m}|},\ y_m a_{\overline{m}|})$.

Coordinates of this type are called 'reinvestment coordinates' and 'reinvestment charts' which plot the position of all the stocks in the market on this basis are sometimes useful in identifying switching opportunities.

So far all the analytical methods considered have been for comparing one stock with a single alternative. We shall now switch our attention to two methods of a more global nature which compare individual stocks against the market as a whole: yield curve analysis and price model analysis. The first of these is considered in the following paragraphs, whilst the next section is devoted to the second.

Yield Curve Analysis

The concept of a yield curve has been around for many years. Essentially it is the shape or curve formed by plotting a graph of yields (nearly always gross redemption yields) on a graph's *y*-axis against some function of life to maturity on its *x*-axis. Traditionally it was normal for liquidity preference considerations to keep short-dated yields low, for the curve to rise towards the medium sector of the market before flattening out in the longs and approaching the irredeemables almost horizontally. J. M. Brew, in an article entitled 'Gilt-edged Yield Curves', published in *The Investment Analyst*, No. 16, December 1966, demonstrated that straight lines drawn on a 'reinvestment chart' of the sort mentioned earlier transform back into curves of this traditional shape, thus supporting the view that this was the naturally correct form for the yield curve to take.

During the early 1980s, however, funding policy caused the yield curve to have a pronounced hump in the medium-dated area and a downward-sloping tail at the long end, as Fig. 7.7 illustrates.

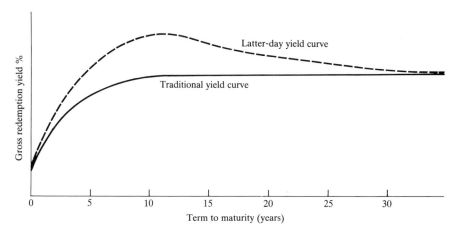

Fig. 7.7 *Traditional and latter-day yield curve shapes*

Prior to the advent of readily accessible computer power, the yield curve was more conceptual than in daily practical use. It was just possible to fit a curve to the points representing stocks' yields and lives to maturity, using mechanical hand calculators and/or seven-figure logarithms, but the sheer volume of the arithmetical calculations involved and the time taken to complete them made this an infrequently performed task. However, by the late 1950s and early 1960s computer power was starting to become available to the investment analyst, and this obstacle to progress started to disappear. The method was first brought into public prominence as a result of a paper delivered by G. T. Pepper to the Institute of Actuaries in 1963. Today there are probably as many (if not more) different forms of yield curve as there are major gilt-edged dealers, each with its own particular *modus operandi* but all basically doing the same thing – providing a measure of the central market yield level at any specified maturity, against which yields of individual stocks can be measured. This value is normally called the 'yield curve value', and the difference between the yield of an actual stock and the yield curve value for the same maturity is normally referred to as the stock's 'yield curve deviation'. When first introduced in the early 1960s, yield curve analysis appeared to be manna from heaven. Instead of having to keep a multitude of records of yield differences between innumerable pairs of stocks, all that seemed necessary was to record the daily yield curve deviations of each stock against the overall market, as in Fig. 7.8

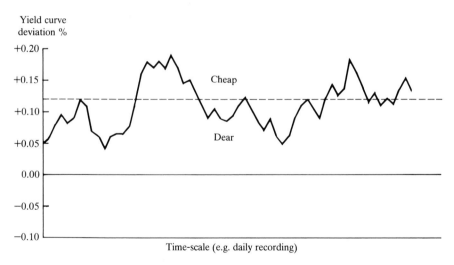

Fig. 7.8 *Hypothetical yield curve deviation chart of a single gilt-edged stock*

But life wasn't quite that easy. Fund managers who had grown up with and had cut their teeth on price ratios and yield differences were loath to give up using those tools of their trade, which they themselves could calculate, for the new statistics which, of necessity, they had to take on trust from whichever source they were supplied. Furthermore, rival brokers using marginally different curve-fitting methods might quite easily produce differing assessments of cheapness and dearness, and as a result in the early days it was felt that, whilst yield curve analysis was extremely quick and good at spotting potential anomalies, one should use the older methods to double-check its recommendations before embarking on a switch. It has to be realised that at this time institutions were not subject to capital gains tax but were very risk averse, so that a large proportion of gilt-edged business then was anomaly-switching between stocks of very similar date and coupon. It is also a fact that at that time the range of coupons on gilt-edged issues was very narrow. For example, on 1 January 1964 there was just one gilt-edged stock with a coupon of 6% (Conversion 6% 1972), whilst at the other end of the range the lowest coupon rate was $2\frac{1}{2}$% (Savings $2\frac{1}{2}$% 1964/67, Treasury $2\frac{1}{2}$% 1975/after, and Consol $2\frac{1}{2}$%. With only a limited coupon range in existence, the spread between the highest and lowest yields in the market was also small, as the scatter diagram for 2 January 1963 in Fig. 7.9 demonstrates. With data packed as closely as this, it was not difficult to obtain curves which fitted the market structure very satisfactorily.

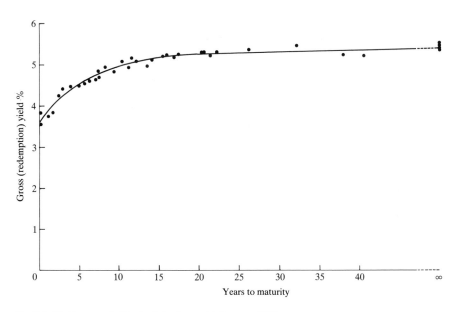

Fig. 7.9 *Yield curve of gilt-edged stocks as at 2 January 1963*

Problems started to occur with yield curve analysis in the latter part of the 1960s and early 1970s, as interest rates and yields rose and stocks of steadily increasing coupon rates were issued. The gilt-edged market has always had a yield to coupon rate correlation, with high-coupon stocks tending to yield considerably more than lower-coupon issues, and the effect of the creation of a plethora of (higher-yielding) high-coupon issues caused yield curve values to rise faster than the general level of actual yields. This tended to invalidate the system, since current deviations could not be compared with their past histories on a like-for-like basis. By the end of 1976 the coupon spread had widened to one of 15½% (Treasury 15½% 1998) to 3% (or 2½% if one counts the irredeemables Treasury 2½% 1975/after and Consol 2½%) – a range almost four times as wide as had existed thirteen years before – and the search was on to find a further form of global market analysis that would compensate for coupon variations as well as maturity differences in estimating central market values. This led to the advent of three-dimensional price models, of which more will be found in the next section. But, before leaving the concept of the yield curve behind, it is valuable to show how it can be used in its broader aspect – to provide simple descriptions of market yield-to-term relationships, etc., and a basis for observing macro changes in the market's overall yield structure.

To do this on a consistent basis requires the yield curves to be drawn at the various different times to be wholly comparable with one another. Since it is normally the high-coupon stocks that set the going market rates at any given time, it is advisable to restrict the stocks contributing to yield curve computations to those in the higher-coupon bracket. The choice is essentially one for each individual analyst to decide for himself, but 12% to 9% is, currently (1986), a not unreasonable selection.

Figure 7.10 shows some sample yield curves 'drawn' on a comparable basis, and the reader will see how easy it is to observe changes both in the level and shape of the market's yield structure, and how they provide a framework through which the investor can, if he is brave enough, make his own forecasts of future yield levels right across the maturity spectrum.

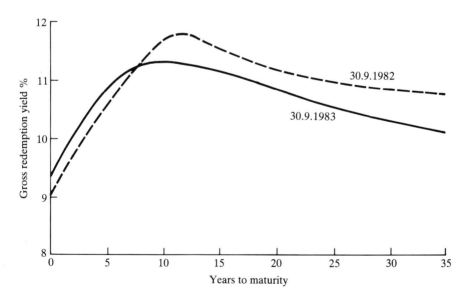

Fig. 7.10 *Yield curves formed by stocks in the 15½%–10% coupon range as at 30 September 1982 and 30 September 1983*

Some yield curve terminology has grown up over the years, and the gilt-edged practitioner should be conversant with the following pieces of jargon.

1. The yield curve is said to be 'positively sloped' when yields rise as maturities lengthen.
2. If yields fall as maturities lengthen the yield curve is said to be 'reverse sloped', or 'negatively sloped'.
3. If, over a period of time, shorter-dated yields fall faster than longer-dated ones, the yield curve is said to 'steepen'.
4. If the reverse happens, i.e. longer yields fall faster than shorter yields, the yield curve is said to 'flatten'.
5. If medium-dated yields exceed the average of short and long yields, the yield curve is said to be 'humped', and the maturity area coinciding with the highest yields is often called the 'hump' of the yield curve.

Price Model Analysis

As outlined in the previous section, price model analysis came about as a result of the need to find an analytical system that would relate stocks' valuations, not simply as a function of maturity (as in the two-dimensional yield–maturity yield curve method), but to take into account coupon variations as well. Essentially it was to find a form of equation

$$P = P(g, n)$$

where g represents coupon and n term to maturity.

There have been a number of varying approaches to solving this problem, some of which are well documented by virtue of having been the subject of public discussion in actuarial or Bank of England papers. Other work has been performed by stockbrokers for more private circulation and application.

Early work in this field was done at the Bank of England by J. P. Burman and W. R. White (see *Bank of England Quarterly Bulletin* for December 1972, September 1973, June 1976 and June 1982), using the expectational theory of interest rates at specified time horizons to obtain hypothetical equilibrium prices for gilt-edged stocks. In their work they segmented the gilt-edged market and in effect produced two market models, one for the short end of the market and another for the long, with an overlapping mid section in which values are blended. The main application of their work appears to have been the construction of the 'Bank of England par yield curve' which is believed to have been used to a considerable extent in fixing the terms of new gilt-edged issues. It is also the basis of the statistical yield series published regularly by the Bank in their *Quarterly Bulletin*. The concept of a par yield curve gets over some of the problems associated with yield curves mentioned in the previous section, but a small caveat regarding its use is in place.

Par yield curve values are obtained by solving the equation

$$P = P(g, n)$$

where n denotes number of half-years to maturity along the length of the maturity range to find the values of *g* (coupon) to make *P* (price) equal to 100, at which level coupon and yield obviously equate. If, as has happened in the past, most or all gilt-edged stocks are priced below par, the par yield value will then relate to a hypothetical coupon rate higher than those existing in the actual market. This can make the par yield curve value exceed the actual yields of the individual stocks. There is nothing statistically wrong with this, but the par yield curve is often (wrongly) considered to be a sort of average market yield for a given maturity from which other yields can be measured, which it is not.

To make this point abundantly clear, consider what would happen using a par yield curve to measure the apparent cheapness or dearness of, say, a 9% stock over a short period of time, in which the par yield value for the same maturity as the stock rose from 11% to 12%. At the initial point of time, the comparison would be one between a 9% stock and an 11% stock of the same maturity. At the later point, the comparison would be between a 9% stock and a 12% stock, and since a 12% stock can (usually) be expected to yield more than an 11% stock, the basis of comparison is invalidated.

Similarly, the use of par yield curves to measure movements in the level of yields in the market as a whole is of dubious validity. Imagine an instantaneous change in the market so that all yields rise by 1%. For the purposes of argument, let us say the par yield curve value at the twenty-year maturity point starts at 11%, meaning that 'on average' an 11% stock should be yielding 11%. A 12% stock at that time might thus be expected to yield, say, 11.1%, since higher yields are usually associated with higher-coupon rates. The subsequent movement upwards in all yields of 1% would carry the 11% coupon stock on to a yield of 12%, and the 12% coupon stock to a yield of 12.1%. Simple extrapolation of these figures would suggest that the new par yield curve for this maturity would be 12.11%. Thus, although in these circumstances the change in every single stock's yield was precisely 1%, the par yield curve value would rise not by 1% but by 1.11%. It is for this sort of reason that par curve values are not always the ideal implement for measuring broad changes in market yield structures.

An alternative approach to three-dimensional market building was introduced in a paper by Dr K. S. Feldman, BSc, PhD, FIA, entitled 'The Gilt-edged Market Reformulated', published in the *Journal of the Institute of Actuaries* (Vol. 104 II, dated September 1977). The essence of the Feldman approach (and also that behind a similar model built by R. T. Eddleston, MA, FIA, is that, at any particular time, there exist implicitly two discounting functions $A(n)$ and $V(n)$ (both functions of term to maturity, n), the former for discounting income items, and the latter for discounting capital payments. At any particular time the co-efficients of these two functions are found by applying a 'least-squares' fit to the observed prices of stocks in the market, and from these coefficients hypothetical model prices can be deduced. Both the Feldman and Eddleston models are fundamentally linear in coupon (though Eddleston makes special adjustments for low-coupon stocks), the Feldman version taking on a basic form of equation

$$P(g, n) = \frac{g}{2} A(n) + 100 V(n)$$

so that the model price for, say, 6% coupon stock would be exactly the average of the model prices for a 3% stock and a 9% stock of the same maturity. There is considerable intellectual purity in this approach, but it suffers from the not inconsiderable drawback that investors tend to place price premiums on stocks at the extremities of the coupon spectrum – especially the effect of higher rate tax payers upon the low coupon stocks – and that, in practice, the price/coupon relationship is curvilinear rather than linear more often than not.

The approach of R. S. Clarkson, BSc, FFA, to this question provoked widespread interest in the whole subject of three-dimensional price modelling when his paper, 'A Mathematical Model for the Gilt-edged Market', was read first to the Faculty of Actuaries in Edinburgh in February 1978, and subsequently to the Institute of Actuaries in London in January 1979. Clarkson uses a curvilinear model in which he eschews the normal compound interest functions such as $A(n)$ and $V(n)$, mentioned earlier, and establishes relationships instead between the flat yield, g/P, and the proportionate capital gain to redemption, $1/P$, for all stocks.

The actual *modus operandi* of the Clarkson method is set out in great detail in the *Journal of the Institute of Actuaries* (Vol. 106 II, September 1979), together with transcripts of the verbal discussion meeting which followed it. The *aficianados* of this subject are well advised to study it.

It is worth considering at this point the essential differences between linear and curvilinear models. Figure 7.11 shows constant-term price curves representative of the two methods. A stock of this term whose coupon and price can be represented by the point X would appear to be intrinsically cheap on the linear model, but correctly priced by the curvilinear one. Which of the two is correct? Does the (lower) valuation of X and the mid-coupon area in general represent a total market anomaly, or is it simply that the curve is the natural shape of the market at that moment? To this thorny question there is no definitive answer. A lot depends upon the use to which the price model is to be put. The most usual use of a price model (or yield curve, for that matter) is to produce theoretical model values for price (or yield) that fit the overall market structure, to compare actual prices (or yields) with them, and measure the deviations of price (or yield) day by day. Such deviations are then compared with their past histories (typically against some form of moving average) to see whether the current deviation is abnormal. Used in this way, the linear and the curvilinear models will often produce similar indications of cheapness or dearness, unless and until some form of fundamental market distortion takes place so as to change the relationship between the two types of model in an irreversible way. (The impact on low-coupon long-dated stocks of allowing index-linked stocks to be bought by all classes of investors in 1982 is a good example of such event.)

However, it is in the field of projective analysis that the real value of market modelling lies. A well-designed and flexible market modelling structure gives the gilt-edged analyst the opportunity to input his own (subjective) judgements about future market levels, yield patterns and relative stock valuations and produce prospective rates of return to some specified time horizon. Used intelligently, such a tool can be of immense value to a fund manager, enabling him if he

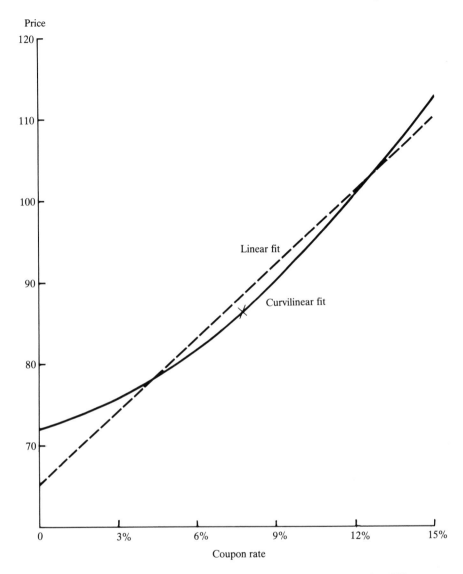

Fig. 7.11 *Linear and curvilinear price curves for five-year maturity as at 1 September 1983*

wishes to investigate the potential results of varying investment strategies and the effects of different forward market assumptions. Obviously the old computer adage, 'Garbage in – garbage out' is equally relevant here, but it also must be realised that to be properly effective in this role the price model structure needs to be very malleable. In this context, a curvilinear model, with its greater flexibility, is considerably more suitable than a linear one.

At this point the author has to declare a proprietory interest. The needs of his own firm for a flexible and adaptable price modelling and forward projective system led him to research and design his own curvilinear model and projection programs, examples of which appear below.

Firstly, let us have a look at how this newer model describes the structure of the market. This is probably more easily displayed in yield rather than price terms, and Fig. 7.12 shows the yield contours for stocks of 3%, 6%, 9%, 12% and 15% along the maturity range as at 22 December 1983. This graphically illustrates not only the differences in the levels of the various yield contours but also in their shapes – a feature which is not always apparent from the older form of yield curve analysis.

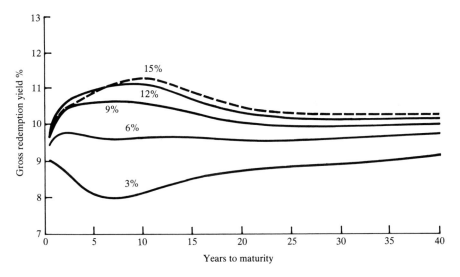

Fig. 7.12 *Three-dimensional yield structure of the gilt-edged market as at 22 December 1983*

Now let us see how this model can be used prospectively to provide an investor with a series of projected rates of return. In each case the projections are made using the gilt-edged market structure as at 30 December 1983 as a starting point, and projecting one year forward to January 1985. In the first example (Table 7.5 on pages 92 and 93) a neutral view of interest rates is taken; i.e. the basic assumption is that the level and shape of the market at the forward date will be the same as that at the outset. However, during the intervening period, stocks' maturities will have shortened by a year, and it is further assumed that all stocks' deviations revert to their (current) historical average at the forward date. Given these assumptions and applying them to the price model makes it possible to make projections of forward prices from which prospective performance yields at any required rate of tax (in this case 30% income tax) can be derived.

In the second and third examples (Table 7.6 on pages 94 and 95 and Table 7.7 on pages 96 and 97) the method is repeated, but the forward model structure is adjusted to allow for a change in the general level of the market and/or the slope of the yield curve. In Table 7.6 a reduction in short-term interest rates of 2%, and in long-term yields of 1%, has been imposed, whilst in the third example a rise of 1% in both short- and long-term rates is assumed.

The advantages of this type of projective analysis are considerable. It allows all sorts of investors with all sorts of tax positions and preferred time horizons to observe which stocks should serve them best on any given forward view of yields and interest rates. The problem is, of course, the formation of the correct strategic view for the period concerned; but once an investor has made his decision on this item, projective analysis regularly performed offers him an effective way of monitoring price movements – in the market in general, or between maturity sectors, or between individual stocks – all against his own expectations of future levels, and highlights switching opportunities consistent with his chosen strategy. If and when an investor wishes to change his strategic stance, a new projection made on the basis of his revised parameters will quickly indicate what portfolio adjustments should be made.

Table 7.5 *Projected rates of return of gilt-edged stocks by price model analysis (neutral assumption)*

SUBJECT TO INCOME TAX @ 30% NO CAPITAL GAINS TAX		CURRENT QUOTED PRICE	LIFE	3.3.1986 GROSS YIELD	FOR-WARD CLEAN PRICE	LIFE	3.3.1987 GROSS YIELD	GROSS REC. INC.	GROSS CAP. GAIN	NET PERF. YIELD
EXCH	10.50 1987	99.188XD	1.09	11.34	99.85	.09	12.23	10.50	.66	8.08
FUND	6.50 85/87	95.750	1.16	10.50	99.15	.16	12.06	6.50	3.40	8.26
TREAS	10.00 1987	98.750	1.27	11.06	99.44	.27	12.15	10.00	.69	7.80
TREAS	3.00 1987	93.125	1.36	8.46	97.10	.36	11.41	3.00	3.98	6.46
TREAS	12.00 1987	101.375	1.66	11.08	99.97	.66	12.05	12.00	− 1.41	6.97
TREAS	7.75 85/88	95.313	1.89	10.55	97.00	.89	11.37	7.75	1.69	7.44
EXCH	10.50 1988	99.438	2.18	10.80	98.96	1.18	11.47	10.50	− .48	6.95
TYCON	9.75 1988	97.750	2.28	10.88	97.99	1.28	11.48	9.75	.24	7.25
TRANS	3.00 78/88	88.500	2.33	8.56	91.98	1.33	9.59	3.00	3.48	6.25
TREAS	9.50 1988	96.750	2.64	10.94	97.24	1.64	11.39	9.50	.49	7.41
TREAS	11.50 1989	101.750	2.97	10.81	100.34	1.97	11.30	11.50	− 1.41	6.56
TYCON	9.50 1989	96.313	3.12	10.92	97.10	2.12	11.07	9.50	.79	7.75
TREAS	3.00 1989	85.000	3.20	8.45	88.06	2.20	9.12	3.00	3.06	6.02
TREAS	10.50 1989	99.250	3.28	10.77	98.69	2.28	11.17	10.50	− .56	6.88
EXCH	10.00 1989	98.063	3.41	10.70	97.68	2.41	11.12	10.00	− .39	6.76
EXCH	11.00 1989	101.000XD	3.57	10.66	99.83	2.57	11.08	11.00	− 1.17	6.50
TREAS	5.00 86/89	86.625	3.62	9.45	89.24	2.62	9.76	5.00	2.62	7.03
EXCON	10.25 1989	99.875	3.70	10.29	100.35	2.70	10.10	10.21	.48	7.66
TREAS	13.00 1990	107.313	3.86	10.65	104.97	2.86	10.93	13.00	− 2.34	6.35
EXCH	11.00 1990	101.188	3.94	10.63	100.33	2.94	10.86	11.00	− .85	6.79
EXCH	12.50 1990	106.125XD	4.05	10.61	104.14	3.05	10.87	12.50	− 1.99	6.41
TREAS	3.00 1990	81.125	4.18	8.46	84.03	3.18	8.88	3.00	2.91	6.13
TREAS	8.25 87/90	92.750	4.28	10.39	93.94	3.28	10.48	8.25	1.19	7.50
TYCON	10.00 1990	97.625	4.64	10.66	98.00	3.64	10.68	10.00	.38	7.59
EXCH	2.50 1990	77.281	4.72	8.44	80.81	3.72	8.65	2.49	3.53	6.76
TREAS	11.75 1991	104.313	4.85	10.59	103.34	3.85	10.67	11.75	− .97	6.99
FUND	5.75 87/91	87.375XD	5.09	8.89	88.72	4.09	9.12	5.75	1.35	6.13
EXCH	11.00 1991	102.313CD	5.64	10.44	101.74	4.64	10.52	11.00	− .57	7.02
EXCH	11.00 1991	102.438XD	5.64	10.42	101.74	4.64	10.52	10.98	4.79	6.91
TREAS	12.75 1992	110.250	5.88	10.38	108.49	4.88	10.48	12.75	− 1.76	6.54
TREAS	10.00 1992	98.625	5.97	10.32	98.66	4.97	10.35	10.00	.03	7.14
TYCON	10.50 1992	100.625	6.18	10.36	100.42	5.18	10.39	10.50	− .20	7.15
EXCH	12.25 1992	108.375	6.48	10.45	107.18	5.48	10.49	12.25	− 1.20	6.83
EXCH	13.50 1992	113.625XD	6.55	10.57	112.29	5.55	10.52	13.50	− 1.34	7.17
TREAS	10.00 1993	23.750	7.12	10.35	98.30	6.12	10.38	8.61	.05	7.16
TREAS	12.50 1993	110.250	7.36	10.47	109.62	6.36	10.40	12.50	− .63	7.39
FUND	6.00 1993	83.750XD	7.53	9.02	84.66	6.53	9.17	6.00	.91	6.09
TREAS	13.75 1993	116.750	7.72	10.53	115.66	6.72	10.45	13.75	− 1.09	7.36
TREAS	14.50 1994	121.625	8.00	10.43	120.27	7.00	10.36	14.50	− 1.36	7.25
EXCH	13.50 1994	115.750CD	8.15	10.57	114.87	7.15	10.49	13.50	− .88	7.46
EXCH	13.50 1994	115.875XD	8.15	10.55	114.87	7.15	10.49	13.48	5.72	7.37
EXCH	12.50 1994	111.125	8.47	10.49	110.32	7.47	10.47	12.50	− .80	7.17
TREAS	9.00 1994	92.625	8.70	10.31	93.87	7.70	10.17	9.00	1.24	8.15
TREAS	12.00 1995	108.500	8.89	10.51	107.99	7.89	10.49	12.00	− .51	7.29
GAS	3.00 90/95	71.625	9.16	7.30	73.44	8.16	7.39	3.00	1.82	5.44
EXCH	10.25 1995	98.875	9.38	10.44	99.21	8.38	10.39	10.25	.33	7.60
TREAS	12.75 1995	113.625	9.70	10.48	112.85	8.70	10.46	12.75	− .78	7.22
TREAS	14.00 1996	120.500	9.88	10.61	119.52	8.88	10.56	14.00	− .98	7.35
TREAS	9.00 92/96	92.375XD	10.03	10.23	93.20	9.03	10.17	9.00	.82	7.70
TREAS	15.25 1996	128.625	10.16	10.59	127.32	9.16	10.53	15.25	− 1.30	7.35
EXCH	13.25 1996	117.500	10.20	10.42	116.42	9.20	10.43	13.25	− 1.08	7.03

continued

Table 7.5   *continued*

						FOR-			GROSS	GROSS	NET
SUBJECT TO			CURRENT		3.3.1986	WARD		3.3.1987	GROSS	GROSS	NET
INCOME TAX @ 30%			QUOTED		GROSS	CLEAN		GROSS	REC.	CAP.	PERF.
NO CAPITAL GAINS		TAX	PRICE	LIFE	YIELD	PRICE	LIFE	YIELD	INC.	GAIN	YIELD
RED	3.00	86/96	77.375XD	10.58	5.91	78.56	9.58	5.97	3.00	1.18	4.23
TREAS	13.25	1997	117.875	10.88	10.46	116.75	9.88	10.49	13.25	− 1.13	6.94
EXCH	10.50	1997	100.750	10.97	10.39	100.59	9.97	10.40	10.50	− .16	7.15
TREAS	8.75	1997	90.375	11.50	10.18	90.88	10.50	10.18	8.75	.51	7.33
EXCH	15.00	1997	128.500CD	11.65	10.67	127.15	10.65	10.67	15.00	− 1.35	7.19
EXCH	15.00	1997	128.625XD	11.65	10.65	127.15	10.65	10.67	14.98	6.01	7.11
EXCH	9.75	1998	96.375	11.88	10.29	96.14	10.88	10.35	9.75	− .23	6.86
TREAS	6.75	95/98	77.625	12.16	9.97	79.51	11.16	9.81	6.75	1.88	8.50
TREAS	15.50	1998	133.875XD	12.57	10.57	132.17	11.57	10.61	15.50	− 1.70	6.86
EXCH	12.00	1998	111.375	12.71	10.37	110.10	11.71	10.48	12.00	− 1.27	6.45
TREAS	9.50	1999	95.250	12.86	10.17	95.34	11.86	10.19	9.50	.09	7.09
EXCH	12.25	1999	113.500XD	13.06	10.35	112.15	12.06	10.46	12.25	− 1.39	6.35
TREAS	10.50	1999	101.875	13.21	10.24	101.18	12.21	10.33	10.50	− .69	6.58
CONV	10.25	1999	100.000	13.72	10.25	99.49	12.72	10.32	10.25	− .51	6.70
TREAS	13.00	2000	119.375	14.36	10.38	118.14	13.36	10.45	13.00	− 1.24	6.62
TREAS	10.00	2001	99.750	14.98	10.04	98.89	13.98	10.15	10.00	− .86	6.18
TREAS	14.00	98/01	123.375	12.22	10.55	122.00	11.22	10.60	14.00	− 1.37	6.88
CONV	9.75	2001	98.000	15.44	10.01	97.16	14.44	10.13	9.75	− .84	6.12
EXCH	12.00	99/02	111.875	12.88	10.32	110.49	11.88	10.44	12.00	− 1.39	6.30
CONV	10.00	2002	99.750CD	16.10	10.03	99.05	15.10	10.12	10.00	− .70	6.36
CONV	10.00	2002	99.875XD	16.10	10.02	99.05	15.10	10.12	9.99	4.16	6.23
TREAS	9.75	2002	98.000	16.48	10.00	97.53	15.48	10.07	9.75	− .47	6.50
TREAS	13.75	00/03	124.625	14.39	10.41	123.29	13.39	10.48	13.75	− 1.34	6.68
TREAS	10.00	2003	41.750	17.51	9.97	99.70	16.51	10.04	9.34	− .55	6.40
TREAS	11.50	01/04	110.625XD	15.04	10.11	109.31	14.04	10.24	11.50	− 1.31	6.11
TREAS	10.00	2004	99.875	18.21	10.02	99.80	17.21	10.02	10.00	− .07	6.97
FUND	3.50	99/04	53.250	18.36	8.62	54.81	17.36	8.54	3.50	1.56	7.49
CONV	9.50	2004	96.000CD	18.64	9.98	95.91	17.64	10.00	9.50	− .09	6.87
CONV	9.50	2004	96.125XD	18.64	9.96	95.91	17.64	10.00	9.49	4.52	6.75
CONV	9.50	2005	96.375CD	19.12	9.93	96.10	18.12	9.97	9.50	− .27	6.66
CONV	9.50	2005	96.500XD	19.12	9.91	96.10	18.12	9.97	9.49	4.34	6.53
CONV	9.50	2005A	20.563	19.12	9.85	96.55	18.12	9.91	8.02	− .51	6.25
EXCH	10.50	2005	104.875XD	19.54	9.93	104.41	18.54	9.97	10.50	− .47	6.58
TREAS	12.50	03/05	119.375	17.71	10.13	118.59	16.71	10.16	12.50	− .78	6.72
TREAS	8.00	02/06	84.625XD	20.59	9.75	84.84	19.59	9.75	8.00	.22	6.88
TREAS	11.75	03/07	113.500	16.88	10.07	112.35	15.88	10.17	11.75	− 1.15	6.26
TREAS	13.50	04/08	127.875XD	18.06	10.11	126.94	17.06	10.15	13.50	− .93	6.68
TREAS	5.50	08/12	62.625XD	26.52	9.33	63.17	25.52	9.30	5.50	.55	7.01
TREAS	7.75	12/15	83.125	28.89	9.47	82.55	27.89	9.55	7.75	− .57	5.86
EXCH	12.00	13/17	121.000	27.77	9.79	120.95	26.77	9.78	12.00	− .05	6.92
CONS	4.00	57/—	40.875	.00	9.79	40.68	.00	9.83	4.00	− .20	6.39
WAR	3.50	52/—	36.500	.00	9.59	36.24	.00	9.66	3.50	− .26	6.02
CONV	3.50	61/—	47.625XD	.00	7.35	46.33	.00	7.55	3.50	− 1.30	2.44
TREAS	3.00	66/—	30.750XD	.00	9.76	30.72	.00	9.77	3.00	− .03	6.73
CONS	2.50	23/—	25.875XD	.00	9.78	25.88	.00	9.66	2.50	.01	6.85
TREAS	2.50	75/—	25.625XD	.00	9.76	25.75	.00	9.71	2.50	.13	7.33

Source: Barclays de Zoete Wedd

Note: Where the period of the projection is longer than six months in duration, the projected returns are expressed as (net) performance yields per cent/per annum. When the period is six months or less the projected returns are expressed in non-annualised percentage form.

Table 7.6   *Projected rates of return of gilt-edged stocks by price model analysis (bull assumption)*

SUBJECT TO INCOME TAX @ 30% NO CAPITAL GAINS TAX	CURRENT QUOTED PRICE	LIFE	3.3.1986 GROSS YIELD	FOR-WARD CLEAN PRICE	LIFE	3.3.1987 GROSS YIELD	GROSS REC. INC.	GROSS CAP. GAIN	NET PERF. YIELD
EXCH 10.50 1987	99.188XD	1.09	11.34	100.02	.09	10.24	10.50	.84	8.25
FUND 6.50 85/87	95.750	1.16	10.50	99.45	.16	10.10	6.50	3.70	8.56
TREAS 10.00 1987	98.750	1.27	11.06	99.95	.27	10.19	10.00	1.20	8.31
TREAS 3.00 1987	93.125	1.36	8.46	97.73	.36	9.54	3.00	4.60	7.12
TREAS 12.00 1987	101.375	1.66	11.08	101.19	.66	10.11	12.00	− .19	8.16
TREAS 7.75 85/88	95.313	1.89	10.55	98.50	.89	9.54	7.75	3.19	8.98
EXCH 10.50 1988	99.438	2.18	10.80	100.96	1.18	9.62	10.50	1.52	8.94
TYCON 9.75 1988	97.750	2.28	10.88	100.10	1.28	9.67	9.75	2.35	9.36
TRANS 3.00 78/88	88.500	2.33	8.56	93.86	1.33	7.97	3.00	5.36	8.31
TREAS 9.50 1988	96.750	2.64	10.94	99.81	1.64	9.63	9.50	3.06	10.01
TREAS 11.50 1989	101.750	2.97	10.81	103.45	1.97	9.54	11.50	1.70	9.55
TYCON 9.50 1989	96.313	3.12	10.92	100.24	2.12	9.37	9.50	3.93	10.94
TREAS 3.00 1989	85.000	3.20	8.45	90.77	2.20	7.64	3.00	5.77	9.12
TREAS 10.50 1989	99.250	3.28	10.77	102.08	2.28	9.46	10.50	2.83	10.22
EXCH 10.00 1989	98.063	3.41	10.70	101.16	2.41	9.45	10.00	3.10	10.24
EXCH 11.00 1989	101.000XD	3.57	10.66	103.59	2.57	9.40	11.00	2.59	10.13
TREAS 5.00 86/89	86.625	3.62	9.45	92.47	2.62	8.26	5.00	5.85	10.65
EXCON 10.25 1989	99.875	3.70	10.29	104.25	2.70	8.46	10.21	4.37	11.47
TREAS 13.00 1990	107.313	3.86	10.65	109.25	2.86	9.25	13.00	1.94	10.27
EXCH 11.00 1990	101.188	3.94	10.63	104.48	2.94	9.22	11.00	3.30	10.79
EXCH 12.50 1990	106.125XD	4.05	10.61	108.57	3.05	9.21	12.50	2.44	10.50
TREAS 3.00 1990	81.125	4.18	8.46	87.47	3.18	7.51	3.00	6.34	10.23
TREAS 8.25 87/90	92.750	4.28	10.39	98.08	3.28	8.94	8.25	5.33	11.84
TYCON 10.00 1990	97.625	4.64	10.66	102.69	3.64	9.12	10.00	5.06	12.27
EXCH 2.50 1990	77.281	4.72	8.44	84.49	3.72	7.35	2.49	7.20	11.34
TREAS 11.75 1991	104.313	4.85	10.59	108.48	3.85	9.09	11.75	4.16	11.79
FUND 5.75 87/91	87.375XD	5.09	8.89	93.22	4.09	7.71	5.75	5.85	11.13
EXCH 11.00 1991	102.313CD	5.64	10.44	107.47	4.64	9.00	11.00	5.16	12.49
EXCH 11.00 1991	102.438XD	5.64	10.42	107.47	4.64	9.00	10.98	10.52	12.40
TREAS 12.75 1992	110.250	5.88	10.38	114.77	4.88	8.95	12.75	4.52	12.10
TREAS 10.00 1992	98.625	5.97	10.32	104.48	4.97	8.87	10.00	5.85	12.85
TYCON 10.50 1992	100.625	6.18	10.36	106.51	5.18	8.90	10.50	5.88	13.03
EXCH 12.25 1992	108.375	6.48	10.45	113.87	5.48	8.99	12.25	5.49	12.83
EXCH 13.50 1992	113.625XD	6.55	10.57	119.30	5.55	9.00	13.50	5.68	13.17
TREAS 10.00 1993	23.750	7.12	10.35	104.96	6.12	8.93	8.61	6.71	14.80
TREAS 12.50 1993	110.250	7.36	10.47	117.14	6.36	8.91	12.50	6.89	14.01
FUND 6.00 1993	83.750XD	7.53	9.02	90.59	6.53	7.87	6.00	6.84	12.93
TREAS 13.75 1993	116.750	7.72	10.53	123.79	6.72	8.96	13.75	7.04	14.14
TREAS 14.50 1994	121.625	8.00	10.43	128.87	7.00	8.87	14.50	7.25	14.10
EXCH 13.50 1994	115.750CD	8.15	10.57	123.27	7.15	9.01	13.50	7.52	14.53
EXCH 13.50 1994	115.875XD	8.15	10.55	123.27	7.15	9.01	13.48	14.13	14.47
EXCH 12.50 1994	111.125	8.47	10.49	118.68	7.47	9.01	12.50	7.55	14.44
TREAS 9.00 1994	92.625	8.70	10.31	101.24	7.70	8.78	9.00	8.61	15.82
TREAS 12.00 1995	108.500	8.89	10.51	116.47	7.89	9.04	12.00	7.97	14.85
GAS 3.00 90/95	71.625	9.16	7.30	79.11	8.16	6.32	3.00	7.48	13.08
EXCH 10.25 1995	98.875	9.38	10.44	107.36	8.38	8.98	10.25	8.49	15.55
TREAS 12.75 1995	113.625	9.70	10.48	122.12	8.70	9.02	12.75	8.50	15.14
TREAS 14.00 1996	120.500	9.88	10.61	129.31	8.88	9.12	14.00	8.81	15.21
TREAS 9.00 92/96	92.375XD	10.03	10.23	101.23	5.03	8.69	9.00	8.85	16.04
TREAS 15.25 1996	128.625	10.16	10.5?	137.73	9.16	9.09	15.25	9.11	15.22
EXCH 13.25 1996	117.500	10.20	10.42	126.20	9.20	9.00	13.25	8.70	15.10

continued

Table 7.6 *continued*

	SUBJECT TO INCOME TAX @ 30% NO CAPITAL GAINS TAX		CURRENT QUOTED PRICE	LIFE	3.3.1986 GROSS YIELD	FOR-WARD CLEAN PRICE	LIFE	3.3.1987 GROSS YIELD	GROSS REC. INC.	GROSS CAP. GAIN	NET PERF. YIELD
RED	3.00	86/96	77.375XD	10.58	5.91	85.27	9.58	4.95	3.00	7.90	12.61
TREAS	13.25	1997	117.875	10.88	10.46	126.86	9.88	9.08	13.25	8.99	15.24
EXCH	10.50	1997	100.750	10.97	10.39	109.59	9.97	9.02	10.50	8.84	15.75
TREAS	8.75	1997	90.375	11.50	10.18	99.30	10.50	8.85	8.75	8.93	16.27
EXCH	15.00	1997	128.500CD	11.65	10.67	138.20	10.65	9.28	15.00	9.70	15.53
EXCH	15.00	1997	128.625XD	11.65	10.65	138.20	10.65	9.28	14.98	17.05	15.49
EXCH	9.75	1998	96.375	11.88	10.29	105.12	10.88	9.00	9.75	8.75	15.84
TREAS	6.75	95/98	77.625	12.16	9.97	87.15	11.16	8.56	6.75	9.52	17.91
TREAS	15.50	1998	133.875XD	12.57	10.57	143.83	11.57	9.25	15.50	9.95	15.29
EXCH	12.00	1998	111.375	12.71	10.37	120.38	11.71	9.13	12.00	9.00	15.40
TREAS	9.50	1999	95.250	12.86	10.17	104.55	11.86	8.87	9.50	9.30	16.39
EXCH	12.25	1999	113.500XD	13.06	10.35	122.61	12.06	9.12	12.25	9.11	15.31
TREAS	10.50	1999	101.875	13.21	10.24	110.93	12.21	9.01	10.50	9.05	15.84
CONV	10.25	1999	100.000	13.72	10.25	109.22	12.72	9.02	10.25	9.22	16.11
TREAS	13.00	2000	119.375	14.36	10.38	129.32	13.36	9.15	13.00	9.95	15.68
TREAS	10.00	2001	99.750	14.98	10.04	108.83	13.98	8.88	10.00	9.08	15.78
TREAS	14.00	98/01	123.375	12.22	10.55	132.93	11.22	9.23	14.00	9.55	15.47
CONV	9.75	2001	98.000	15.44	10.01	107.03	14.44	8.88	9.75	9.03	15.84
EXCH	12.00	99/02	111.875	12.88	10.32	120.84	11.88	9.10	12.00	8.96	15.25
CONV	10.00	2002	99.750CD	16.10	10.03	109.17	15.10	8.89	10.00	9.42	16.19
CONV	10.00	2002	99.875XD	16.10	10.02	109.17	15.10	8.89	9.99	14.28	16.05
TREAS	9.75	2002	98.000	16.48	10.00	107.59	15.48	8.84	9.75	9.59	16.37
TREAS	13.75	00/03	124.625	14.39	10.41	134.82	13.39	9.18	13.75	10.20	15.62
TREAS	10.00	2003	41.750	17.51	9.97	110.08	16.51	8.83	9.34	9.83	17.08
TREAS	11.50	01/04	110.625XD	15.04	10.11	120.04	14.04	8.96	11.50	9.41	15.48
TREAS	10.00	2004	99.875	18.21	10.02	110.28	17.21	8.83	10.00	10.41	17.08
FUND	3.50	99/04	53.250	18.36	8.62	61.45	17.36	7.51	3.50	8.20	19.31
CONV	9.50	2004	96.000CD	18.64	9.98	106.13	17.64	8.81	9.50	10.13	17.14
CONV	9.50	2004	96.125XD	18.64	9.96	106.13	17.64	8.81	9.49	14.74	17.05
CONV	9.50	2005	96.375CD	19.12	9.93	106.41	18.12	8.79	9.50	10.04	16.99
CONV	9.50	2005	96.500XD	19.12	9.91	106.41	18.12	8.79	9.49	14.65	16.87
CONV	9.50	2005A	20.563	19.12	9.85	106.91	18.12	8.73	8.02	9.84	18.53
EXCH	10.50	2005	104.875XD	19.54	9.93	115.46	18.54	8.79	10.50	10.59	16.71
TREAS	12.50	03/05	119.375	17.71	10.13	130.41	16.71	8.96	12.50	11.03	16.28
TREAS	8.00	02/06	84.625XD	20.59	9.75	94.37	19.59	8.60	8.00	9.75	17.68
TREAS	11.75	03/07	113.500	16.88	10.07	123.58	15.88	8.94	11.75	10.08	15.82
TREAS	13.50	04/08	127.875XD	18.06	10.11	139.42	17.06	8.95	13.50	11.55	16.09
TREAS	5.50	08/12	62.625XD	26.52	9.33	70.77	25.52	8.27	5.50	8.15	18.59
TREAS	7.75	12/15	83.125	28.89	9.47	92.54	27.89	8.45	7.75	9.42	17.41
EXCH	12.00	13/17	121.000	27.77	9.79	135.36	26.77	8.60	12.00	14.36	18.34
CONS	4.00	57/—	40.875	.00	9.79	45.32	.00	8.83	4.00	4.44	17.28
WAR	3.50	52/—	36.500	.00	9.59	40.36	.00	8.67	3.50	3.86	16.93
CONV	3.50	61/—	47.625XD	.00	7.35	51.61	.00	6.78	3.50	3.98	13.25
TREAS	3.00	66/—	30.750XD	.00	9.76	34.22	.00	8.77	3.00	3.47	17.65
CONS	2.50	23/—	25.875XD	.00	9.78	28.83	.00	8.67	2.50	2.95	17.86
TREAS	2.50	75/—	25.625XD	.00	9.76	28.69	.00	8.71	2.50	3.06	18.29

Source: Barclays de Zoete Wedd

Note: Where the period of the projection is longer than six months in duration, the projected returns are expressed as (net) performance yields per cent/per annum. When the period is six months or less the projected returns are expressed in non-annualised percentage form.

Table 7.7 *Projected rates of return of gilt-edged stocks by price model analysis (bear assumption)*

SUBJECT TO INCOME TAX @ 30% NO CAPITAL GAINS TAX			CURRENT QUOTED PRICE	LIFE	3.3.1986 GROSS YIELD	FOR-WARD CLEAN PRICE	LIFE	3.3.1987 GROSS YIELD	GROSS REC. INC.	GROSS CAP. GAIN	NET PERF. YIELD
EXCH	10.50	1987	99.188XD	1.09	11.34	99.76	.09	13.25	10.50	.57	7.99
FUND	6.50	85/87	95.750	1.16	10.50	99.00	.16	13.05	6.50	3.25	8.11
TREAS	10.00	1987	98.750	1.27	11.06	99.18	.27	13.15	10.00	.43	7.54
TREAS	3.00	1987	93.125	1.36	8.46	96.79	.36	12.36	3.00	3.66	6.13
TREAS	12.00	1987	101.375	1.66	11.08	99.35	.66	13.05	12.00	−2.03	6.36
TREAS	7.75	85/88	95.313	1.89	10.55	96.24	.89	12.32	7.75	.93	6.66
EXCH	10.50	1988	99.438	2.18	10.80	97.92	1.18	12.44	10.50	−1.52	5.92
TYCON	9.75	1988	97.750	2.28	10.88	96.90	1.28	12.45	9.75	− .85	6.15
TRANS	3.00	78/88	88.500	2.33	8.56	90.10	1.33	10.44	3.00	2.50	5.17
TREAS	9.50	1988	96.750	2.64	10.94	95.90	1.64	12.33	9.50	− .85	6.04
TREAS	11.50	1989	101.750	2.97	10.81	98.71	1.97	12.26	11.50	−3.04	4.96
TYCON	9.50	1989	96.313	3.12	10.92	95.44	2.12	12.00	9.50	− .87	6.05
TREAS	3.00	1989	85.000	3.20	8.45	86.61	2.20	9.93	3.00	1.61	4.35
TREAS	10.50	1989	99.250	3.28	10.77	96.89	2.28	12.10	10.50	−2.36	5.07
EXCH	10.00	1989	98.063	3.41	10.70	95.82	2.41	12.05	10.00	−2.25	4.88
EXCH	11.00	1989	101.00XD	3.57	10.66	97.82	2.57	12.01	11.00	−3.18	4.52
TREAS	5.00	86/89	86.625	3.62	9.45	87.50	2.62	10.60	5.00	.87	5.06
EXCON	10.25	1989	99.875	3.70	10.29	98.26	2.70	11.01	10.21	−1.62	5.59
TREAS	13.00	1990	107.313	3.86	10.65	102.65	2.86	11.88	13.00	−4.66	4.19
EXCH	11.00	1990	101.188	3.94	10.63	98.09	2.94	11.79	11.00	−3.10	4.58
EXCH	12.50	1990	106.125XD	4.05	10.61	101.73	3.05	11.81	12.50	−4.39	4.15
TREAS	3.00	1990	81.125	4.18	8.46	82.15	3.18	9.65	3.00	1.03	3.85
TREAS	8.25	87/90	92.750	4.28	10.39	91.67	3.28	11.36	8.25	−1.08	5.09
TYCON	10.00	1990	97.625	4.64	10.66	95.41	3.64	11.58	10.00	−2.21	4.96
EXCH	2.50	1990	77.281	4.72	8.44	78.77	3.72	9.40	2.49	1.49	4.17
TREAS	11.75	1991	104.313	4.85	10.59	100.49	3.85	11.59	11.75	−3.82	4.27
FUND	5.75	87/91	87.375XD	5.09	8.89	86.20	4.09	9.94	5.75	−1.17	3.28
EXCH	11.00	1991	102.313CD	5.64	10.44	98.50	4.64	11.42	11.00	−3.81	3.86
EXCH	11.00	1991	102.438XD	5.64	10.42	98.50	4.64	11.42	10.98	1.55	3.74
TREAS	12.75	1992	110.250	5.88	10.38	104.92	4.88	11.41	12.75	−5.33	3.31
TREAS	10.00	1992	98.625	5.97	10.32	95.34	4.97	11.25	10.00	−3.29	3.80
TYCON	10.50	1992	100.625	6.18	10.36	96.94	5.18	11.30	10.50	−3.69	3.69
EXCH	12.25	1992	108.375	6.48	10.45	103.32	5.48	11.42	12.25	−5.06	3.29
EXCH	13.50	1992	113.625XD	6.55	10.57	108.24	5.55	11.45	13.50	−5.39	3.62
TREAS	10.00	1993	23.750	7.12	10.35	94.41	6.12	11.29	8.61	−3.84	2.59
TREAS	12.50	1993	110.250	7.36	10.47	105.20	6.36	11.33	12.50	−5.05	3.40
FUND	6.00	1993	83.750XD	7.53	9.02	81.15	6.53	10.00	6.00	−2.60	1.93
TREAS	13.75	1993	116.750	7.72	10.53	110.85	6.72	11.40	13.75	−5.90	3.25
TREAS	14.50	1994	121.625	8.00	10.43	115.16	7.00	11.31	14.50	−6.46	3.07
EXCH	13.50	1994	115.750CD	8.15	10.57	109.86	7.15	11.44	13.50	−5.89	3.13
EXCH	13.50	1994	115.875XD	8.15	10.55	109.86	7.15	11.44	13.48	.71	3.02
EXCH	12.50	1994	111.125	8.47	10.49	105.31	7.47	11.43	12.50	−5.82	2.67
TREAS	9.00	1994	92.625	8.70	10.31	89.41	7.70	11.08	9.00	−3.22	3.37
TREAS	12.00	1995	108.500	8.89	10.51	102.85	7.89	11.44	12.00	−5.65	2.58
GAS	3.00	90/95	71.625	9.16	7.30	69.95	8.16	8.11	3.00	−1.67	.60
EXCH	10.25	1995	98.875	9.38	10.44	94.22	8.38	11.34	10.25	−4.65	2.59
TREAS	12.75	1995	113.625	9.70	10.48	107.15	8.70	11.43	12.75	−6.47	2.20
TREAS	14.00	1996	120.500	9.88	10.61	113.49	8.88	11.53	14.00	−7.01	2.36
TREAS	9.00	92/96	92.375XD	10.03	10.23	88.23	9.03	11.10	9.00	−4.15	2.36
TREAS	15.25	1996	128.625	10.16	10.59	120.85	9.16	11.50	15.25	−7.74	2.33
EXCH	13.25	1996	117.500	10.20	10.42	110.36	9.20	11.40	13.25	−7.14	1.86

continued

Table 7.7 *continued*

SUBJECT TO INCOME TAX @ 30% NO CAPITAL GAINS TAX			CURRENT QUOTED PRICE	LIFE	3.3.1986 GROSS YIELD	FOR-WARD GROSS CLEAN PRICE	LIFE	3.3.1987 GROSS YIELD	GROSS REC. INC.	GROSS CAP. GAIN	NET PERF. YIELD
RED	3.00	86/96	77.375XD	10.58	5.91	74.33	9.58	6.67	3.00	−3.05	−1.24
TREAS	13.25	1997	117.875	10.88	10.46	110.40	9.88	11.46	13.25	−7.47	1.56
EXCH	10.50	1997	100.750	10.97	10.39	94.93	9.97	11.36	10.50	−5.82	1.54
TREAS	8.75	1997	90.375	11.50	10.18	85.52	10.50	11.12	8.75	−4.85	1.43
EXCH	15.00	1997	128.500CD	11.65	10.67	120.13	10.65	11.65	15.00	−8.37	1.70
EXCH	15.00	1997	128.625XD	11.65	10.65	120.13	10.65	11.65	14.98	−1.01	1.59
EXCH	9.75	1998	96.375	11.88	10.29	90.40	10.88	11.31	9.75	−5.97	.90
TREAS	6.75	95/98	77.625	12.16	9.97	74.59	11.16	10.71	6.75	−3.04	2.21
TREAS	15.50	1998	133.875XD	12.57	10.57	124.64	11.57	11.58	15.50	−9.24	1.23
EXCH	12.00	1998	111.375	12.71	10.37	103.45	11.71	11.46	12.00	−7.93	.43
TREAS	9.50	1999	95.250	12.86	10.17	89.35	11.86	11.14	9.50	−5.90	.80
EXCH	12.25	1999	113.500XD	13.06	10.35	105.26	12.06	11.44	12.25	−8.24	.30
TREAS	10.50	1999	101.875	13.21	10.24	94.81	12.21	11.29	10.50	−7.07	.29
CONV	10.25	1999	100.000	13.72	10.25	93.08	12.72	11.29	10.25	−6.92	.26
TREAS	13.00	2000	119.375	14.36	10.38	110.68	13.36	11.42	13.00	−8.70	.35
TREAS	10.00	2001	99.750	14.98	10.04	92.22	13.98	11.11	10.00	−7.53	− .54
TREAS	14.00	98/01	123.375	12.22	10.55	114.98	11.22	11.58	14.00	−8.39	1.17
CONV	9.75	2001	98.000	15.44	10.01	90.47	14.44	11.09	9.75	−7.51	− .72
EXCH	12.00	99/02	111.875	12.88	10.32	103.76	11.88	11.41	12.00	−8.12	.26
CONV	10.00	2002	99.750CD	16.10	10.03	92.15	15.10	11.08	10.00	−7.60	− .62
CONV	10.00	2002	99.875XD	16.10	10.02	92.15	15.10	11.08	9.99	−2.74	− .76
TREAS	9.75	2002	98.000	16.48	10.00	90.63	15.48	11.02	9.75	−7.36	− .56
TREAS	13.75	00/03	124.625	14.39	10.41	115.60	13.39	11.45	13.75	−9.03	.49
TREAS	10.00	2003	41.750	17.51	9.97	92.51	16.51	10.99	9.34	−7.74	−1.31
TREAS	11.50	01/04	110.625XD	15.04	10.11	102.10	14.04	11.20	11.50	−8.52	− .44
TREAS	10.00	2004	99.875	18.21	10.02	92.48	17.21	10.98	10.00	−7.40	− .41
FUND	3.50	99/04	53.250	18.36	8.62	50.24	17.36	9.35	3.50	−3.01	−1.06
CONV	9.50	2004	96.000CD	18.64	9.98	88.73	17.64	10.96	9.50	−7.27	− .66
CONV	9.50	2004	96.125XD	18.64	9.96	88.73	17.64	10.96	9.49	−2.65	− .80
CONV	9.50	2005	96.375CD	19.12	9.93	88.84	18.12	10.93	9.50	−7.54	− .94
CONV	9.50	2005	96.500XD	19.12	9.91	88.84	18.12	10.93	9.49	−2.92	−1.09
CONV	9.50	2005A	20.563	19.12	9.85	89.25	18.12	10.87	8.02	−7.81	−2.73
EXCH	10.50	2005	104.875XD	19.54	9.93	96.58	18.54	10.93	10.50	−8.30	− .92
TREAS	12.50	03/05	119.375	17.71	10.13	110.35	16.71	11.12	12.50	−9.02	− .24
TREAS	8.00	02/06	84.625XD	20.59	9.75	78.05	19.59	10.70	8.00	−6.57	−1.17
TREAS	11.75	03/07	113.500	16.88	10.07	104.60	15.88	11.13	11.75	−8.90	− .61
TREAS	13.50	04/08	127.875XD	18.06	10.11	118.20	17.06	11.10	13.50	−9.68	− .19
TREAS	5.50	08/12	62.625XD	26.52	9.33	57.52	25.52	10.21	5.50	−5.11	−2.05
TREAS	7.75	12/15	83.125	28.89	9.47	75.10	27.89	10.53	7.75	−8.03	−3.21
EXCH	12.00	13/17	121.000	27.77	9.79	110.34	26.77	10.81	12.00	−10.66	−1.91
CONS	4.00	57/—	40.875	.00	9.79	36.90	.00	10.84	4.00	−3.98	−2.95
WAR	3.50	52/—	36.500	.00	9.59	32.87	.00	10.65	3.50	−3.63	−3.33
CONV	3.50	61/—	47.625XD	.00	7.35	42.02	.00	8.33	3.50	−5.60	−6.83
TREAS	3.00	66/—	30.750XD	.00	9.76	27.86	.00	10.77	3.00	−2.89	−2.63
CONS	2.50	23/—	25.875XD	.00	9.78	23.48	.00	10.65	2.50	−2.40	−2.60
TREAS	2.50	75/—	25.625XD	.00	9.76	23.36	.00	10.70	2.50	−2.26	−2.06

Source: Barclays de Zoete Wedd

Note : Where the period of the projection is longer than six months in duration, the projected returns are expressed as (net) performance yields per cent/per annum. When the period is six months or less the projected returns are expressed in non-annualised percentage form.

8

Speciality analysis

All the foregoing has been concerned with the analytical methods used to assess the merits of 'conventional' gilt-edged stocks. But, as outlined in Chapter 5, there are several varieties of gilts that have peculiar characteristics that render them incapable of being analysed by 'conventional' methods, namely the following:

1. Variable-rate stocks.
2. Convertible stocks.
3. Index-linked stocks.

Variable-rate Stocks

Up to the end of 1985 there have only been three issues of variable-rate stocks made by the British Government:

£400 million	Variable-rate Treasury Stock 1981	issued on 27 May 1977
£400 million	Variable-rate Treasury Stock 1982	issued on 1 July 1977
£400 million	Variable-rate Treasury Stock 1983	issued on 26 Jan 1979

All of these have by now been redeemed, but it is possible that at some future date further issues of this sort may reappear. Thus a short note regarding suitable analytical methods for them is applicable.

The coupon payments made on these stocks were determined by taking the interest that would accrue on a daily basis at an indicator rate equal to the weekly Treasury bill tender rate (which is, incidentally, a rate of discount, as opposed to a rate of interest) plus $\frac{1}{2}\%$, the reference period for calculation purposes normally being that between the two relevant ex-dividend dates. Given this formula, it was always possible to know the gross accrued interest on a particular day, even if the final half-yearly coupon rate was not established until the ex-dividend date immediately preceding it.

Thus it was possible to use clean price ratios as a method of comparing these stocks with one another or with conventional gilts; but precisely the same qualifications about the validity of price ratios as an analytical method that were mentioned in Chapter 7 also apply in this instance. Furthermore, since the half-yearly coupon payments varied, and the accrued interest did not accumulate linearly, it was not possible to make the necessary trend compensations to overcome the income flow differentials. Price ratios were, however, undoubtedly used for this purpose by some investors in ignorance of their unsuitability. History does not relate whether disastrous losses resulted or accidental profits were made as a result.

The system of performance ratios had no such problems in coping with variable coupons, and proved to be adequate for historical price comparisons.

Yields were not capable of being computed on a conventional compound interest basis, unless assumptions were made as to the future course of the Treasury bill rate. The most widely used assumption was that it should remain constant at the most recent weekly tender rate. Not surprisingly, this gave the intelligent investor no guidance whatsoever about the absolute valuation of these stocks, but when subtracted from the assumed future Treasury bill *yield* gave the investor an approximate measure of the additional yield to be obtained from holding these stocks to redemption, as opposed to holding a rolling portfolio of Treasury bills for the same period.

Note: It is important to appreciate fully the difference between a rate of interest and a rate of discount in these matters. The Treasury bill rate is a rate of discount, d, such that applying it for, say, 91-day bills

$$\text{current price, } P = 100 - \left(d \times \frac{91}{365} \right)$$

$$\text{i.e.} \quad d = (100 - P) \times \frac{365}{91}.$$

The equivalent simple interest yield is related not to the redemption value of 100, but to the current price, P, such that

$$y = \frac{100 - P}{P/100} \times \frac{365}{91}.$$

Whilst this difference may seem trifling, it is salutary to observe the margin between the two, especially at times of higher (crisis-related) interest rates.

For example, when Treasury bill rate $= 16\%$, the price of 91-day bills would be 96.01096. This produces a corresponding yield of 16.66%; whilst at lower levels a 10% bill rate equated with a 10.26% yield basis.

Thus, the linking of the coupons of the variable-rate stocks to the (discount) rate on Treasury bills, plus $\frac{1}{2}\%$, was not quite as generous as it ostensibly seemed, and the real attraction of the variable-rate stocks came in being able to acquire them at below par.

Convertible Stocks

The archetypal convertible gilt-edged is a short-dated (nil to five years to maturity) stock offering the holder the right to convert into a longer issue on various terms at a finite number of dates in the future. Sometimes the 'convert-into' stock is an existing one; alternatively, it may be a new stock which will be created wholly by the exercise of the conversion option.

There is, in principle, no reason why the 'convert-from' stock need not be a medium- or long-dated stock converting into something shorter, but this has not been the way of things in practice. There is, however, one index-linked stock which carried the right to convert into a conventional fixed-coupon issue with the same redemption date, and one conventional stock with options to convert into either of two other issues. It would be a brave man who would be prepared to state that no further conversion innovations will be forthcoming!

Convertible stocks need, therefore, to be assessed on both a 'non-converted' and an 'if-converted' basis. Of these, the former presents little problem, since all the conventional methods can be applied. Viewing a convertible on an 'if-converted' basis, however, is more complex – not least for the reason that most stocks have a range of differing conversion dates and terms.

As an example, consider Treasury $10\frac{1}{4}\%$ Convertible 1987. For every £100 nominal of this stock the holder had the option to convert, if he should so wish, into Conversion $9\frac{3}{4}\%$ 2001 on the following terms:

On 10 February 1984 into	£100	nominal	Conversion $9\frac{3}{4}\%$	2001		
On 10 August 1984	,,	£97	,,	,,	,,	,,
On 10 February 1985	,,	£94	,,	,,	,,	,,
On 10 August 1985	,,	£91	,,	,,	,,	,,
On 10 February 1986	,,	£88	,,	,,	,,	,,

After 10 February 1986 no further conversion options exist, and if not converted by that date the stock will be redeemed in the normal way on 10 February 1987.

Thus, it can be seen that on an 'if-converted' basis there are potentially five different bases of valuation for this stock, depending on which conversion option is likely to be exercised. In this case, the conversion terms have been deliberately chosen so as to deteriorate as time progresses, and it soon becomes apparent that nearest conversion is the most attractive. This is demonstrated by an analysis of the gross redemption yields relating to each differing conversion option.

Calculation of such yields is simply a matter of establishing which dividends and capital repayments will be obtained from each option, and applying the compound interest techniques of Chapter 6 to them. The schedule in Table 8.1 shows how these vary with the various options.

Table 8.2 shows the range of gross redemption yields of the stocks, based on a market price of $96\frac{3}{16}$ (+ 1.272 gross accrued interest) on 30 August 1983.

Having calculated these yields, the potential investor is then faced with the problem of seeing how they compare with those of conventional stocks in the market. This is normally done by making assessments of what the 'correct' yields of the stock should be, either as a short-dated stock (without a conversion option), or as a pure long-dated stock. Such yields are normally found by reference to existing stocks with similar coupon rates and maturities, but where the

Table 8.1 *Dividends and capital repayments for various conversion options Treasury $10\frac{1}{4}$% Convertible 1987*

Interest payments	Not converted	Converted 10 Feb. 84	Converted 10 Aug. 84	Converted 10 Feb. 85	Converted 10 Aug. 85	Converted 10 Feb. 86
10 Feb. 84	5.8499	5.8499	5.8499	5.8499	5.8499	5.8499
10 Aug. 84	5.125	4.875	5.125	5.125	5.125	5.125
10 Feb. 85	5.125	4.875	4.72875	5.125	5.125	5.125
10 Aug. 85	5.125	4.875	4.72875	4.5825	5.125	5.125
10 Feb. 86	5.125	4.875	4.72875	4.5825	4.43625	5.125
10 Aug. 86	5.125	4.875	4.72875	4.5825	4.43625	4.290
10 Feb. 87	5.125	4.875	4.72875	4.5825	4.43625	4.290
10 Aug. 87	—	4.875	4.72875	4.5825	4.43625	4.290
10 Feb. 88	—	4.875	4.72875	4.5825	4.43625	4.290
. . . .	. . . . . .	. . . . . .	. . . . . .	. . . . . .	. . . . . .	. . . . . .
Redemption	. . . . . .	. . . . . .	. . . . . .	. . . . . .	. . . . . .	. . . . . .
10 Feb. 87	100.000	. . . . . .	. . . . . .	. . . . . .	. . . . . .	. . . . . .
		. . . . . .	. . . . . .	. . . . . .	. . . . . .	. . . . . .
10 Aug. 2001 (dividend)		4.875	4.72875	4.5825	4.43625	4.290
10 Aug. 2001 (redemption)		100.000	97.000	94.000	91.000	88.000

Note: The figure of 5.8499 for 10 February 1984 is in no way connected with the conversion options. It is a non-standard first interest payment as described in Chapter 5.

Table 8.2 *Gross redemption yields as at 30 August 1983. Treasury $10\frac{1}{4}$% Convertible 1987. Market price = $96\frac{3}{16}$*

		Gross redemption yield %
Unconverted	Redeemable 10 Feb. 1987	11.606
Converted 10 Feb. 1984	Redeemable 10 Aug. 2001	10.289
Converted 10 Aug. 1984	,,	9.933
Converted 10 Feb. 1985	,,	9.650
Converted 10 Aug. 1986	,,	9.389
Converted 10 Feb. 1986	,,	9.147

'convert-into' stock is one which is already quoted in the market, comparisons are even simpler.

In the example above the investor would need to estimate the gross yields upon which a non-convertible $10\frac{1}{4}$% 1987 stock and a conventional $9\frac{3}{4}$% 2001 stock would be neutrally valued relative to existing stocks in the market at that time (in this case 11.70% and 10.75% respectively). Once such values have been determined it is then possible to calculate the premium being paid for the conversion option and assess whether it is justifiable or not.

A convenient method of performing this analysis is to create a graph plotting the convertible stock's gross redemption yield if converted to a 'long' against its 'unconverted' yield as a 'short'. In Fig. 8.1, showing the position at at 30 August 1983, the slanted lines represent the relationships between these two yields for each of the conversion options available, whilst the horizontal line, *OL*, and the

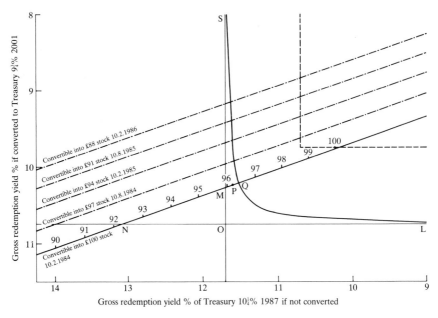

Fig. 8.1 *Analysis of conversion options for Treasury 10¼% Convertible 1987 as at 30 August 1983*

vertical line *OS*, represent the estimated 'correct' yield levels for 10¼% 1987 and 9¾% 2001 stocks respectively. (Note that the axes have been inverted so that the price of the stock rises as one moves along the slanted lines from bottom-left to top-right.) Logic dictates that the convertible should not yield more than these levels, since if it did switching into it from comparably dated non-convertible stocks could be expected to occur. It therefore follows that the point *P* representing the market value of the convertible should, theoretically, always be in the upper right-hand segment of such diagrams.

The conversion premium is the amount by which the market price is within the area bounded by the lines *OL* and *OS*. In this particular case the convertible's price is very close to its intrinsic value as a 'short' (represented on the graph by the point *M*) and some four points greater than its alternative value as a 'long' (represented by the point *N*). If there were now to be a sudden fall of 1% in yields across all sectors of the market, moving the horizontal and vertical to those dotted on the graph, the price of the convertible would then be more determined by long-yield comparisons.

This analysis illustrates clearly the alternative nature of a convertible stock's valuation and the size of the premium element involved. What it does not do is assess whether the premium is worth paying for or not. There is obviously a relationship between the 'dearness of the stock as a short' (*PM*) and its 'dearness as a long' (*PN*) which holds the stock in equilibrium at any particular time. Extreme values of either of these 'dearnesses' can only be justified when the alternative 'dearness' is very small, and a strong case can be made for considering that a convertible's equilibrium valuation should lie on an hyperbolic curve tangential to the lines OL and OS of the sort drawn in Fig. 8.1. If so, the convertible's equilibrium price will be represented by the point Q where the hyperbola intersects the relevant slanted line, and its current over- or under-valuation by the difference in price PQ.

The exact form of this curve will very much depend on the individual analyst's view of prospective movements in short- and long-term yields, but is also a function of the length of the time period to the date of conversion. The longer the option period the further away the curve will pass from the point O. Conversely, as a stock approaches a conversion date the hyperbola will progressively resemble the lines OL and OS themselves.

The diminishing nature of the conversion premium is not always properly appreciated by many in the market and investors should be wary of propositions based solely on the fact that 'the premium is at a historically low level', and of comparisons made between convertibles with differing conversion periods by reference to the relative size of their conversion premiums alone.

Furthermore, it may sometimes be necessary to look beyond the most immediate conversion date to observe the true value to an investor of all a stock's conversion options. This may occur if a stock's conversion terms deteriorate only very gradually at each consecutive conversion date or not at all. This would cause the family of slanted lines representing the various conversion options to be very compact, and the hyperbola for some forward conversion date may intersect the relevant slanted line at a higher implied price level than that pertaining to the nearest conversion date.

Index-linked Stocks

To appreciate the problems concerned with, and the methods of valuing index-linked stocks, it is imperative to understand exactly how they work.

Index-linked gilt-edged stocks have dividend payments and capital redemption payments that are compensated for inflation by being *linked* to the General Index of Retail Prices, hereafter referred to as the RPI.

For reasons explained in Chapter 4, the RPI figure relevant to any particular dividend or capital payment is that of the month eight months prior to that in which the benefit (dividend or capital) is to be received. To be consistent with this, the Base RPI from which value benefits are adjusted is that relating to eight months prior to the month of issue.

For example, the very first of these issues, 2% Index-linked Stock 1996, was issued on 27 March 1981. Counting back eight months from March 1981 takes one to July 1980, the RPI for which was 267.9. This, therefore, was established as the Base RPI for this stock.

The actual gross dividend payments for this stock are indexed to this value. For example, the half-yearly dividend due on 16 September 1990 will be linked to the RPI for January 1990 (eight months before the payment date), and calculated as

$$\tfrac{1}{2} (2 \times \text{RPI for January } 1990/267.9).$$

Likewise, the capital redemption payment on 16 September 1996 will be calculated as

$$100 \times \text{RPI for January } 1996/267.9.$$

This form of lagged indexation is needed so as to enable each successive dividend to be known at the commencement of the time period to which it relates, but it produces somewhat peculiar side-effects which are not always fully appreciated by investors.

Most importantly, it means that the inflation experience over the last eight months of a stock's life will not be reflected in capital and dividend indexation, but, by the reverse token, the impact of whatever inflation existed in the eight months before the date of issue will be felt instead. This has somewhat bizarre effects. For instance, imagine what would happen in the hypothetical case of there being no inflation whatsoever after March 1981. The RPI would thus be stuck at its March 1981 value of 284.0; successive half-yearly coupons (except the first one of 0.80 on 16 September 1981, which was indexed to the January 1981 RPI, but also reflected the fact that the stock was issued partly paid) would thus be constant, and equal to

$$\tfrac{1}{2}\,(2 \times 284.0/267.9) = 1.06$$

and the eventual capital repayment would be

$$100 \times 284.0/267.9 = 106.00$$

i.e., despite the fact that no inflation 'took place' during the life of the stock, its dividends would be above the 2% nominal coupon rate, and the capital redemption value above par.

The rough rule of thumb is that if inflation proves to have been higher in the eight months before issue than it is in the last eight months of the stock's life, the investor will benefit and vice versa.

The schedule in Table 8.3 gives an idea of how index-linked payments will vary under different assumptions of (uniform) inflation for the period July 1983 until 1996, starting from an actual RPI figure of 336.5 for July 1983.

A word about the definition of inflation is needed here. Inflation is normally measured, talked about, and compensated for, in annual terms. To say that inflation over the past year has run at 10% implies that general prices are now 10% higher than they were a year ago. However, gilt-edged yields, etc., are normally computed on a semi-annual compounding basis, i.e. a yield of 12% is in reality a return of 6% per half-year. When the first index-linked stocks were issued, there was a school of thought that felt that inflation should be treated likewise, i.e. that when talking of 8% inflation, one really meant 4% per half-year.

This definition failed to gather any real support, and the alternative convention – 'Inflation, annual; yields semi-annual' – has become established and is the basis upon which the figures in Table 8.3 have been calculated.

How should index-linked stocks be assessed? There are basically two main methods: money yields and real yields. In both cases an assumption about the future rate of inflation is involved. This is an item about which each individual

Table 8.3   *Index-linked 2% Stock 1996 as viewed from August 1983*

Payment date	RPI month	Assumed inflation rate July 1983–January 1996					
		0.0%	2.5%	5.0%	7.5%	10.0%	12.5%
Dividends (gross)							
16 Sep. 81	Jan. 81	0.80	0.80	0.80	0.80	0.80	0.80
16 Mar. 82	July 81	1.10	1.10	1.10	1.10	1.10	1.10
16 Sep. 82	Jan. 82	1.15	1.15	1.15	1.15	1.15	1.15
16 Mar. 83	July 82	1.20	1.20	1.20	1.20	1.20	1.20
16 Sep. 83	Jan. 83	1.21	1.21	1.21	1.21	1.21	1.21
16 Mar. 84	July 83	1.25	1.25	1.25	1.25	1.25	1.25

Items above this line will be known at the time in question.

- -

Items below this line have been projected at the relevant rate.

16 Sep. 84	Jan. 84	1.25	1.27	1.28	1.30	1.31	1.33
16 Mar. 85	July 84	1.25	1.28	1.31	1.35	1.38	1.41
16 Sep. 85	Jan. 85	1.25	1.30	1.35	1.40	1.44	1.49
and so on	. . . .	. . . .	. . . .	. . . .	. . . .	. . . .	. . . .
until	. . . .	. . . .	. . . .	. . . .	. . . .	. . . .	. . . .
16 Mar. 96	July 95	1.25	1.68	2.25	2.99	3.94	5.16
16 Sep. 96	Jan. 96	1.25	1.71	2.31	3.10	4.13	5.47
Redemption 16 Sep. 96	Jan. 96	125.60	171.03	231.13	310.19	413.43	547.55

Note: In the above schedule dividend and redemption values have been shown rounded down to two decimal places. This is in accordance with the terms detailed in the prospectus for this stock. Similar payments for Index-linked 2% Stock 2006 and Index-linked 2½% Stock 2011 are also rounded down to two decimal places. *All subsequent issues* (to date) *have provisions for payments to be rounded down to four decimal places.*

investor must make up his own mind. This single factor swamps all other prospective considerations, and to try and value index-linked stocks without first having a view on this item is to court disaster. What the investor needs to do here is to be able to forecast the progress of the RPI so that he can compute the future values of dividends and the capital redemption payment. For practical purposes, it is most usual to decide upon a central 'core' rate of inflation, which it is estimated may be the average rate over the years to redemption, and project values forward on that constant basis. It may be that some investors feel they wish to make more intricate or flexible assumptions. If so – no bother. As long as one can postulate the future RPI figures, one can forecast the money values of the stock's benefits.

Once, therefore, a view of future inflation has been made, and the prospective values of dividends and capital calculated, orthodox compound interest techniques can then be applied to compute the redemption yields relating to that particular inflation assumption. These are often referred to as 'money' yields and as such can be compared directly with the redemption yields on conventional gilts.

The other widely used method is to compute so-called 'real yields' – yields in 'real' (i.e. inflation-adjusted) rather than 'money' terms. This method has acquired a certain amount of its popularity partly because some of its users (wrongly) think that it obviates the need to make an inflation forecast. (It is a fact, however, that real yields vary quite substantially depending on the prospective rate of inflation assumed, as later examples will show.) The only really correct way to calculate 'real' yields is first to compute the money values on the given inflation assumption, then deflate them to real terms as at the bargain's settlement date, and finally to discount these 'real' values on a compound interest basis to find the 'real' yield.

For example, consider Index-linked 2% Stock 1988, as at Monday, 29 March 1982 (for settlement 30 March 1982). At this time the most recently published RPI was that for January 1982 = 310.6. The Base RPI for this stock = 297.1 (July 1981). Assuming (for the purposes of this example) forward inflation of 8% per annum, it is possible to build up a schedule of prices, calls, dividends and redemption values, in both money and real terms, as in Table 8.4.

Table 8.4   *Schedule for calculation of total market price to give 3% real gross yield at 29 March 1982: Index-linked 2% Stock 1988*

(1)	(2)	(3)	(4) ·	(5)	(6)	(7)	(8)
						Discounting to give 3% real yield	
Date of Dividends	RPI month	Projected RPI value	Money value	Real conversion value	Real value	Factor	Value
30 Sep. 82	Jan. 82	310.6	0.9996	0.96225	0.96187	0.98522	0.94766
30 Mar. 83	July 82	322.8	1.0865	0.92593	1.00597	0.97066	0.97646
30 Sep. 83	Jan. 83	335.4	1.1291	0.89097	1.00597	0.95632	0.96203
30 Mar. 84	July 83	348.6	1.1734	0.85734	1.00597	0.94218	0.94781
30 Sep. 84	Jan. 84	362.3	1.2194	0.82497	1.00597	0.92826	0.93380
30 Mar. 85	July 84	376.5	1.2672	0.79383	1.00597	0.91454	0.92000
30 Sep. 85	Jan. 85	391.3	1.3169	0.76387	1.00597	0.90103	0.90641
30 Mar. 86	July 85	406.6	1.3686	0.73503	1.00597	0.88771	0.89301
30 Sep. 86	Jan. 86	422.6	1.4223	0.70728	1.00597	0.87459	0.87981
30 Mar. 87	July 86	439.1	1.4781	0.68058	1.00597	0.86167	0.86681
30 Sep. 87	Jan. 87	456.4	1.5361	0.65489	1.00597	0.84893	0.85400
30 Mar. 88	July 87	474.3	1.5964	0.63017	1.00597	0.83639	0.84138
							10.92918
Redemption							
30 Mar. 88	July 87	474.3	159.6355	0.63017	100.59744	0.83639	84.13869
							95.06787
Call due							
29 Apr. 82	—	—	47.5	0.99369	47.20048	0.99756	47.08531
			Partly paid market price to give 3% real yield = 47.983				

To find the total market price on this day to give a gross real yield of 3%, it is necessary to sum the discounted real values of interest and capital, and subtract the discounted *real* value of the call due on 29 April 1982. This is a somewhat laborious process, but it does give one an insight into the key relationship between money yields and real yields.

When the assumed money values of all items in column (4) of the schedule have been established, two factors are applied to columns (5) and (7) to produce the real discounted values in column (8) which form the equation of value.

In this particular case, column (7) is the discounting factor relating to a rate of interest of 3% per annum compounded semi-annually, whilst column (5) is the factor for converting money values into real values at an 8% per annum inflation rate. This is equivalent to discounting at a rate of 7.8461% per annum compounded semi-annually.

Thus the money yield is given by the relationship

$$1 + Y/200 = (1 + 7.8461/200) \times (1 + 3/200)$$

$$Y = 10.9638\%.$$

In more general terms, the relationship between money yields (Y), inflation (J), and real yields (R) is

$$1 + \frac{Y}{200} = \left(1 + \frac{R}{200}\right) \cdot \sqrt{1 + \frac{J}{100}}$$

or, alternatively,

$$R = 200\left(\frac{1 + Y/200}{\sqrt{1 + J/200}} - 1\right).$$

Further mathematical examination of this relationship leads to two important facts:

1. That real yields are NOT simply money yields minus the rate of inflation.
2. That for a given price, but varying inflation assumptions, the derived real yield values decrease as the inflation rate rises.

Table 8.5 is illustrative of these points:

Table 8.5 *Money yields and real yields: Index-linked 2% Stock 1988*

Inflation rate (assumed)	Money yield (%)	Real yield (%)	Money yield – real yield
0	3.638	3.638	0
2	5.498	3.474	2.024
4	7.339	3.313	4.026
6	9.161	3.155	6.006
8	10.964	3.000	7.964
10	12.749	2.848	9.901
12	14.517	2.699	11.818

Index-linked Stocks and Tax Considerations

The next main point to cover is that the attractions of index-linked stocks are much greater for high-rate taxpayers than for the gross funds to whom they were originally restricted. This is because the interest component of an index-linked stock is very small, in relation to the capital part, and in this respect these stocks have a certain amount in common with conventional low-coupon gilts.

Figure 8.2 shows broken parallel lines representing the net (money) redemption yields of Index-linked 2% Stock 1988 as at 29 March 1982, based on a number of inflation assumptions, whilst the two solid lines represent the net redemption yields for a comparable high-coupon and low-coupon stock in the same maturity area, namely Treasury 12% 1987 and Transport 3% 78/88.

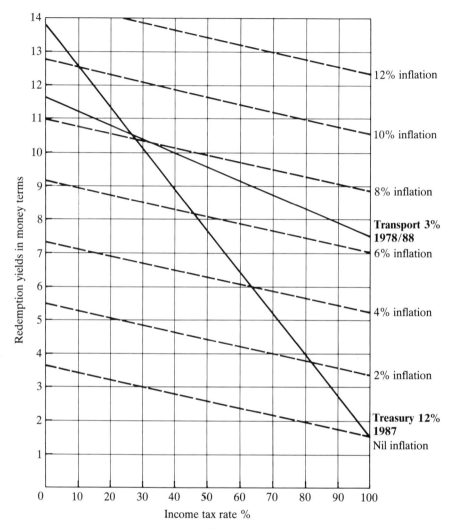

Fig. 8.2 *Comparative net returns from index-linked and conventional gilt-edged stocks as at 29 March 1982*

Index-linked 2% Stock 1988	price 47.983 partly paid
Transport 3% 1978/88	price $63\frac{1}{16}$
Treasury 12% 1987	price $91\frac{7}{8}$

Note: The fact that the net yields at 100% income tax rate on Treasury 12% 1987 and Index-linked 2% Stock 1988 (assuming nil inflation) are equal is purely coincidental and of no particular significance.

What this chart shows is that given a prospective inflation assumption of, say, 8%, a taxpayer at below the standard rate of 30% would do better in either of the two chosen conventional stocks, but that higher-rate taxpayers should prefer the index-linked stock. It also underlines the point made earlier about the overwhelming importance of making a correct judgement about the rate of future inflation in these matters. This fact cannot be over-emphasised.

Other Analytical Methods for Use with Index-linked Stocks

All the usual problems associated with price ratios are here compounded by having varying dividend flows, and price ratio techniques cannot be recommended for precise analytical work with index-linked stocks.

On the other hand there are no fundamental problems associated with performance ratios, and this system of historical retrospection is particularly well suited in this field. ·

Money yield differences can be used as long as the basis of yield computation remains consistent. This really means deciding in advance upon a suitable inflation assumption and calculating prospective money yields on this constant basis day by day. If (and this is a big 'if') this assumption is broadly correct, then money yield differences between index-linked stocks and conventional stocks, and between index-linked issues themselves, can be a convenient tool, but only for judging current relative valuations with past history.

Real yield differences are reasonably satisfactory for measuring relativities between index-linked stocks, even if their inflation assumption varies from time to time, as long as both yields are based on a common assumption at any particular time. This comes about by virtue of further consideration of our earlier equation:

$$1 + \frac{Y}{200} = \left(1 + \frac{R}{200}\right) \cdot \sqrt{1 + \frac{J}{100}} \cdot$$

If we substitute $\qquad 1 + \dfrac{Q}{200} \quad$ for $\quad \sqrt{1 + \dfrac{J}{100}}$

i.e. using a semi-annual compounding equivalent inflation rate Q in place of the annual compounding rate J, then the equation becomes

$$1 + \frac{Y}{200} = \left(1 + \frac{R}{200}\right)\left(1 + \frac{Q}{200}\right)$$

$$\left(1 + \frac{Q}{200}\right)\frac{R}{200} = \left(1 + \frac{Y}{200}\right) - \left(1 + \frac{Q}{200}\right)$$

$$R = \frac{Y - Q}{1 + \dfrac{Q}{200}} \cdot$$

Thus, given two index-linked stocks, A and B, with money yields Y_a and Y_b, their real yield difference is

$$\Delta R = (R_a - R_b) = \frac{(Y_a - Q)}{(1 + Q/200)} - \frac{(Y_b - Q)}{(1 + Q/200)}$$

$$= \frac{(Y_a - Y_b)}{\sqrt{(1 + J/100)}} \, .$$

Thus, if the money yield difference $Y_a - Y_b$ remains constant at, say 0.20, and over time the (annual) inflation rate has changed from 12% to 4%, the real yield *difference* will only move from

$$\frac{0.20}{\sqrt{1.12}} \quad \text{to} \quad \frac{0.20}{\sqrt{1.04}}$$

i.e. from 0.189 to 0.196, which is not really significant enough to invalidate the use of the method, provided the analyst knows precisely what he is doing, and the implicit assumptions he is making. However, using differences between real yields on index-linked stocks and redemption yields on conventional stocks is a totally different matter, and should be avoided like the plague.

One perfectly valid method for comparing index-linked and conventional gilts does exist. If one turns the problem around and calculates the rate of future inflation required to make the money yield on an index-linked stock equate to the redemption yield of a gilt, one obtains a measure of their relative valuation *vis-à-vis* the inflationary prospect. This is somewhat akin in character to the system of balance-of-term yields for comparing two conventional stocks, in that not only does the historical sequence describe past relativities, but the current figure can also be assessed by the analyst in absolute terms.

9

Gilt-edged futures and options

In the autumn of 1982, trading commenced on the London International Financial Futures Exchange, known colloquially as LIFFE – pronounced 'life' and never 'liffey' – and one of the initial contracts established, together with currencies, short-term UK interest rate futures, and three-month Eurodollar deposit futures, was a long-dated gilt-edged contract. This was augmented in September 1985 by a short-dated gilt-edged contract. Because of their existence and the fact that market-makers, brokers/dealers, banks, and various other players in the game, have seats on LIFFE, and are active participants in this parallel market, there is a need in this book to cover at least the basic aspects of this subject and its interplay with the gilt-edged market proper (known to futures operators as the 'cash' market).

What exactly are financial futures?

In its broadest sense, a futures contract is an obligation to buy or sell a particular commodity at a specified price on a specified future date. If and when a market is made to deal in these specified futures contracts, instead of the actual commodity itself, this becomes a futures market. Where the underlying commodity to be traded is a physical entity, such as gold, copper, zinc, grain, pork bellies, or even potatoes, it is not too difficult to envisage the concept. With financial futures, the underlying commodity is less tangible, being perhaps a foreign currency exchange rate, an interest rate, or, in the case in which this book is most interested, the price(s) of some gilt-edged stock.

How the Gilt Futures Market Works

Obviously, there has to be some link between values in the 'cash' market and the prices in the equivalent future. The mechanism that links the two is the process of delivery by which, at the end of the time period specified for the particular futures contract, the *sellers* have the option either to close their position by buying back their contracts, or to deliver the given commodity (through some form of clearing mechanism) to those with open bought positions. In practice, most positions are closed out prior to delivery, but the fact that the seller has the delivery option means that the relative prices in the two markets have to converge as the contracts mature.

The long gilt-edged contract is formally specified as the price of £50,000 nominal of a notional 12% twenty-year British Government stock, but the terms of the contract actually permit the seller to deliver any gilts (subject to certain specific provisos – see later) with maturities in the fifteen- to twenty-five-year range. Obviously the seller, unless he is either insane or has some special reason of his own, will choose to deliver whichever of these eligible stocks conveys the least value. Thus, the futures price will normally 'track' the 'cheapest deliverable instrument'.

The short gilt-edged contract differs slightly from the long one. Its unit of trading is £100,000 nominal (twice the size of the long contract), the maturity range of its deliverable stocks is three to four-and-a-half years and the notional coupon rate is 10%.

In the LIFFE market there are a number of separate contracts traded for each 'commodity', each relating to different delivery months, each spaced three months apart running on a March, June, September, December cycle. The contract month nearest to the current date is usually referred to as the 'nearby' month, though once that contract month has begun it is known as the 'spot' month. Experience so far in London has been that the vast majority of business transacted is done in the 'nearby' contract.

In complete contrast with the gilt-edged market, the dealing method is by 'open outcry', whereby traders meet in recessed octagonal 'pits' and shout out their bids or offers in order to match buyer with seller. Once transactions have been made, they are recorded in writing by both parties and reported to the market officials, and quickly fed into the market's computer. This computer in turn links with the futures market price display system, and those of commercial information providers such as Reuters and Telerate, and it is no exaggeration to say that the price at which a trade is done will be public knowledge across the world in a matter of seconds after it is transacted.

Prices of gilt-edged futures contracts are quoted by reference to discrete minimum price movements called 'ticks', the size of which varies between contracts. For the long gilt-edged contract the tick size is $\frac{1}{32}$nd of a point, whilst for the short contract it is $\frac{1}{64}$th. This inconsistency sometimes causes trouble for the unwary, since it means that a price quotation of, say, 102–27 means two different values, depending upon the contract to which it relates. 102–27 for the long contract means a price of $102\frac{27}{32} = 102.84375$, but 102–27 for the short contract equals $102\frac{27}{64} = 102.421875$. One of the reasons for this differentiation was that by so doing the cash value of a single tick movement in the two contracts ($\frac{1}{32}$ on £50,000 nominal of the long and $\frac{1}{64}$ on £100,000 nominal of the short) would be equal. Whilst recognising that this makes lif(f)e easier for market professionals it is often a cause of confusion to other investors.

The next major dissimilarity between futures and the 'cash' gilt market is that futures are always dealt in on margin, by which it is meant that only a small proportion of the quoted futures price needs to be paid by the futures trader. There are two forms of margin, known as 'initial' (or 'original') margin and 'variation' margin, both of which are settled with International Commodities Clearing House (ICCH), which is the clearing house for LIFFE contracts. The clearing house acts as guarantor of the contracts, and, once a trade has been registered, each party then has an open position with the clearing house rather than with its original counterparty.

Initial margin, which varies according to the individual contract in question, is the amount required to be paid when an investor originally takes out a futures contract, whether buying or selling. The purpose of initial margin is to provide a cash buffer against which a potential loss can be put.

The concept of variation margin becomes clear when one realises the mechanism by which futures bargains are settled. Unlike securities markets, in which profits and losses are only taken when positions are finally closed out, in the futures markets all positions are valued daily on the basis of the exchanges' closing official settlement price – a process known as 'marking to market' – and profits or losses resulting from the day's change in prices are credited or debited to the investor's account. In an adverse trading situation, an investor will be called upon to put up further 'variation' margin in order to preserve a solvent account. This *modus operandi* means that an investor with a continuing adverse trading position has a continuing day-by-day negative cash flow, and as such is forced to face the reality of his loss-making situation very quickly. This feature, combined with the cushion provided by initial margins, is singularly effective in preventing overstretched debt positions from arising.

In order to get an idea of the cash flows involved, consider the progress of a single transaction in the long gilt future.

> Date: 4 July 1983
> Action: Buy one Sept. 1983 long gilt contract @ 104 – 15
>   (*Note:* in this case prices are quoted as integers + $\frac{1}{32}$nd, i.e. 104 – 15
>   denotes $104\frac{15}{32}$.)
> Valuation of this contract = £52,234.37
> Initial margin paid to clearing house = £1,500.

> Date: 4 July 1983
> Closing settlement price = 104 – 07 (down $\frac{8}{32}$ on the day)
> Valuation of this contract = £52,109.37, therefore variation margin required
> to be paid to clearing house = £125.

> Date: 5 July 1983
> Closing settlement price = 103–23
> Valuation of contract = £51,859.37
> Change on the day = $-$£250, to be settled with clearing house, and so on.

Now let us look at the situation when the contract runs through to delivery, because it is the possibility of this happening that links prices in the cash and futures markets together.

For the gilt-edged futures contracts there is no unique settlement day. The seller can choose to deliver stock on any business day in the required delivery month. The choice of date and the choice of stock (within the eligible list) belong to the seller, who is required to give notice of his intention to deliver prior to the close of business on LIFFE two business days before his chosen delivery date. The amount to be paid to the seller for the stock delivered is determined by the closing settlement price on notification day. The cash sum due to change hands obviously varies, depending on which stock the seller has opted to deliver, and is based on a stock price factor system which is explained below.

In the case of the long gilt-edged future the notional contract specifies a 12% coupon rate, and thus the stock price factor is determined as the clean price of each (deliverable) stock to give a gross redemption yield of 12% on the first day of the delivery month. Deliverable stocks are those whose lives to *earliest* maturity on the first day of the delivery month lie between fifteen and twenty-five years, and exclude convertible, variable-rate, index-linked stocks, or any stock not paying interest semi-annually. In addition, partly-paid stocks are ineligible for delivery if they are partly paid at any time in the delivery month, and otherwise eligible stocks may not be delivered during their three-week special ex-dividend periods.

Table 9.1 shows the list of deliverable stocks in existence on 1 July 1983, and their stock factors for the five futures contracts, September 1983 through to September 1984. It will be noticed that individual stocks' factors vary for different contracts, and that not all the stocks shown are deliverable for all contract months.

Table 9.1   *Stock price factors for long gilt contracts as at 1 July 1983*

	Sept. 1983	Dec. 1983	Mar. 1984	June 1984	Sept. 1984
Treasury 15½% 1998	1.241763				
Exchequer 12% 1998	0.999076				
Treasury 9½% 1999	0.825746	0.827841			
Exchequer 12¼% 1999	1.017713	1.017093	1.017509		
Treasury 10½% 1999	0.894213	0.895661	0.895989		
Treasury 13% 2000	1.070768	1.071879	1.070780	1.071140	1.069326
Exchequer 12% 99/02	0.999212	1.000630			
Treasury 13¾% 00/03	1.124602	1.125659	1.124134	1.124378	1.122087
Treasury 11½% 01/04	0.962312	0.962001	0.962540	0.961606	0.962782
Funding 3½% 99/04	0.353652	0.355878	0.357577	0.359740	
Treasury 12½% 03/05	1.036756	1.037675	1.037204	1.036757	1.036268
Treasury 8% 02/06	0.689520	0.689571	0.690877	0.690966	0.692313
Treasury 11¾% 03/07	0.979759	0.981188	0.980485	0.981259	0.979928
Treasury 13½% 04/08	1.113929	1.113020	1.113246	1.111584	1.112523
Treasury 5½% 08/12		0.477153	0.477875	0.477982	0.479045

The invoice price for settlement by delivery of a single contract is calculated thus:

(Stock factor × Settlement price on notification day)

plus

Gross accrued interest to delivery day

multiplied by

500

Let us assume that, in this case, the seller opted to deliver £50,000 nominal of Treasury 15½% 1998 on 9 September 1983. He would have to give notice on Wednesday, 7 September, for which day the official LIFFE settlement price was 102–20 (102.625). This, multiplied by the stock factor of 1.241763, comes to 127.43592, and to this is added the gross accrued interest relating to *settlement* day (9 September) of −0.89178. Since the contract relates to £50,000 nominal stock, this total is multiplied by 500 to produce a contract invoice value of £63,272.07.

The choice of which stock to deliver is crucial in these matters. Because the price structure of the gilt-edged market (the 'cash' market') puts a premium on the lower coupon stocks, but the futures market does not, large discrepancies between the 'cash' market price and the equivalent futures delivery value often exist, and a seller choosing to settle by delivery should take particular care not to give away value by delivering the wrong stock.

Once again, it may be instructive to examine a table of values taken towards the end of the delivery month. Table 9.2 shows that the futures price has converged to within 0.079 of that of Treasury 15½% 1998, which is therefore perfectly suitable for delivery, but it also shows how dear all the other gilts are in relation to the futures market and just how much value would be thrown away if they were delivered instead.

Table 9.2   *Comparison of futures delivery values with cash market prices for September 1983 long gilt contract*
Futures price 26 September 1983 = 105–16

Delivery 28.9.1983	Stock factor	Clean price	Gross accrued interest	Invoice price	Gilt market price 26.9.1983	Relative dearness of stock
Treasury 15½% 1998	1.241763	131.006	−0.085	130.921	131.000	0.079
Exchequer 12% 1998 is not deliverable as it is specially ex-dividend on this day						
Treasury 9½% 1999	0.825746	87.116	1.952	89.068	95.500	6.432
Exchequer 12¼% 1999	1.017713	107.369	0.067	107.436	110.875	3.439
Treasury 10½% 1999 is not deliverable as it is specially ex-dividend on this day						
Treasury 13% 2000	1.070768	112.966	2.707	115.673	119.750	4.077
Exchequer 12% 1999/2002	0.999212	105.417	2.236	107.652	111.750	4.098
Treasury 13¾% 2000/03	1.124602	118.645	2.449	121.094	125.000	3.906
Treasury 11½% 2001/04	0.962312	101.524	0.284	101.808	108.625	6.817
Funding 3½% 1999/2004	0.353652	37.310	0.729	38.039	49.250	11.211
Treasury 12½% 2003/05 is not deliverable as it is specially ex-dividend on this day						
Treasury 8% 2002/06	0.689520	72.744	−0.153	72.591	83.500	10.909
Treasury 11¾% 2003/07	0.979759	103.365	2.189	105.554	112.875	7.321
Treasury 13½% 2004/08	1.113939	117.519	0.074	117.593	124.500	6.907

Uses of the Gilt Futures Market

What are the uses to which gilt futures can be put that cannot be found in the 'cash' market? These divide broadly into two categories: speculative or trading activities on the one hand, and hedging operations on the other.

Because of the gearing available, by virtue of futures being dealt in on margin, futures are an attractive vehicle for use by speculators and market traders. Since initial margins on gilt futures are low it is easily possible for speculators to open highly geared positions, if they are brave (or foolhardy) enough. But it should be remembered that if prices subsequently move against them, they will experience immediate variation margin calls, and bearing this in mind it would probably be imprudent to commit themselves to too high a level of gearing.

The next point to make is that futures markets allow one to back one's view that the market may move *downwards* as well as upwards. In the gilt-edged market itself it is difficult for traders to open outright bear positions, unless they have access to some stock borrowing facility. No such problem exists with futures.

Futures can also be used advantageously to advance an investment fund's cash flows. Take the case where a fund manager knows that he has new money due to arrive in the coming months, but is fully invested at the current moment. If he feels that the market is going to rise substantially before his new money arrives he can, for a modest outlay, take up a bull position in the futures market, which – if his view is correct – will produce a profit equivalent to that which he would have been able to obtain by early investment in the cash market.

Hedging Operations

Hedging is the name used to describe taking a position in futures contrary to that of a (roughly) equal position in another market (in this case, the 'cash' gilt market). In fact, the 'advancing cash flow' example mentioned above is an illustration of an 'anticipatory hedge'. Hedging is really a matter of taking out some form of insurance against a feared market movement, when, for some reason or other, the investor does not want to liquidate, or is precluded from selling, his principal investment. A good example might be that of a holder of a gilt-edged stock who needs to hold on to his stock in order to obtain a specific dividend payment but fears the market may collapse. Futures give him the opportunity to insure his position now, by selling an equivalent number of futures contracts. If the market reverse that he fears comes about, it will affect the value of his gilt-edged holding adversely, but he will make a compensating profit from his bear position in the futures market.

'CASH-AND-CARRY OPERATIONS'

This delightful phraseology is used to describe a combined futures and cash market arbitrage strategy, whereby an investor runs a matched position holding gilts and at the same time being short of an equal nominal amount of futures. Even when this involves a *long* gilt-edged stock and *long*-dated futures, it is still essentially a short-term money operation, the overall return of which is the balance of the profits/losses on the two offsetting positions taken between instigation and the chosen delivery date. This is generally known as the 'implied repurchase rate', or 'implied repo-rate'.

Because of the uneven yield structure in the gilt-edged market, it is normally found that only one or two gilt-edged stocks are priced cheaply enough relative to futures to produce high enough 'implied repo-rates' to make these strategies attractive.

When implied repo-rates are all markedly below money market rates for the period to delivery, the opposite operation can be considered. This can be termed a 'reverse cash-and-carry', as it involves selling the relevant gilt-edged stock and buying futures. This releases cheap cash to the investor which he can place in money markets at the higher rate. A certain element of danger is involved in this strategy, since the investor is *no longer the seller of the futures, and therefore does not control the timing or the choice of stock to be delivered.* If, however, there is only a single clearly distinguishable cheapest deliverable stock that the futures market is 'tracking' and if the implied repos on this stock to all possible delivery dates are still below money market rates, it should be possible to profit from this type of operation.

One has to be very careful when talking about 'implied repo-rates'. There is a popular misconception that there is a unique 'implied repo-rate' associated with a given pair of gilt and futures prices, and that the operation is insulated from variations in the level of the market at delivery, or the choice of delivery date during the delivery month. This is a very dangerous fallacy, as the next few examples will now show.

Table 9.3 shows the implied repo-rates existing on 11 July 1983 for cash-and-carry strategies against September 1983 futures, based on the (neutral) view that futures price at delivery would be the same as that ruling at that date. Two main facts are quickly apparent. Firstly, the implied repo-rates increase as the delivery date extends to the end of the month, and secondly, the only practical strategy of this kind would be one using Treasury $15\frac{1}{2}$% 1998. A less obvious fact that shows up in the table is that three stocks, Exchequer 12% 1998, Treasury $10\frac{1}{2}$% 1999, and Treasury $12\frac{1}{2}$% 03/05, are not eligible for delivery on the final delivery date (30.9.1983) by virtue of the fact that they are within their three-week special ex-dividend periods on that date.

Next, let us compare the values in Table 9.3 with those in Table 9.4, in which similar calculations are made, but based this time on an assumption that September 1983 futures prices will be rather higher (105–10) at delivery. It can be seen quite clearly that in this case implied repo-rates of stocks with factors in excess of unity are increased, whilst those on stocks with factors below 1 are diminished. When one thinks about it, this is hardly surprising as a cash-and-carry strategy involves equal *nominal* amounts of stock and futures, which will favour higher-priced stocks in a rising market, and vice versa.

The relationships between all the various parameters can be put into focus by the following analysis of a cash-and-carry operation subsequently closed by delivery through LIFFE.

If S represents the stock factor of the gilt for this contract

    g represents the gilt's coupon rate

    P_0 represents the initial purchase price of the gilt

    P_1 represents the disposal price of the gilt

    F_0 represents the initial futures price

F_1 represents the final futures price

t_0 represents the time period between the last coupon payment and the purchase date

t_1 represents the time period from the last coupon payment and delivery

m represents the initial margin on the future

the profit from the operation has two components:

(i) the profit from holding the gilt $= P_1 - P_0$;

(ii) the profit from the bear operation in futures $= F_0 - F_1$.

The initial outlay is P_0 plus the initial margin on the futures contract of m. The simple interest return derived from the operation, r, can thus be defined as

$$r = \frac{(P_1 - P_0) + (F_0 - F_1)}{P_0 + m} \times \frac{100}{t_1 - t_0} \tag{9.1}$$

Now the invoice price P_1 is related to the delivery future price F_1 by the relationship

$$P_1 = (F_1 \times S) + gt_1$$

$$\text{thus} \quad r = \frac{F_1 S + gt_1 - P_0 + F_0 - F_1}{P_0 + m} \times \frac{100}{t_1 - t_0}$$

$$= \frac{[F_1(S-1) + gt_1] - (P_0 - F_0)}{P_0 + m} \times \frac{100}{t_1 - t_0} \tag{9.2}$$

If we now use C_0 to denote the initial clean price of the stock, so that

$$P = C_0 + gt_0$$

$$= \frac{[F_1(S-1) + g(t_1 - t_0)] - (C_0 - F_0)}{P_0 + m} \times \frac{100}{t_1 - t_0} \tag{9.3}$$

the numerator between the square brackets has three components relating to

(i) final futures price, F_1, multiplied by the stock factor minus 1;

(ii) the accrued interest, $g(t_1 - t_0)$ over the period of the operation;

(iii) the difference between the initial clean price, C_0, and the initial futures price, F_0.

The most usual cash-and-carry assumption is the neutral one that the delivery futures price F will be the same as the initial one, i.e. $F_1 = F_0$, so that deviations in actuality from that assumption cause the realised cash-and-carry rate to rise by an amount

$$= \frac{(F_1 - F_0)(S-1)}{P_0 + m} \times \frac{100}{t_1 - t_0}.$$

When a stock has a coupon rate equal to the notional coupon rate of the relevant future, its stock factor will be 1 (or so close to 1 as not to matter) and this

Table 9.3 *Implied repurchase rates on cash-and-carry strategies: September 1983 long gilt contract (neutral assumption)*

September 1983 futures	Price 11.7.1983	First delivery day 1.9.1983		Middle delivery day 15.9.1983		Final delivery day 30.9.1983	
	101–25	101–25		101–25		101–25	
		Delivery value	Repos %	Delivery value	Repos %	Delivery value	Repos %
Treasury 15½% 1998	131.375	125.157XD	7.93	125.751XD	8.87	126.388XD	9.51
Exchequer 12% 1998	106.125	105.106	– 7.04	105.567	– 3.20	Not deliverable	
Treasury 9½% 1999	90.250XD	85.295	–37.86	85.659	–28.15	86.050	–21.27
Exchequer 12¼% 1999	109.750	102.745XD	– 6.18	103.215XD	– 2.43	103.718	0.16
Treasury 10½% 1999	97.000	94.035	–21.30	94.437	–14.76	Not deliverable	
Treasury 13% 2000	112.250XD	110.729	–10.06	111.228	– 5.44	111.762	– 2.27
Exchequer 12% 1999/2002	104.750XD	103.049	–11.98	103.509	– 7.00	104.002	– 3.57
Treasury 13¾% 2000/03	117.000XD	115.895	– 7.12	116.422	– 3.07	116.987	– 0.30
Treasury 11½% 2001/04	107.500	97.378XD	–28.00	97.819XD	–20.13	98.292	–14.47
Funding 3½% 1999/2004	46.750XD	36.465	< –100.00	36.599	< –100.00	36.743	–86.20
Treasury 12¼% 2003/05	113.625	109.050	–27.58	109.529	–19.82	Not deliverable	
Treasury 8% 2002/06	82.375	69.435XD	–67.89	69.742XD	–53.83	70.071XD	–43.38
Treasury 11¾% 2003/07	105.750XD	101.041	–31.16	101.492	–22.53	101.975	–16.47
Treasury 13½% 2002/08	123.625	112.452XD	–24.88	112.970XD	–17.53	113.525	–12.27

Note: This table makes no allowance for taxation.

Table 9.4 *Implied repurchase rates on cash-and-carry strategies in September 1983 long gilt contract (bull assumption)*

September 1983 futures	Price 11.7.1983 101–25	First delivery day 1.9.1983 105–10		Middle delivery day 15.9.1983 105–10		Final delivery day 30.9.1983 105–10	
		Delivery value	Repos %	Delivery value	Repos %	Delivery value	Repos %
Treasury 15½% 1998	131.375	129.542XD	12.62	130.136XD	12.52	130.773XD	12.43
Exchequer 12% 1998	106.125	108.634	− 7.21	109.095	− 3.37	Not deliverable	
Treasury 9½% 1999	90.250XD	88.211	−42.30	88.575	−31.85	88.965	−24.41
Exchequer 12¼% 1999	109.750	106.339XD	− 5.92	106.809XD	− 2.26	107.312	0.27
Treasury 10½% 1999	97.000	97.192	−23.98	97.595	−16.97	Not deliverable	
Treasury 13% 2000	112.250XD	114.510	− 8.62	115.009	− 4.33	115.543	− 1.39
Exchequer 12% 1999/2002	104.750XD	106.577	−12.15	107.038	− 7.17	107.531	− 3.75
Treasury 13¾% 2000/03	117.000XD	119.866	− 4.54	120.394	− 1.06	120.959	1.31
Treasury 11½% 2001/04	107.500	100.776XD	−28.93	101.217XD	−20.92	101.690	−15.15
Funding 3½% 1999/2004	46.750XD	37.714	< −100.00	37.848	< −100.00	37.992	−99.99
Treasury 12¼% 2003/05	113.625	112.711	−26.97	113.190	−19.36	Not deliverable	
Treasury 8% 2002/06	82.375	71.870XD	−74.96	72.177XD	−60.01	72.505XD	−48.79
Treasury 11¾% 2003/07	105.750XD	104.501	−31.74	104.951	−23.04	105.434	−16.92
Treasury 13½% 2004/08	123.625	116.386XD	−22.87	116.904XD	−15.93	117.459	−10.97

Note: This table makes no allowance for taxation.

divergence will be equal to zero. But for all other stocks this potential divergence is important.

The second point is to realise from looking at equation (9.3) that the realised simple rate of return is equal to

$$\frac{g}{P_0 + m} \quad \text{(approximately the flat yield of the stock)}$$

$$\text{plus} \quad \frac{F_1(S-1)-(C_0-F_0)}{P_0 + m} \times \frac{100}{t_1 - t_0}.$$

For any given value of F_1 (the projected futures price) the absolute value of the second element diminishes as the time period $(t_1 - t_0)$ lengthens. Thus, when this factor is positive, the best delivery option is the earliest date, and if it is negative a cash-and-carry operation will show the highest return by being left open until the last possible opportunity.

In all of the above theory one factor has been omitted in order to keep the mathematics as straightforward as possible, which in real life cannot be ignored, and that is the cost or profit to the investor of the variation margin cash flows during the life of a cash-and-carry operation. If the general market rises, his futures position will go into a loss situation and his total outlay will increase, thus diminishing the eventual overall return. If markets fall, this element will work to his advantage. It also makes a difference when these movements occur, since the investor may, in theory, obtain (pay) interest on the positive (negative) variation margin cash flows, and these amounts will be greater or lesser, depending on exactly how these price movements occur. The normal assumption of most commercial computations is that the price movement from F_0 to F_1 takes place evenly over the time period.

OTHER HEDGING ACTIVITIES

In the cash-and-carry operations discussed above, it was important that the total position could be closed by making delivery. This meant that a holding of a gilt-edged stock would be matched by an equal and opposite *nominal* amount of 'stock' in the futures market. But this would most often mean that in value terms the position would be under-hedged if the clean price, C_0, of the stock was greater than the futures price, F_0, or over-hedged if C_0 was less than F_0.

If, therefore, an investor were to use the futures market to hedge a position in the gilt market itself without using the delivery mechanism, how should he gear his hedge? If he follows the following procedure, he should not go far wrong; though it cannot be stated too forcibly that there is no such thing as the perfect guaranteed hedge.

First of all, he should quantify the extent and time period of the stock price movement against which he wishes to seek protection.

Secondly, he must make an assessment as to which of the eligible stocks is likely to be the cheapest deliverable stock at the *future date*, and through this stock estimate the likely prospective futures price, should the market movement he wishes to hedge against take place.

Thirdly, he should form the ratio of the change in value of the stock (allowing, if necessary, for the receipt of dividends *en route*) to the change in the futures price. This is called the 'hedge ratio' and should be applied to the size of his gilt holding to determine the number of futures contracts that will best 'insure' him against that particular eventuality. For this method to be effective requires there to be some reasonably close correlation between movements in the prices of the stock to be hedged and the cheapest deliverable gilt. Where these are disparate, such close correlation may not exist, and the reader is warned against being tempted to think that, say, medium-dated gilts can be exactly hedged by a combination of the short and long futures contracts. If the shape or slope of the yield curve alters, even hedges worked out on a weighted average volatility basis could be dangerously inaccurate.

Gilt-edged Traded Options

As derivative instruments of the gilt-edged market, financial futures and traded options are often classed together in the minds of investors, but in practice they serve quite significantly different purposes. Whereas in the case of a futures contract it is mandatory for the seller to deliver stock or close out his position, an option (as its name suggests) conveys upon its owner the right (but not the obligation) to exercise his option to buy (or sell) a given stock or alternatively let it lapse. It follows therefore that the most a purchaser of an option stands to lose if prices of the underlying stock move against him is the price paid for the option, whilst his potential gain is unlimited. This contrasts clearly with the situation in futures where the price movement is theoretically unlimited in either direction.

There are two types of gilt-edged traded options: call options and put options.

A traded call option is a negotiable contract that enables the buyer to purchase (call) a specified amount of the given gilt-edged stock (£50,000 nominal) at a predetermined clean price (the exercise price) plus gross accrued interest throughout a given time period. The price that the buyer of the option pays for this right is known as the 'option premium'.

The counterparty to this bargain is the call option seller (or 'writer' as he is often called). This person receives the option premium but stands committed to sell the relevant amount of stock to the buyer at the exercise price at any time up to the date of expiry of the option. If he already owns the stock he is called a 'covered' writer; if he does not he is called an 'uncovered' or (rather more exotically) a 'naked' writer.

A traded put option entitles the buyer of the option to sell (put) a specified amount of stock (£50,000 nominal) at the predetermined exercise price plus gross accrued interest during the period of the option, and the writer of a put option pockets the option premium in return for his obligation to buy the stock at the exercise price (plus gross accrued interest) during that period if requested.

The first gilt-edged traded option contracts to come into existence were based upon the short-dated stock Exchequer 10% 1989. These started life on 10 January 1985 and were followed on 25 June that year by similar options linked to the long-dated Treasury 11¾% 2003/07. The market is normally arranged so that there will be a choice of three different expiry dates spaced at three-monthly intervals on (for gilts) a February, May, August, November cycle; and a range of no less than three exercise prices at two-point price intervals. Every so often it is necessary to change the underlying stock when the passage of time means that it is no longer representative of the relevant maturity area. For example, options on Exchequer 10% 1989 ceased after the February 1986 series to be replaced by those based on Treasury 11¾% 1991.

As with many other markets the traded option market has its own jargon and nomenclature. All options of the same nature (i.e. calls or puts) relating to the same underlying security form what is called an 'option class'; and all options of the same class with the same exercise price and the same expiry date form an 'option series'.

If the stock's price in the market is higher than the exercise price of a call option (or if the stock price is lower than the exercise price of a put option) the option in question is termed to be 'in the money'.

If the stock's price equals the exercise price the option is said to be 'at the money'.

If the stock's price is lower than the exercise price of a call option (or is higher than the exercise price of a put option) the option is considered to be 'out of the money'.

When option prices are being considered, expressions such as 'intrinsic value' and 'time premium' will be encountered. For an option that is 'in the money' the intrinsic value is the absolute value of the difference between the underlying stock price and the exercise price, and for 'out of the money' options the intrinsic value is zero. The 'time premium' is the amount by which the actual option price exceeds the intrinsic value. Figure 9.1 illustrates these in the case of call option with an exercise price of 96.

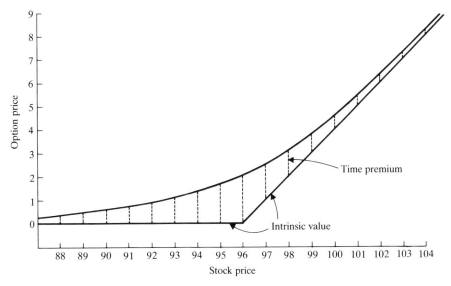

Fig. 9.1 *Call option – exercise price 96*

Gilt-edged traded option bargains are transacted on the floor of The Stock Exchange by an open outcry method, and are settled through the London Options Clearing House (LOCH), a subsidiary of The Stock Exchange, which places itself as the official counterparty to both buyer and seller (writer). This obviates the necessity for the two parties to have any further dealings with each other in respect of that bargain. All business in options is transacted for cash settlement on the next day. For an option buyer this means making available the option premium to the broker for payment to LOCH by 10.00 a.m. the following day. In the case of a writer he must either deposit with LOCH a confirmation by an approved authority that that authority holds in its nominee company sufficient stock to cover the contract, or deposit cash margin or some other form of collateral whose value equals or exceeds the margin requirements as detailed in the contract specification. This is subject to daily adjustment as the price of the underlying stock changes.

Exercising or Closing Out a Traded Option

The initiative in exercising a traded option position lies wholly with the buyer – the writer has no control of whether or when an option is exercised. The buyer can exercise his option at any time during its life by giving notice to his broker so as to enable the broker to inform LOCH of his intentions in writing by 5.00 p.m. that day (6.00 p.m. on the expiry day, which in the case of the gilt-edged contracts is the last business day of the expiry month). Once such notice has been given, LOCH – using a random selection process – chooses a counterparty from the pool of outstanding writers of that particular option series, and on the next business day a bargain representing the exercise of the option is conducted between these two parties. The consideration for such bargains is based on the exercise price plus gross accrued interest relating to the next subsequent business day and is settled accordingly; that is, two business days after notice is given to LOCH.

If rather than exercise an option the buyer chooses to close out his position by making an equal and opposite bargain in that option series, this must be designated as a closing bargain and LOCH must be notified accordingly. Without such specification the two positions would remain independently in the clearing system instead of cancelling each other out. This could easily lead to the written option being matched by LOCH against an exercise of an option by a totally unrelated party, thereby leaving the original buyer with an unwanted open position.

Traded Option Pricing

The pricing of traded options is an area of investment where probability theory comes into its own. This is perhaps hardly surprising when one considers that the essential determinants of value are the probability that a given stock will reach or exceed certain price targets within a specified time frame. It is important to realise right from the beginning that the calculation of these probabilities is highly subjective and that the whole business of valuing option premiums is far from precise. However, there are certain limiting boundaries within which option values are constrained which provide a basic framework for price analysis.

It is probably most instructive to start by examining a simple call option, as depicted by Figure 9.2. In this case the option premium is plotted against the *y*-axis and the stock price against the *x*-axis. The exercise price (E) is represented by the point *E* on that axis.

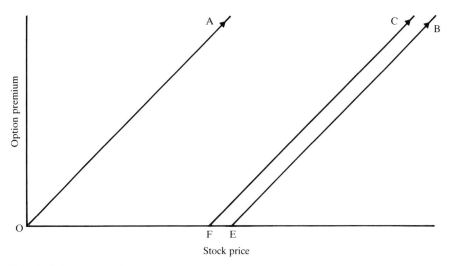

Fig. 9.2 *Call option boundaries*

The first point to make is a rather obvious one. Since nobody in his right mind should pay more for a call option (irrespective of exercise price) than the current stock price, the point in the option/stock price diagram representing their relationship must always be below and to the right of the 45° line *OA*.

Secondly, the price of an option can never be negative for this would imply that the option represented a liability to its owner; and since at worst an option can always be abandoned this can never be the case.

Next, consider the 45° line *EB* drawn through the point *E* on the *x*-axis representing the exercise price. If by any chance the option/stock price point were to be to the right of this line, this would imply that it would be possible to make a riskless profit by selling the underlying stock, buying the call option, and closing the position by immediately exercising that option. The efficiency of the market and the alertness of those who operate in it normally preclude this from happening!

It would thus appear that by combining these three logical considerations we have established the boundaries of valid call option pricing, i.e. within the parallelogram *AOEB*. But no. There is a further refinement which is often neglected by those more used to dealing with equity traded options but which is of not insignificant importance for options on instruments where interest accrues on a day-to-day basis. In considering the riskless arbitrage above it was only examined in the case of the option being exercised immediately. But gilt-edged options are exerciseable at any time up to their expiry date. If in that period the rate of interest that can be earned on the proceeds of the sale of the underlying stock less the cost of the call option is greater than the rate at which the stock is accruing, then it would be possible to make an even bigger arbitrage profit by delaying the exercise of the option until just before expiry. This means that in such circumstances the really accurate boundary of valid option pricing will not be the line *EB* but another line, *FC*, parallel and a little way to the left of it.

This can perhaps best be illustrated by some mathematical analysis.

Let P_0 represent the current stock price

a_0 represent the current gross accrued interest

Z_0 represent the current traded option price

E represent the exercise price of the option

q represent the time period until exercise

a_q represent the gross accrued interest at exercise

v^q represent the discounting factor at the going rate of interest for the period until exercise

and d represent the present value of any dividends due on the underlying stock in this period.

Let us now examine the strategy discussed above whereby the holder of the underlying stock sells his stock and covers his position by buying an option and subsequently exercises it. As we have already said, market forces will determine that this can never be done to make a profit, so that, *for all values of q,*

$$Z_0 + v^q(E + a_q) \geqslant (P_0 + a_0) - d$$

$$\text{or} \quad Z_0 \geqslant (P_0 + a_0) - v^q(E + a_q) - d.$$

Put in words this says that a valid call option price should always be greater or equal to the current *total* price less the sum of the discounted value of the *total* future exercise price and the discounted value of any dividend payments due in the period.

If one rewrites the equation as

$$Z_0 \geqslant P_0 - (v^q[E + a_q] - d)$$

this establishes the value on the *x*-axis of the point *F* as the term in brackets. If one takes the case of a call option on a 10% stock with an exercise price of 96 and expiry in three months' time, where the initial accrued interest is, say, 0.625 and that at expiry 3.125, and where three-month money rates are, say, 12%, then

$$F = v^q(E + a_q) - a_0$$

$$= 0.971286(96 + 3.125) - 0.625$$

$$= 95.65$$

and the theoretical value of such a call option can be represented by a monotonic increasing curve which starts off passing through the point O and eventually becomes asymptotic to the line FC.

Three crucial factors need to be stressed:

1. The line FC will tend towards EB as the option expiry date approaches.
2. The size of the time premium (which is at its greatest when the option is 'at the money') decreases in proportion to the square root of the period to expiry.
3. The size of option premiums are in general closely related to the magnitude of underlying stock's potential price variability. This item is, regrettably, in option circles referred to as 'volatility' and is most usually defined as the standard deviation of the price of the underlying stock. It should not be confused with the mathematical volatility of Chapter 6.

The whole business of obtaining theoretical option prices owes a great deal to the work of Fischer Black and Myron Scholes, whose pioneering work has established industry standards in this field, but it is open to argument whether the application of the Black and Scholes model to gilt-edged traded options is really valid. The Black and Scholes method is based upon assumptions that the expected price of the underlying stock at expiry is lognormally distributed about the current price, and that the stock's 'volatility' is both accurately quantifiable and stable. Unfortunately there is little hard evidence to support the stability assumption and there are practical difficulties in establishing satisfactory prospective 'volatility' figures simply from analysing historic price movements. In the first instance one can quite easily get radically different 'volatility' figures depending on the retrospective time period chosen for analysis, and, secondly, because the life to maturity of the stock is reducing day by day these will tend to reflect the 'volatility' of a stock somewhat longer than that in question. Nevertheless, many adapted versions of this basic method can be found in use today, and perhaps their most advantageous usage is in making comparative judgements of different option series within the same option class.

PUT OPTION PRICING

Very similar considerations to those above apply to the pricing of put options. Except in the case of the riskless arbitrage, this now consists of an initial purchase of both the put option and the underlying stock, and the closing of the arbitrage is effected by the exercise of the put option. Using the same notation as before it is possible to establish the basic relationship for put options,

$$Z_0 \geqslant v^q(E + a_q) + d - (P_0 + a_0).$$

Once again the fundamental principle that the option price cannot be negative applies, but the other basic pricing boundary is determined by the fact that it would be illogical for the put option price to exceed the exercise price. This leads to a diagrammatical representation of a put option, as shown in Fig. 9.3.

Following very much the same thought processes as before, it is clear that valid put option values must at least fall within the area $ABEX$, and that *if the rate at which the underlying stock accrues exceeds money rates* for the period to expiry

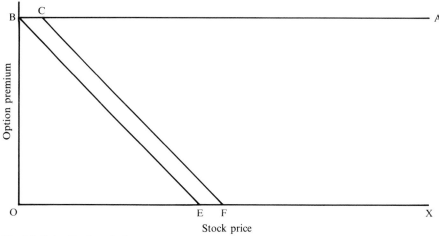

Fig. 9.3 *Put option boundaries*

then they must be further constrained to fall within the area *ACFX*. In which case *F* takes the value

$$F = v^q(E + a_q) - a_0$$

just as before.

THE RELATIONSHIP BETWEEN PUT AND CALL OPTION PRICES

There is a tidy price relationship between the price of a put option and that of the call option of the same series. This comes about by virtue of the equivalence of two option strategies, the first to hold a portfolio consisting of both stock and a put option, and the second to hold the relevant amount of cash plus a call option. That these two strategies are equivalent can be argued thus. If, at expiry, the stock price has risen above the exercise price, the owner of the first portfolio can abandon the put option and end up simply holding the stock, whilst the owner of the second portfolio will exercise his call option using his cash to finance acquiring stock in this way. Likewise, if the stock price at expiry is below the exercise price the first investor can exercise his put option against his holding of stock, whilst the second will just abandon the call option. In the first instance both portfolios end up holding an equal amount of stock, and in the second they end up holding the same amount of cash.

Thus, call option price minus put option price

$$= (P_0 + a_0) - v^r(E + a_r)$$

where *r* denotes the period to expiry and the other symbols take the same meanings as in previous examples.

Option Trading Strategies

The ability to combine limited liability instruments like traded options with physical stock positions or with other options opens up a vast new area of potential for the adept investor. People venturing into this area for the first time are sometimes confused and uncertain as to the precise results of combining various options. This problem can most often be overcome by considering the potential levels of profit or loss at expiry for a full range of prices of the underlying stock at that time. This is not as difficult as it might seem, since there are only four basic option actions: buy calls, write calls, buy puts and write puts. Each of these has a profit profile which is shown in Fig. 9.4, and where options are combined the profile of the aggregated profit or loss quickly discloses the character of the combined strategy.

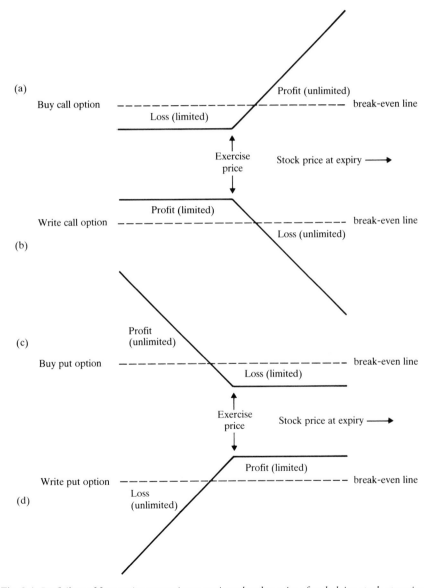

Fig. 9.4 *Profit/loss of four option strategies at expiry related to price of underlying stock at expiry*

As an example of this technique consider the result of simultaneously buying 96 puts at 2 and writing 96 calls at 1. This is portrayed in Fig. 9.5 in which the profit profiles for both options are shown individually, together with the overall profit of the combined strategy. Ignoring for the moment the (minuscule) costs of financing the cash flow deficit of 1 and any other expenses, this clearly breaks even if the stock price at expiry is 95 and makes a further one-point profit for every point the stock price falls below that level. One has thus effectively created a synthetic short sale of the stock at price of 95.

There are quite obviously very many different stock and option combinations that can be constructed for a variety of investment purposes, many of which are quite sophisticated and deserve a book in their own right. However, it is important not to lose sight of the main purposes to which traded options are put. Just like futures they can be used for both speculation and hedging, but, unlike futures when options are used as hedging instruments there is no convenient constant hedge ratio between the size of the stock position to be hedged and the number of option contracts required to do it. The reason for this is that the rate at which the option price rises or falls with respect to changes in the price of the underlying

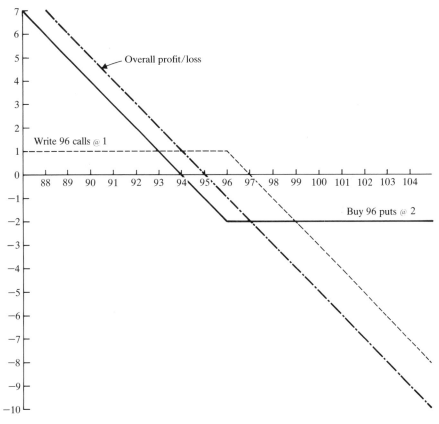

Fig. 9.5 *Profit profile for a strategy of simultaneously buying put options and selling call options*

stock is virtually always less than unity. This relative rate of change of option price to stock price is the gradient of the option price curve shown in the earlier examples and is known in the business as the 'delta'. Simple observation of the option price curve shows how the delta itself varies from close to zero in the case of deep out-of-the-money options to approaching unity in the instance of heavily in-the-money ones. It is therefore understandable why option hedges require rather more careful management than those involving futures.

Finally, the point at which futures and options really met and became completely intertwined was reached in March 1986 when LIFFE introduced options on three of its futures contracts, including the long gilt future and the US Treasury bond future, a point at which the author is inclined to feel that financial innovation, at least in this sphere, has gone far enough for the time being.

10

Taxation of gilt-edged stocks and associated instruments

Historically the incidence of tax in one form or another has given rise to many of the price anomalies that occur in the gilt-edged market, and the interplay between funds with differing tax positions has created a considerable proportion of the market's turnover. It has thus always been important for those involved in the market to have a full understanding of the taxation implications. However, in a rare reversal of the law of maximum perversity, the taxation changes announced in the 1985 Budget (and becoming effective in 1986) have, on balance, simplified the taxation environment for gilts. The major fiscal gluepot had always been capital gains tax, where an accumulation of successive pieces of legislation from 1965 onwards created a veritable tangle of rules for stock identification, index-ation, loss offsetting and so on. Capital gains tax on gilt-edged stocks was also just not a revenue producer – in fact some would argue that it was a net revenue loser. This possibility arose from the basic principle emanating from the 1968 Budget of the then Labour Chancellor of the Exchequer, Mr Roy Jenkins, that gilt-edged stock should be exempt from capital gains if held for more than one year, and that losses on gilt-edged stock realised within one year from purchase could be offset not only against similar short-term gilt gains, but also against any other chargeable gains that an investor might have from equities, property, etc. This meant that a taxed gilt-edged investor was given an option to run his profitable holdings until he had held them for more than a year and they had become free of capital gains tax, or to cut his losses by selling within the one-year period and effectively obtaining 30% tax relief on those losses. Many large funds found this option highly advantageous and some considered it sufficient justifi-cation for holding a larger proportion of their total assets in gilts than they would otherwise have done. This situation ceased to exist on 2 July 1986 when capital gains tax on gilt-edged (and certain other fixed-interest) stocks was abolished in its entirety. By contrast the extension of the system of taxation of income from gilts to include accrued interest and which became effective on 28 February 1986 did introduce some new complexities in this field; but taken as an overall package the net effect has been to create an environment where there are no longer any artificial restraints on dealing and where stock values can now freely find their own levels under the basic forces of supply and demand.

In the post-2 July 1986 environment the only taxation about which an investor need be concerned is that on income. This can be subdivided into that emanating directly from dividends and that derived from the differences in accrued interest at purchase and disposal.

The Taxation of Dividends

Interest payments (dividends) on gilt-edged stocks are normally paid after deduction at source of the basic rate of income tax, currently (1986/87) 29%. There are some exceptions to this rule.

Firstly, dividends on War $3\frac{1}{2}$% 1952/after ('War Loan') are always paid gross, whether to residents of the United Kingdom or to non-residents.

Secondly, the Bank of England maintains a register of holders of stocks who are exempt from tax – pension funds, charities, etc. – and dividends to these holders on these stocks can be paid gross. The process of registering an exempt holding is cumbersome, and if a total holding is disposed of and reacquired later the process has to be repeated. It is not unknown, however, for a tax-exempt fund to acquire and register a series of minuscule holdings, say £10 nominal, of all gilt-edged stocks, and to maintain these as permanent minimum holdings.

The third category is the payment of gross dividends on certain specified gilt-edged stocks to non-residents of the United Kingdom upon application. The list of stocks to which this facility is applicable is relatively limited. They are mostly the older gilt-edged stocks issued pre-1980 and formally designated as tax free to non-residents in the Stock Exchange Official List, and often referred to as 'FOTRA' (Free Of Tax Residents Abroad) stocks.

As at the end of March 1986 they comprised the following:

Treasury $8\frac{1}{2}$% 1984/86	Treasury $12\frac{3}{4}$% 1995
Funding $6\frac{1}{2}$% 1985/87	Treasury 9% 1992/96
Treasury $7\frac{3}{4}$% 1985/88	Treasury $15\frac{1}{4}$% 1996
Treasury 13% 1990	Exchequer $13\frac{1}{4}$% 1996
Exchequer 11% 1990	Treasury $13\frac{1}{4}$% 1997
Treasury $8\frac{1}{4}$% 1987/90	Treasury $8\frac{3}{4}$% 1997
Funding $5\frac{3}{4}$% 1987/91	Treasury $6\frac{3}{4}$% 1995/98
Treasury $12\frac{3}{4}$% 1992	Treasury $15\frac{1}{2}$% 1998
Treasury $10\frac{1}{2}$% Convertible 1992	Treasury $9\frac{1}{2}$% 1999
Treasury 10% 1993	Conversion 9% 2000
Treasury $12\frac{1}{2}$% 1993	Treasury 8% 2002/06
Funding 6% 1993	Treasury $5\frac{1}{2}$% 2008/12
Treasury $13\frac{3}{4}$% 1993	Treasury $7\frac{3}{4}$% 2012/15
Treasury $14\frac{1}{2}$% 1994	War $3\frac{1}{2}$% 1952/after
Treasury 9% 1994	

In order for a non-resident to obtain payment of dividends on these stocks in gross form, or to be able to claim back tax already deducted at source, he must first make application to the Inspector of Foreign Dividends on Form A3 (Inland

Revenue). For exemption to be granted it is necessary for the investor to declare that he is a bona-fide non-resident of the United Kingdom, and that he is the beneficial owner of the relevant stock. Whilst this may not present many difficulties for individuals, insurance companies, pension funds and banks, it does pose acute problems for overseas investment funds/trusts who cannot give guarantees that none of their beneficiaries is a UK resident. In fact, even if they knew this to be the fact, it would still be necessary for each beneficiary to lodge a form A3 application and be approved for the fund/trust to benefit in this way. Since this is not a practical proposition, overseas mutual funds and the like have, historically, eschewed investment in the gilt-edged market, except for War $3\frac{1}{2}\%$, where dividends are paid gross to all and sundry without any formalities being required. Partly because of this factor, War $3\frac{1}{2}\%$ has often stood at a premium valuation to other undated stocks, and was once the subject of the following epithet at a Scottish actuarial meeting: 'War Loan is an investment for widows and orphans who could do better, and for foreigners who wish to remain anonymous.' There is, actually, a second way for a non-resident to obtain dividends on FOTRA stocks by use of a so-called 'E' arrangement under which procedure the investor normally is saved from completing any form for the Inland Revenue himself.

It is also possible for a non-resident to obtain tax exemption from gilts through the operation of double taxation agreements with some overseas countries. Non-resident investors wishing to make use of such facilities should approach the Inspector of Foreign Dividends in the normal way. Tax exemptions granted under this aegis are not necessarily restricted to the normal list of 'tax free to non-resident' stocks.

There are, however, some important considerations relating to such dividends paid abroad. In its strictest sense, the legislation requires the non-resident to be the beneficial owner of the stock in question on the day the dividend is paid. Since this is normally some five weeks and two days after going ex-dividend, this, if rigidly applied, locks an overseas investor into a holding for that period. Accordingly, the Inland Revenue has declared that the policy of the Inspector of Foreign Dividends is to allow claims wherever the overseas resident has been a bona-fide holder of the stock for a reasonable period of time, and has sold the stock between the ex-dividend date and the dividend payment date. There is no formal definition of what constitutes a reasonable period, but it is thought that any period shorter than one month would *not* be deemed 'reasonable'.

The one thing which is emphatic is that when an overseas resident sells stock in the special ex-dividend form during the twenty-one-day period prior to becoming officially ex-dividend, no claim for repayment of tax will be considered whatsoever, except possibly under certain double taxation arrangements.

The Accrued Interest Scheme

The whole basis of taxation of gilt-edged income changed radically on 28 February 1986. Hitherto only actual dividend payments received counted as taxable income, but the introduction and operation of the accrued interest scheme from that date has widened the tax net. Under this scheme the gross accrued interest at the time of sale is considered to be a receipt of income and as such becomes chargeable to income tax. As a natural offset to this the accrued interest content of the purchase consideration is treated as negative income deductable from the investor's total income aggregation. The overall result of these arrangements is to make the total taxable income derived from a gilt-edged holding proportional to the time it is held, rather than have it incremented in lumps every time a dividend is paid. It thereby eliminated, at a stroke, the previously highly advantageous situation whereby income could be converted into capital gain by judicious sales of stock shortly before they went ex-dividend. For such a capability to have been allowed to persist in a market not subject to capital gains would, in theory, have allowed an investor prepared to pursue this tactic to the nth degree to escape all taxation on his gilt investments. Clearly such a prospect did not appeal to the Inland Revenue and it is this aspect of the matter that is the link which ties these two pieces of legislation together.

Technically, the tax relating to accrued interest items becomes payable (or, in the case of a purchase, creditable) on the date of the immediately following dividend payment, but in practice may not be settled until perhaps as long as a year later when the annual tax return is made. This allows a modest cash flow strategy to exist by which taxed investors making sales just before stocks become ex-dividend and repurchases just afterwards obtain a cash flow approximating to the gross dividend instead of the net dividend from which tax has been deducted at source at standard rate. Admittedly they will have to pay the same amount of total tax in the final analysis, but they will have the use of the larger amount for some reasonable time which will be of value to them.

Dealing Restraints

The restrictions on dealing in stocks at or near ex-dividend dates have not always been limited to overseas investors; UK investors too have been governed by legislation controlling their ability to receive excess dividends, but the advent of the accrued interest scheme appears to make much of that redundant. In the past when bargains were performed specially ex-dividend a broker had to certify that:

either, for sales ex-dividend:

Certificate A

'We [the broker] have made all enquiries necessary to satisfy ourselves, including obtaining a written assurance from our principal that the principal has been the beneficial owner of this stock for more than one month prior to the date of this sale, or that he has bought the stock ex-dividend previously during the current three-week period.'

or, for sales ex-dividend:

Certificate A1

'We have obtained a written assurance from our principal that the stock was beneficially owned by the principal who is a member of the London Discount Market Association.'

or, for purchases ex-dividend:

Certificate B

'We have made all enquiries necessary to satisfy ourselves, including obtaining a written assurance from our principal that this purchase neither reverses a cum-dividend short sale already effected, nor will be reversed by a cum-dividend sale done simultaneously or yet to be effected before the payment of the dividend.'

The operation of these certificates was one of the main methods by which the Inland Revenue enforced the provisions of sections 471–475 of the Income and Corporation Tax Acts 1970, of which s.471(2) specifically penalised investors who bought stock cum-dividend and subsequently sold it ex-dividend within one month. Under the accrued interest scheme there is no longer any disadvantage to the Inland Revenue brought about by such transactions, and paragraph 2 of schedule 17 of the 1986 Finance Act provides for securities covered by the accrued interest scheme to be excluded from the 'claws' of s.471(2). What this all means is that from 19th March 1986 investors have been free to buy gilts cum-dividend and sell ex-dividend without having to worry about how long they held them. It also made Certificates A and A1 redundant.

The Inland Revenue, however, remains very sensitive to the basic question of manufactured dividends and the provisions of Certificate B remain. Furthermore, when the bargain is a specially ex-dividend purchase of £50,000 or more in nominal value the relevant transfer form is placed in temporary 'cold storage' by being required to be lodged with The Stock Exchange until the official ex-dividend date. Should the purchaser wish to resell this stock before that date, he would be required to sell it in the same nominal amount(s) and through a registered market-maker in the London market.

The reasons for most of this legislation have been to preclude the infamous practice of 'bond washing'. Before these regulations were framed, it was quite possible for someone to buy stock ex-dividend and match it with a corresponding sale cum-dividend. The buyer on the other side of the cum-dividend transaction, being entitled to a dividend, would claim the net value of the coupon from the first buyer. Since the first buyer had bought the stock ex-dividend, he had no actual dividend to pass on and would settle the account by passing a cash payment equal to the net dividend – which he was happy to do since this would normally have been less than the actual profit on the buying and selling operation. If, however, the second buyer was a gross (tax-exempt) fund, he would then ask the Inland Revenue for a repayment of basic-rate tax on his dividend. But, in reality, this dividend had never existed; it had, in effect, been 'created' by the operation of buying XD and selling CD. It does not need much imagination to understand the consternation of the Inland Revenue at the prospect of paying out tax relief on non-existent dividends, and the above rules were framed so as to prevent such happenings occurring.

Taxation of Gilt-edged Futures and Options

As from 2 July 1986 these derivative instruments have been free from capital gains tax where the underlying security is a gilt-edged stock.

In the year between the 1985 Budget – when the intention to abolish capital gains tax on gilts was first indicated – and the 1986 Budget, there was considerable speculation that an anomalous situation would be created if, after 2 July 1986, gilt-edged financial futures and traded options were to continue to be subject to capital gains tax whilst the underlying stocks themselves were tax free. This would have allowed buyers of these instruments to play a new variation of the 'if it goes up – it's capital gains tax free, if it goes down – it's allowable for tax' game. In the case of a rising market they could demand delivery of stock or exercise their option to buy stock which would give them capital gains tax exemption, but if the market fell they could establish tax losses by selling their futures contract or by selling or abandoning their call options. Once again this prospect did not appeal to the tax authorities and the 1986 Budget contained provisions to extend the capital gains tax exemption to gilt-edged futures and options where disposal takes place on or after 2 July 1986. Since neither options nor futures generate any accrued interest this leaves these instruments as the only totally tax-free investments available to the UK domestic investor.

11

Gilt-edged indices and performance measurement considerations

Virtually every securities market in the world has some published indicator or index (many have more than one) by which its aggregate progress can be monitored. The gilt-edged market is no exception to this rule. There are two main indices, both published by the *Financial Times* newspaper (*FT*) on a daily basis, and no book on this subject would be complete without reference to them.

The older of the two is the *Financial Times* Government Securities Index, and comes, so to speak, from the same stable as the *Financial Times* Industrial Ordinary Share Index. Both date from before World War II – the Ordinary Share Index having a base date of 1 July 1935, whilst the Government Securities Index goes back to 18 January 1926. Both of them are geometric averages of prices of a 'representative' selection of stocks or shares in their respective markets.

At 15 March 1986, the eleven constituent members of the *FT* Government Securities Index were:

Transport 3% 1978/88	Exchequer 12% 1999/2002
Treasury 11½% 1989	Treasury 12½% 2003/05
Treasury 11¾% 1991	Treasury 5½% 2008/12
Funding 6% 1993	War 3½% 1952/after
Treasury 15¼% 1996	Consol 2½% 1923/after
Treasury 9½% 1999	

It was stated above that the index was a geometric average; by this it is meant that the index figure is found by multiplying together the constituent prices and taking the eleventh root of this product. This process ensures that percentage movements in all stocks, whether they are high-priced or low-priced stocks, are given equal weightings in the averaging process. In this index the relevant prices are clean prices, and the index ignores the incidence of dividends. As such, it is of use only as a broad indicator of changes in market levels, and should not be used for any sophisticated form of performance comparison (on which subject more will be found later on in this chapter). In fact, there follows below an analysis of this index, which has a lot in common mathematically with the analysis of price ratios in Chapter 7.

In this analysis, q represents the *FT* Government Securities Index, formed from stocks whose *total* prices are $P_1, P_2, \ldots, P_m$ and whose coupon rates are $g_1, g_2, \ldots, g_m$ respectively.

Using this notation,

$$q = [(P_1 - g_1 t_1) \cdot (P_2 - g_2 t_2) \ldots (P_m - g_m t_m)]^{1/m}.$$

Taking logarithms of both sides of this equation,

$$m \log q = \log (P_1 - g_1 t_1) + \log (P_2 - g_2 t_2) + \ldots + (P_m - g_m t_m).$$

Differentiating with respect to time, t,

$$\frac{m}{q} \frac{dq}{dt} = \frac{-g_1}{P_1 - g_1 t_1} + \frac{-g_2}{P_2 - g_2 t_2} + \ldots + \frac{-g_m}{P_m - g_m t_m}$$

$$\frac{1}{q} \frac{dq}{dt} = -\frac{f_1 + f_2 + \ldots + f_m}{m}.$$

If one compares this with a similar analysis for a single stock's clean price, c,

$$c = P - gt$$

$$\log c = \log (P - gt)$$

$$\frac{1}{c} \frac{dc}{dt} = \frac{-g}{P - gt} = -f$$

it can be seen that the *geometrically* averaged *FT* Government Securities Index acts like a stock with the same flat yield as the *arithmetical* average of the flat yields of its constituent parts.

It thus follows that the trends shown up by this index will overstate the market's progress if the index's average flat yield is below the 'going market rate', and understate it if the average flat yield exceeds it.

If the 'going market rate' is deemed to be, say, the average gross redemption yield of the index's constituents – a not perfect, but far from impractical assumption – then the size of the bias in this index becomes determined by the difference between its average flat yield and its average gross redemption yield at any particular time.

On 15 March 1986 these values were as in Table 11.1, from which it can be deduced that at that time the index would have had a small propensity to overstate the performance of the market.

Like all indices of this sort, it also suffers from the problem of discontinuities. These normally arise when one of its constituents approaches redemption and has to be replaced with another (obviously) longer stock. In an index with a relatively small number of constituents, this can cause the 'average life' of the index to increase suddenly, and if the flat yields of the outgoing and incoming constituents differ to any great degree this will also affect the passage-of-time

Table 11.1   FT *Government Securities Index: average flat yield and gross redemption yield, 15 March 1986*

Stock	Flat yield	Gross redemption yield
Transport 3% 1978/88	3.37	8.30
Treasury 11½% 1989	11.18	10.33
Treasury 11¾% 1991	11.06	10.05
Funding 6% 1993	6.94	8.46
Treasury 15¼% 1996	11.44	9.96
Treasury 9½% 1999	9.55	9.56
Exchequer 12% 1999/2002	10.33	9.76
Treasury 12½% 2003/05	10.06	9.61
Treasury 5½% 2008/12	8.22	8.72
War 3½% 1952/after	9.00	9.00
Consol 2½% 1923/after	9.05	9.05
Average	9.11	9.35

trends outlined above. It can be argued that the effects of these discontinuities are only small and can normally be ignored, but the fact remains that, rightly or wrongly, a number of technical analysts (chartists) all over the world use this index as the basis for their gilt-edged charts, and they need to be aware of any distortions, large or small, that are built into their data.

By contrast, the newer set of indices, the *FT*–Actuaries British Government Price Indices, is riddled with discontinuities, and revels in it. These indices were designed to act as far as possible like individual stocks, so that the price indices are like *total* prices, and discontinuities occur as prices drop whenever a constituent member goes ex-dividend. To compensate for this, each of these indices has a second component which is incremented by the appropriate amount of dividend at the time of going ex-dividend.

Again in contrast to the *FT* Government Securities Index, the *FT*–Actuaries Indices take into account the (total) prices of all stocks in the gilt-edged list, and weight them by market capitalisation. The full details of the methods used for computing both these indices and the average gross redemption yields of certain defined market sectors which accompany them daily in the *Financial Times* can be found in the *Journal of the Institute of Actuaries* (Vol. 105, parts 15 and 27) or the *Transactions of the Faculty of Actuaries* (Vol. 36, part 3).

In presentation the *FT*–Actuaries Gilt Indices, and two other indices for Debentures and Loans and for Preference Shares computed on a similar basis, follow the style shown in Table 11.2. The key values on any one day, however, are the first and last columns of the left-hand table, the first column being the *total* price component of the index, and the last column being the accumulated amount of dividend relating to stocks that have *gone ex-dividend* so far in the calendar year.

Because of the very obvious discontinuities of the price components of these indices, they should not be used for chart purposes, but they are ideal (and were specifically designed) for performance measurement.

Table 11.2 FT–Actuaries Gilt, Debentures and Loans, and Preference Share Indices, 31 March 1983

FIXED INTEREST

PRICE INDICES	Thur. 31 March	Day's change %	Wed. 30 March	XD adj. today	XD adj. 1983 to date
British Government					
1 5 years	116.59	+0.23	116.32	—	2.92
2 5–15 years	128.68	+0.55	127.97	—	3.69
3 Over 15 years	138.40	+0.71	137.43	—	2.49
4 Irredeemables	148.12	+0.75	147.02	—	1.62
5 All Stocks	127.72	+0.51	127.08	—	3.10
6 **Debentures and Loans**	101.71	+0.39	101.31	—	2.90
7 **Preference**	80.10	—	80.10	—	2.28

AVERAGE GROSS REDEMPTION YIELDS

	Thur. 31 March	Wed. 30 March	Year ago (approx.)	Highs	Lows
British Government				1982/83	
1 Low 5 years	9.42	9.45	11.66	13.49 (5/1/82)	7.89 (2/11/82)
2 Coupons 15 years	10.24	10.29	12.68	14.28 (5/1/82)	9.25 (11/11/82)
3 25 years	10.24	10.29	12.53	14.17 (12/1/82)	9.47 (2/11/82)
4 Medium 5 years	11.47	11.50	13.79	16.41 (12/1/82)	9.89 (11/11/82)
5 Coupons 15 years	11.09	11.17	13.67	16.10 (5/1/82)	10.32 (3/11/82)
6 25 years	10.61	10.69	13.21	15.46 (12/1/82)	10.01 (19/10/82)
7 High 5 years	11.47	11.54	13.78	16.30 (8/1/82)	9.96 (3/11/82)
8 Coupons 15 years	11.31	11.39	13.84	16.28 (5/1/82)	10.55 (2/11/82)
9 25 years	10.71	10.79	13.27	15.76 (12/1/82)	10.14 (2/11/82)
10 Irredeemables	10.06	10.12	12.16	13.64 (12/1/82)	9.31 (3/11/82)
11 Debs 5 years	12.28	12.40	14.70	17.07 (12/1/82)	11.11 (12/11/82)
12 and 15 years	12.33	12.38	14.62	16.85 (12/1/82)	11.35 (12/11/82)
13 Loans 25 years	12.34	12.38	14.58	16.72 (12/1/82)	11.49 (15/11/82)
14 **Preference**	12.26	12.26	15.18	16.24 (11/1/82)	12.20 (18/3/83)

Source: *Financial Times.*

The divided nature of these indices often confuses people when they come to use them. The example that follows shows how they should be correctly used for that purpose (reference should be made to Table 11.3).

Table 11.3   FT–*Actuaries Gilt Indices, 31 March and 30 September 1983*

PRICE INDICES	Thur. 31 March	Day's change %	Wed. 30 March	XD adj. today	XD adj 1983 to date	PRICE INDICES	Fri. 30 Sept.	Day's change %	Thurs. 29 Sept.	XD adj. today	XD adj. 1983 to date
British Government						**British Government**					
1 5 years	116.59	+ 0.23	116.32	—	2.92	1 5 years	117.36	+ 0.08	117.27	—	8.44
2 5–15 years	128.68	+ 0.55	127.97	—	3.69	2 5–15 years	130.29	+ 0.02	130.27	—	10.70
3 Over 15 years ..	138.40	+ 0.71	137.43	—	2.49	3 Over 15 years ..	140.44	− 0.01	140.44	—	10.29
4 Irredeemables ..	148.12	+ 0.75	147.02	—	1.62	4 Irredeemables ..	152.73	—	152.73	—	8.90
5 All Stocks	127.72	+ 0.51	127.08	—	3.10	5 All Stocks	129.16	+ 0.03	129.12	—	9.86

Source: *Financial Times.*

To compute the performance of any given sector of the market over a specified period, it is necessary to obtain:

(a) the change in the (total) price index over the period, and
(b) the income payments received or due in respect of stocks going ex-dividend during the period,

and then divide the sum of these two elements by the initial (total) price index, e.g.

For the All Stocks Index (assuming no tax) between 31 March 1983 and 30 September 1983,

$$(a) = 129.16 - 127.72 = 1.44$$
$$(b) = \quad 9.86 - \quad 3.10 = 6.76$$
$$(a) + (b) \qquad\qquad\quad = 8.20$$

Divide by 127.72   = 6.42% over the six months.

The two-part nature of these indices often tempts people to add the two components together and consider the percentage change in this composite figure to be the relevant performance. *This method is totally incorrect,* since in this method the divisor is not the initial price index, but that figure plus the dividends accumulated to date for the year. If the starting date for the period of measurement is the beginning of the year, this latter item will be zero, and arithmetically the result will be accidentally correct, but for all other starting dates it will cause the performance figure to be understated.

A further complication occurs when the performance measurement period spans a calendar year end. The XD adjustments run as cumulative totals, and their 'meters' are reset to zero at the beginning of each new year. In such cases, item (b) will have two parts:

(i) relating to the period from the starting date in the earlier year to 31 December of that year, and

(ii) the XD adjustment at the end of the performance period in the later year.

These two elements need to be added together to form the total income relevant to the measurement period.

The essential separation of income and capital elements in these indices makes it very easy to calculate net of tax performance figures, too. If in the case of the All Stocks Index used earlier, income was subject to tax at, say, $37\frac{1}{2}\%$, the net performance would be

$$\frac{(129.16 - 127.72) + (1 - 0.375)(9.86 - 3.10)}{127.72}$$

$$= 4.44\% \text{ net of income tax at } 37\frac{1}{2}\%$$

and if it were subject to income tax at $37\frac{1}{2}\%$ and capital gains tax at 30%, the net performance would be

$$\frac{(1 - 0.3)(129.16 - 127.72) + (1 - 0.375)(9.86 - 3.10)}{127.72}$$

$$= 4.10\%.$$

These figures, and others calculated on a comparable basis, can be described as '*simple* performance figures', since they measure the simple interest return on the relevant index, with no allowance made for the compounding of interest (which is an integral part of gilt-edged portfolio management). However, they do provide a series of standard yardsticks against which actual portfolio experience can be compared. For comparisons like this to be meaningful, it is necessary for the actual and comparative portfolio performances be computed on an exactly similar basis, i.e. capital gain plus income flow added together, and the total divided by the initial capital value.

However, very few gilt-edged funds are totally static. Most will experience new money inflows from time to time (and quite possibly outflows as well) as their investment managers allocate new funds or change their overall asset distributions. It is when new money gets involved with performance calculations that problems start to arise.

There are two principal ways of looking at this subject: by (a) money-weighted rates of return (sometimes referred to as the 'internal rate of return'), or (b) time-weighted rates of return.

In the case of a portfolio initially valued at V_0 receiving income payments of D after time t_1 (measured in half-years), new money for investment of N after time t_2, and being finally valued at V_n after time t_n, the internal rate of return can be defined as the rate of interest $r\%$ per annum such that

$$V_0\left(1 + \frac{r}{200}\right)^{t_n} + D\left(1 + \frac{r}{200}\right)^{(t_n - t_1)} + N\left(1 + \frac{r}{200}\right)^{(t_n - t_2)} = V_n.$$

This is a highly satisfactory measure of an individual fund's performance taken in isolation; but it must be realised that the internal rate of return thus produced will be highly dependent upon the fortuitous timing of any new money flows. As such, it does not represent a tool for making performance comparisons between different funds whose new money may become available for investment at different times. For the performance measurement industry, which is extremely partial to compiling league tables of comparative fund performances, this obviously will not do, and the alternative 'time-weighted rate of return' has evolved to meet their requirements.

The essence of 'time-weighted rates of return' is to break the period over which performance is to be measured into segments bordered by the occasions when dividends or new money flows take place, to compute a succession of simple interest returns for each segment, and to chain-multiply them together to form an overall return.

The problem with this method is that – to be done properly – it requires the portfolio to be valued each and every time a dividend or injection of new money occurs.

Using the same notation as in the previous example, and designating the portfolio values V_1 and V_2 at times t_1 and t_2 respectively,

$$\text{the rate of return between time } t_0 \text{ and } t_1 = \frac{(V_1 - V_0 + D)}{V_0}$$

$$\text{the rate of return between time } t_1 \text{ and } t_2 = \frac{(V_2 - V_1)}{V}$$

$$\text{the rate of return between time } t_2 \text{ and } t_3 = \frac{(V_3 - [V_2 + N])}{(V_2 + N)}$$

and the time-weighted rate of return (w) is defined by the equation

$$\left(1 + \frac{w}{200}\right)^{t_3} = \frac{V_1 + D}{V_0} \times \frac{V_2}{V_1} \times \frac{V_3}{V_2 + N}$$

Both these examples have been deliberately simplified to allow for the incidence of one dividend payment and one new money injection only. In practice, there will tend to be a far greater number of such occurrences and this can become administratively cumbersome. To overcome this, certain systems of computing time-weighted rates of return choose to aggregate dividends and new money inflows, and deem them to be made at average market values and at mean times within certain periods, say, monthly. Whilst this may suffice within the tolerances acceptable for equity performance measurement, the imprecisions inherent in such approximations are incompatible with those involved in the gilt-edged market, where margins of over- or under-performance are measured in tenths and hundredths of percentage points.

There are sometimes further complications with such systems when a fund manager sells a gilt-edged holding, and does not immediately invest in another stock. In some time-weighted measurement systems, this is treated as the obverse of a new money inflow, and if the subsequent reinvestment takes place in a later aggregation period, performance figures can easily result that are certainly misleading and sometimes bizarre.

Moving away from the area of inter-fund performance comparison to that of monitoring the stewardship of an individual fund's manager, there is a lot to be said for the 'notional' fund approach. In this method, a notional portfolio is selected before the start of the respective period of measurement on the basis that if the fund were not to be actively managed, but were to remain totally passive, the notional portfolio would be the one chosen to meet the fund's needs. As and when new money is invested in the actual portfolio, the notional portfolio is also augmented by a similar cash amount (net of expenses), increasing all its holdings proportionately. The two portfolios – the original and the notional – can thus be compared on a like-for-like basis in cash terms, to see whether the active management of the fund has created added value over and above that which would have occurred naturally. This method has the additional advantage that it can be adapted without difficulty to take into account interest earned on (a) uninvested cash balances, (b) money reserved for calls on partly-paid stocks, and (c) dividend payments received by portfolios during the measurement period. As such, it is a very true test of an investment manager's capabilities. This sort of comparison is most commonly found in the area of pension fund management, where before 1976 there was a fairly wide diversity of notional portfolios. But the advent of the *FT*–Actuaries Indices in the spring of that year changed things virtually overnight as the Over-15-Year Index became the *de facto* industry standard notional portfolio. Since then, beating the Over-15-Year Index has become a major preoccupation for a great many gilt-edged fund managers.

By contrast, the *FT*–Actuaries Yield Indices remain a trifle under-used. These indices are obtained from taking constant term yield values at the five-, fifteen- and twenty-five-year maturity points on three separate yield curves, for low-, medium- and high-coupon stocks respectively. The basic intention has been to keep the numbers of stocks in each of these coupon bands as nearly equal as possible, and from time to time the coupon boundaries of the bands are adjusted to allow for changes in the composition of the market brought about by redemptions and new issues. The final yield index relates to the irredeemables, and is the easiest of all to calculate, being the simple arithmetic mean of the flat yields of the six undated stocks.

12

The settlement of gilt-edged transactions

Prior to the 1983 decision to subsequently abolish minimum commissions, the gilt settlement system then in use had been in operation since 1979, when it was introduced, as an interim measure, to relieve some of the pressures at periods of peak trading. Those pressures had on occasions threatened an earlier system with partial collapse owing to the sheer volume of paperwork and to the lack of a sufficiently rigid timetable framework. In the breathing space which this system had given the settlement side of the market, a modern 'paperless' type of system was devised and was originally expected to have become operative in the middle of 1985. However, the agreement to abolish minimum commissions and the resulting proposals for the introduction of dual capacity and, therefore, direct trading between new-style market-makers and investors, necessitated significant adjustments to that system and led to the decision to phase the introduction of the full service.

The service arrangements are operated by the Central Gilts Office (CGO) which has been established within the Bank of England and which is responsible jointly to the Bank and The Stock Exchange.

Phase 1 was introduced in January 1986 and phase 2 on 27 October 1986. This chapter explains the settlement procedures in operation on that date and will cover not only the 'paperless' system available to certain parties (known as CGO participants), but also the preceding system still used by institutional and private investors (non-CGO investors).

CGO participants are market-makers, inter-dealer brokers, Stock Exchange money-brokers, discount houses, certain banks and the International Commodities Clearing House.

Settlement

For the moment we will consider only those transactions involving an institutional or private investor. When a bargain is executed the broker/dealer, market-maker or investment house (hereafter referred to as client counterparty) sends a contract note, plus a stock transfer form in the case of a sale, to the investor, his nominee or the registered holder (or any combination of these). In return, the investor makes payment on the next business day for any stock he has bought, or, if he has sold, sends back the completed stock transfer form, together with the stock certificate, and duly receives payment for the stock.

In principle, therefore, gilt-edged settlement is very simple. However, in practice all sorts of contingencies occur, most – if not all – of which are covered in this chapter.

Gilt-edged securities are normally dealt for settlement on the next Stock Exchange business day ('cash settlement'). Attempts in the past to change this have been strongly resisted by the institutions, whose type of business requires an immediate switch from stock to cash. It is sometimes possible to deal up to 11.00 a.m. for settlement the same day. However, the necessary documents must be available within the time limits – some of which expire *before* 11.00 a.m.

Deferred settlement is also allowed, if arranged at the time of dealing, but only for specific reasons and within defined limits. When buying or selling for forward settlement the agreed interest is calculated up to and including the specified settlement date.

Classes of Stock

Gilt-edged securities are mainly the UK-registered type. A selection of stocks is available in bearer form with coupons attached, whilst some new stocks exist for a month or so in allotment letter form – which is effectively bearer, but without coupons, as although interest is earned, none is paid until after the stock has been changed to registered form. 'Gilt-edged' is a term strictly used to cover only government securities, but is commonly used to include other first-class securities that are dealt for cash settlement. However, since by far the largest part of the market is in government securities, the rest of this chapter refers solely to them, unless otherwise stated.

Bearer Stock

Just over one-third of the government stocks in issue are currently available in bearer form. The maximum denomination varies, according to the stock, between £1,000 and £50,000, whilst the minimum denomination (and therefore the dealing multiple) is either £50 or £100. Stock is convertible free of charge from bearer to registered or vice versa, at any time, but settlement may be delayed if sales of either type are made immediately after conversion. Lack of a free market in bearer (due to the limited amount of stock available) inhibits demand, but the inconvenience of claiming interest on the coupon, plus the inherent problem of safe custody of a bearer bond, are other limiting factors.

Registered Stock

Owing to the restricted demand for bearer, government stocks are therefore dealt in mainly in the registered form. The stock is registered at the Bank of England into the name of the purchaser (or his nominee), who subsequently receives a certificate stating that he is in fact the registered holder. Registration can be carried out by the client, his agent or the client's counterparty. Special registration facilities exist, and should be used (except in the case of very small bargains) where stock is likely to be sold within fourteen days of lodgement. These special facilities separate such stock and allow it to be quickly accessed for matching against a sale, thereby ensuring that (if used by a professional) there is no delay in settlement.

When registered government stock is sold, the registered holder has to sign a stock transfer form, if a single holder, or seal and sign in accordance with the articles, if a corporate body. That transfer form, together with the registered certificate, is forwarded to the client counterparty by a specified time on settlement day.

If for any reason the stock certificate is not available, formalities and deadlines vary according to the circumstances, whilst in some cases settlement may be delayed. Sales by CGO participants are not subject to these settlement delays.

Allotment Letter Stock

When the Government offers stock for sale by application or tender, these stocks are not issued in registered form. Successful applicants for such stocks receive an 'allotment letter', which is itself a document of title, but in bearer form for a limited period, during which further call money may be due. Whilst still in allotment letter form, delivery is simplified in that no signatures or seal are required, but settlement for stock sold may be delayed in the case of part sales, sales when stock bought has not been delivered, or when call money or registration is due or in course. At the end of the allotment letter period, the stock should be registered into the name of the new owner or his nominee. Special registration facilities exist (similar, but not identical, to those applying to registered stocks) and it is important that they are used if an early sale is probable. Once again CGO participants have special facilities which enable them to avoid most of these delays.

Settlement Procedures

Since CGO participants have special facilities, it follows that when an investor buys, unless the market is short of stock, then the stock will be delivered on settlement day and must be paid for value that day; for example, if by cheque, this should be drawn on the City branch of a clearing bank. Sale proceeds will similarly be paid for value the date of delivery of the stock sold.

Because most investors do not have special facilities, it is important that when they buy stock they are aware of the problems attaching to an early sale, and that when they sell they should already have taken such steps as are possible to avoid (expensive) settlement delays. In this respect, it should be noted that the possible delays mentioned here relate to current procedures on government stocks only, and that other erroneously called 'gilt-edged' stocks may be subject to different formalities.

A summary of the salient points and problems of settlement is incorporated in the following sections.

Market-makers Settlement

A market-maker is committed to make markets to users of the market generally and it is one of the fundamental concepts of his trading that he may sell stock which he does not possess (and which he may not acquire for a considerable time). Conversely, he may purchase stock (sometimes in large quantities) for which he has no immediate buyer. The consequences which stem from this situation in fact underpin the basic relationship between investor and the market as follows.

In order to take maximum advantage from, or to correct stock or cash imbalances in, the dealing situations referred to, a market-maker has the choice (subject to availability) of borrowing or depositing money, and borrowing, lending or pledging stock. He may also deal with other Stock Exchange member firms including, therefore, money brokers, and, under some circumstances, with the Bank of England. Indirectly involved are discount houses, banks and institutional investors.

When a market-maker deals with a non-CGO member then a stock transfer form and certificate (or suitable alternative) pass between them. When the market-maker himself has issued the transfer then it is not permitted for that transfer to be passed back to another CGO member; that is, it must be registered into the name of some non-CGO member.

Transfer of stock between CGO members uses the computerised 'paperless' system known as 'book entry transfer' and the facilities provided cover most of the stocks for which the Bank of England acts as registrar. In due course it is hoped to extend the system to include other securities traded in the gilt market. The system permits presentation of a transfer to the CGO where relevant details are captured within the system and against which stock up to that amount (and any other already held) can be transferred. Interest payments are made by the Bank of England in the usual way. All necessary information for participants in the system is available on VDU screens, with immediate printout facilities, and there are identical back-up systems for both the computer and power sources, and security safeguards to protect confidentiality at a variety of levels.

Once stock is held within the system it can be transferred

(a) to any non-CGO member by means of an enfaced stock transfer form ('enfacement' is a statement on the transfer that the underlying stock is held by the CGO for the new owner), or
(b) to another CGO member by book entry transfer, i.e. by an entry being made on a computer terminal – without the need for stock transfer forms or certificates.

At the end of each business day information is passed to the registrar concerning the movement of stock within the CGO system, and the register remains the prime record of legal title.

It is also possible for stock in allotment letter form to be taken within the CGO system and for ownership to be changed by computerised entry, or to be withdrawn, although the registrar will not be advised of such movements of unregistered stock.

An integral part of this computerised system is an assured payments routine such that irrevocable instructions for guaranteed payments are generated simultaneously with movement of stocks between CGO accounts. The buyer and seller of stock are thus equally protected. Banks operating the town clearing and Clearing Houses Automated Payment System (CHAPS) systems participate on appointment by a CGO member. A paying bank's position is that, in exchange, there is either stock held by the CGO for that bank's client or, if sold on, a corresponding irrevocable cash commitment from another settlement bank. The banks are advised by the CGO daily of only the up-to-date net cash position of each client, rather than individual transactions.

This entire concept of computerised transfer is based on the principle of positive acceptance by the taker of both the stock amount and the cash consideration which have been input by the giver. In the case of non-acceptance, neither stock nor cash will move within the system.

Stock movements into and out of the system, and having a cash value of over £100,000, are equally protected by assured payment and there are provisions to protect the banks in the event of the liquidation of a CGO member. Because of the volumes of business and the number of his counterparties, a market-maker will need to know as soon as possible, with as much accuracy as possible, his total stock movements for the day, and he will then need as long a time as possible to deal with the stock/cash adjustments and arrangements. It is for these reasons, and to achieve an orderly settlement, that delivery formalities and deadlines are imposed. From the marker-maker's point of view, one of the most important deadlines is that parties to transactions have until 11.15 a.m. to tell each other what stock they will be delivering that day. It is from this 'call over' that the market-maker projects his stock, and cash requirements and commitments.

Settlement with Investors

The earliest job on settlement day is to contact investors who have sold – firstly in order to arrange collection/receipt of executed transfers and certificates, or other documents, in time to meet the deadlines explained below, and, secondly, in order to advise the market-making departments by 11.15 a.m. of all deliveries that will be made that day. The final time for actual delivery to the market-maker of registered, allotment letter or bearer stock is 12.45 p.m.

The client counterparty will require to receive the transfer before that time in order to process even a straightforward delivery (say 12.15 p.m.), earlier for a Stock Exchange certification (11.45 a.m.), as early as 10.45 a.m. for some Bank of England certifications (registered stock), whilst the earliest could be 10.15 a.m. for recently registered allotment letter stock, although these times could vary slightly either way, depending on how busy the market is.

Sales

An executed transfer in respect of registered stock sold by an investor should, where possible, be accompanied by a stock certificate for the exact amount. However, this is not always possible, because of the following factors:

1. The certificate may be for more than the amount of stock sold, in which case the stock transfer form can be presented with the larger certificate by the client

counterparty to The Stock Exchange, which then forwards details and the certificate to the registrar and certifies on the transfer that it has done so. This certified transfer is then good for delivery. The balance of stock due may be held to the order of any member, for a period of up to two months, during which further sale transfers may be certified at The Stock Exchange (i.e. subject only to the deadline of 12.45 p.m. for subsequent delivery to the jobber). If a 'balance certificate' is requested, this would be issued by the Bank of England in about eight days.

2. The certificate may be in course of preparation:
   (a) where a certificate has been requested, i.e. as in (1) above;
   (b) from a recent registration or after a sale certification against part only of a recent registration;
   (c) from recent registration of an allotment letter; or
   (d) a recently purchased stock transfer form may not yet have been sent for registration.

Provided that special procedures, where applicable, have been followed, the Bank of England will certify executed sold transfers for same-day delivery if lodged

by 11.15 a.m. on or after the first Stock Exchange business day after a registration or certification as in (b) above;

by 10.45 a.m. on or after the first Stock Exchange business day after a registration as in (c) above; or

by 11.15 a.m. on any day in respect of (d) above.

'Certification' is a statement on the transfer that the stock covering the sale has been lodged with the registrar/agent.

Under (a) however, although lodgement has to be made by 11.15 a.m. on or after the first day following the request, there may still be a delay in certification, and therefore in delivery also.

The above deadlines are critical and, since the client counterparty has to process the transfers before taking them to the Bank of England (or The Stock Exchange), it follows that he himself will require the documents up to half an hour before the times given above, perhaps earlier if the market is very busy, and on this basis the deadlines could vary between 10.15 a.m. and 12.15 p.m.

3. Stock sold through one party may have been purchased through another. The basic settlement formalities do not vary, but if the bargains were dealt on different days, there might be a slight further settlement delay when the formalities cannot be completed in time to meet the deadlines.

4. The certificate may be lost, in which case settlement is delayed until a form of indemnity has been completed and lodged with the Bank of England. The entire procedure, including certification of the executed stock transfer form, normally delays settlement between two and five days.

5. Although the foregoing refers to registered stock, it should be mentioned here that there will be a delay in settlement of allotment letter and bearer stock in the case of partial sales or sales to different parties where the denominations

held cannot be matched to the exact amount sold. Allotment letters will then need to be split by the registrar. To instigate this, the allotment letter should be forwarded to the registrar with a note detailing the required splits, which are then normally available within twenty-four hours.

6. Stock purchased may not yet have been delivered by the seller (i.e. the purchase and sale may have been dealt on the same day; the seller may have been short of stock purchased; or the purchase may have been for deferred settlement). When such purchases are due for settlement, like or part sales can normally be 'made up' (i.e. set off against those purchases, so that no stock passes). However, the following points should be noted:

   (a) 'Making up' is not possible when either bargain is a medium- or long-dated gilt which has been dealt specially ex-dividend (Sp. XD) in the three-week period before the stock is normally quoted ex-dividend. Such special ex-dividend bargains are not always permissible, and, separately from the settlement problems, investors dealing in this way are required to sign a declaration which is designed to prevent tax avoidance, as mentioned in Chapter 10.

   (b) Nor can any cum-dividend bargain be made up with any ordinarily ex-dividend bargain.

   (c) Neither is it possible to 'make up' allotment letter bargains if dealt through different market-makers (this also applies equally to bearer transactions). Furthermore, even if the bargains are transacted with the same jobber, there may be difficulty in 'making-up' when the amounts purchased and sold are not identical. These restrictions may not apply to allotment letters when the stock is held within the CGO system.

   (d) When a bargain cannot be 'made up' under (c) above, the investor may be out of money for one day if the first seller does not deliver the stock in time for the second seller to send it out against his sale within the normal time limits.

   (e) When a bargain cannot be 'made up' under (a) and (b) above, then, after paying for the purchase, settlement of stocks sold specially ex-dividend is delayed

      (i) until the next Stock Exchange business day in all cases;

      (ii) until the day after the stock is quoted officially ex-dividend, in cases where the special XD sale cannot be matched exactly with the transfer(s) delivered against the purchase, unless the sale is in excess by an amount which was purchased ordinarily.

   In cases where correct 'shapes' might not be available to cover sales of allotment letters or special ex-dividend bargains, the resulting settlement delay could be avoided by asking for splits at the time of dealing for the purchase.

   The facility to 'make up' afforded by the market-maker is not mandatory; (c) above cites examples where he does not, or may not, provide the facility, whilst (a) and (b) quote instances where 'make-ups' are forbidden under Stock

Exchange rules. If a market-maker should withdraw this facility for any other reason, then the minimum settlement delay would be as in (d) or (e) (i).

Deferred Settlement

Government and other gilt-edged stocks normally dealt in for cash settlement may be dealt in for deferred settlement, if necessary, so as to allow reasonable time for the transit and execution of the required documents, or for the conversion of another currency into sterling. Alternatively, if reported, and if the circumstances were specified at the time of dealing, deferred settlement is permitted if the cost of the purchase is to be financed from the proceeds of any of the following:

1. Any security normally and in fact dealt in for settlement on the current Stock Exchange Account day.
2. The redemption of any gilt and some quasi-gilts, provided the register has finally closed.
3. The repayment of short-term loans to a local government authority, or public boards of Great Britain and Northern Ireland.
4. The repayment of loans or deposits to corporate bodies, including loans or deposits which require notice for repayment.
5. A security sold in an overseas stock exchange not dealt for cash.

Under items (2) to (5), the maximum delay is fourteen days from the date of the bargain, and, additionally under (5), the delay must not exceed the normal settlement period of the overseas stock exchange.

Contingent Bargains

Settlement of a purchase may also be effectively deferred for a maximum period of three weeks, provided that the purchase is financed by a *like amount* of money, being the sale proceeds of another government or 'gilt-edged' stock which was dealt at the same time, for the same investor, with the same market-maker, by the same party, and provided that the 'contingent' (CN) condition was applied at the time of dealing. In these circumstances, for the first three weeks from settlement day, neither party may deliver stock until the other is in a position to do likewise. If the condition 'CN NB' is applied at the time of dealing, then that three-week period is extended indefinitely.

Payment for Stock

When the client counterparty is able to deliver sold government or other 'gilt-edged' stock to the market-maker, or when the bargain is 'made up', the cash proceeds of the sale can be paid to the investor or his agent, either against delivery of the documents or by independent payment. The payment is made either by cheque drawn on the City branch of a clearing bank or, alternatively, by direct credit to a nominated bank account, either by telegraphic transfer or by using CHAPS. If payment is made by direct credit, the recipient has no control over the paying-in, but, equally, saves the administration cost. When an investor is due both to pay and to receive money on the same day in respect of deals with the same broker, he may choose either to pay and receive in full both ways, or to settle simply the final balance.

Payment for such stock purchased may also be made as above to the broker's account. Payment can be made by any party, and may similarly be against delivery of documents or by separate payment.

In some instances one party to a transaction may insist that settlement takes place by exchanging a banker's draft for the relevant stock. Such a draft guarantees to the recipient that payment will be honoured, whereas the ordinary methods of payment fail if there are insufficient funds in the account in question.

Registration of Stock

When government stock purchased is registered into the name of the buyer or his nominee, special procedures are available. The Bank of England has issued a comprehensive notice (dated August 1979) which sets out the various methods and times of registering transfers and allotment letters, and also quotes the methods and times by which (*pending the issue of stock certificates*) sale transfers will be validated – i.e. 'certified' for delivery. If investors wish to handle their own registration, then a detailed knowledge of this document is essential. However, large investors would be well advised to delegate these matters to a professional on the spot.

The following special procedure is intended for use when a sale is anticipated before the stock certificate would otherwise be in the hands of the seller:

1. A special two-part receipt form is available for registration of registered stock. If lodged with a valid transfer form at the Bank of England before 11.15 a.m., then a receipt is given and a sale transfer against all or part of that stock (if similarly lodged before 11.15 a.m., from the next day onwards) will be certified for delivery on that day. When registering stock in this way, care should be taken not to lodge too early in case a sale for same-day settlement should be made (possible up to 11.00 a.m.), in which case –
2. The original purchase deed, without the two-part form, should be presented to the Bank before 11.15 a.m. with the executed sale transfer, for certification and delivery on that day.
3. When allotment letters are presented for registration (the time is normally 3.00 p.m. at the Bank of England) a different 'special' form should be used, but, again, a receipt is issued. In this case, certification and delivery are *not* possible on the next Stock Exchange business day, but would be available one day later.

Sale transfers lodged for certification in other circumstances, or with other supporting documents (e.g. probate or power of attorney), will be subject to varying delays, depending on the method and time of lodgement, for both registration and certification. The Bank of England's notice sets out the problems in concise detail. It is sufficient here to illustrate the complexity by pointing out that, for example, a transfer lodged for registration at the Bank, and received in the second postal delivery at about noon, is in fact deemed to have been received one day later than a transfer received after 3.30 p.m. on the same day in the second delivery bag direct from The Stock Exchange.

Certificates arising from special registrations of registered stock are normally available after eight working days, but quite often take considerably longer when allotment letters are registered. There is frequently a further delay because certificates are despatched by post (except to Stock Exchange members and to others who have made special arrangements).

The Future

Phase 3 of the CGO service (expected early 1987) will involve the provision of agency facilities, and the extension to broker/dealers and institutional clients of membership – which to them would be optional if phase 3 is framed in line with the *original* CGO service.

When the total CGO system is in service the consequent drastic reduction in paperwork, the resulting speed of operation, and the inbuilt protection against defaulters will enable members to concentrate on their function of effectively settling gilt transactions, thus ensuring the liquidity of the market which is provided by the gilt-edged market-makers.

However, it should be remembered that not all institutions will subscribe to membership of the CGO and also that there will be many smaller investors who cannot do so. Settlement of the relevant proportion of transactions will therefore still have to be part-settled outside CGO, i.e. until captured by a member within the CGO.

Thus it will be necessary to operate a second system in order to accommodate that proportion of stock still held in certificate form. It is likely that the old procedure may then be altered in order to dovetail better with the new system; it is possible that the original facilities provided by the Bank of England may be curtailed or withdrawn because of changing priorities, but nevertheless a second system there will be, to cover the contingencies detailed in this chapter.

Operating a settlement department using two different systems is inherently inefficient. Progress cannot be made towards a completely paperless system until (1) all investors can be persuaded to forego possession of a stock certificate, (2) the necessary alterations to the system are in place, and (3) inter-related problems are considered.

Item (1) may seem a matter of education. If it is, then the growing interest in and use of (home) computers should provide self-education. In any event it is always open to the Bank of England to force the issue in due course. Item (2) cannot take place until the full CGO system has been thoroughly tested and the new market structure has settled down, and (3) implies that whatever steps are taken in this direction should be compatible with developments in other areas of the market.

In the final analysis, however, there *will* be a fully certificateless, computerised settlement system.

Appendix

Sample prospectuses for the various types of gilt-edged stock

This appendix comprises specimen prospectuses for a conventional stock (Exchequer 10% 1989) over pages 157–159, a variable-rate stock (Treasury Variable-rate 1981) over pages 160–162, a convertible stock (Treasury Convertible $9\frac{3}{4}$% 1988) over pages 163–165, and an index-linked stock (Treasury Index-linked 2% 1996) over pages 166–169.

TENDERS MUST BE LODGED AT THE BANK OF ENGLAND, NEW ISSUES (A), WATLING STREET, LONDON EC4M 9AA, NOT LATER THAN 10.00 A.M. ON WEDNESDAY, 16TH NOVEMBER 1983, OR AT ANY OF THE BRANCHES OF THE BANK OF ENGLAND, OR AT THE GLASGOW AGENCY OF THE BANK OF ENGLAND, NOT LATER THAN 3.30 P.M. ON TUESDAY, 15TH NOVEMBER 1983.

ISSUE OF £1,150,000,000

10 per cent EXCHEQUER STOCK, 1989

MINIMUM TENDER PRICE £97.00 PER CENT

PAYABLE AS FOLLOWS:

Deposit with tender	£20.00 per cent
On Wednesday, 14th December 1983	£40.00 per cent
On Monday, 16th January 1984	Balance of purchase money

INTEREST PAYABLE HALF-YEARLY ON 1ST FEBRUARY AND 1ST AUGUST

This Stock is an investment falling within Part II of the First Schedule to the Trustee Investments Act 1961. Application has been made to the Council of The Stock Exchange for the Stock to be admitted to the Official List.

THE GOVERNOR AND COMPANY OF THE BANK OF ENGLAND are authorised to receive tenders for £1,000,000,000 of the above Stock; the balance of £150,000,000 has been reserved for the National Debt Commissioners for public funds under their management.

The principal of and interest on the Stock will be a charge on the National Loans Fund, with recourse to the Consolidated Fund of the United Kingdom.

The Stock will be repaid at par on 1st August 1989.

The Stock will be registered at the Bank of England or at the Bank of Ireland, Belfast, and will be transferable, in multiples of one penny, by instrument in writing in accordance with the Stock Transfer Act 1963. Transfers will be free of stamp duty.

Interest will be payable half-yearly on 1st February and 1st August. Income tax will be deducted from payments of more than £5 per annum. Interest warrants will be transmitted by post. The first interest payment will be made on 1st August 1984 at the rate of £6.1421 per £100 of the Stock.

Tenders must be lodged at the Bank of England, New Issues (A), Watling Street, London EC4M 9AA, not later than 10.00 A.M. on WEDNESDAY, 16TH NOVEMBER 1983, or at any of the Branches of the Bank of England or at the Glasgow Agency of the Bank of England, not later than 3.30 P.M. on TUESDAY, 15TH NOVEMBER 1983. Tenders will not be revocable between 10.00 a.m. on Wednesday, 16th November 1983, and 10.00 a.m. on Monday, 21st November 1983.

Each tender must be for one amount at one price. The minimum price, below which tenders will not be accepted, is £97.00 per cent. Tenders must be made at the minimum price or at higher prices which are multiples of 25p. Tenders lodged without a price being stated will be deemed to have been made at the minimum price.

A separate cheque representing a deposit at the rate of £20.00 for every £100 of the *nominal* amount of Stock tendered for must accompany each tender; cheques must be drawn on a bank in, and be payable in, the United Kingdom, the Channel Islands or the Isle of Man.

Tenders must be for a minimum of £100 Stock and for multiples of Stock as follows:

Amount of Stock tendered for	Multiple
£100–£1,000	£100
£1,000–£3,000	£500
£3,000–£10,000	£1,000
£10,000–£50,000	£5,000
£50,000 or greater	£25,000

Her Majesty's Treasury reserve the right to reject any tender or part of any tender and may therefore allot to tenderers less than the full amount of the Stock. Tenders will be ranked in descending order of price and allotments will be made to tenderers whose tenders are at or above the lowest price at which Her Majesty's Treasury decide that any tender should be accepted (the allotment price), which will be not less than the minimum tender price. All allotments will be made at the allotment price: tenders which are accepted and which are made at prices above the allotment price will be allotted in full; tenders made at the allotment price may be allotted in full or in part only. Any balance of Stock not allotted to tenderers will be allotted at the allotment price to the Governor and Company of the Bank of England, Issue Department.

Letters of allotment in respect of Stock allotted, being the only form in which the Stock may be transferred prior to registration, will be despatched by post at the risk of the tenderer, but the despatch of any letter of allotment, and any refund of the balance of the amount paid as deposit, may at the discretion of the Bank of England be withheld until the tenderer's cheque has been paid. In the event of such withholding, the tenderer will be notified by letter by the Bank of England of the acceptance of his tender and of the amount of Stock allocated to him, subject in each case to payment of his cheque, but such notification will confer no right on the tenderer to transfer the Stock so allocated.

No allotment will be made for a less amount than £100 Stock. In the event of partial allotment, the balance of the amount paid as deposit will, when refunded, be remitted by cheque despatched by post at the risk of the tenderer; if no allotment is made the amount paid as deposit will be returned likewise. Payment in full may be made at any time after allotment, but no discount will be allowed on such payment. Interest may be charged on a day-to-day basis on any overdue amount which may be accepted at a rate equal to the London Inter-Bank Offered Rate for seven-day deposits in sterling ('LIBOR') plus 1 per cent per annum. Such rate will be determined by the Bank of England by reference to market quotations, on the due date for the relevant payment, for LIBOR obtained from such source or sources as the Bank of England shall consider appropriate. Default in due payment of any amount in respect of the Stock will render the allotment of such Stock liable to cancellation and any amount previously paid liable to forfeiture.

Letters of allotment may be split into denominations of multiples of £100 on written request received by the Bank of England, New Issues, Watling Street, London EC4M 9AA, or by any of the Branches of the Bank of England, on any date not later than 12th January 1984. Such requests must be signed and must be accompanied by the letters of allotment (but a letter cannot be split if any payment is overdue).

Letters of allotment must be surrendered for registration, accompanied by a completed registration form, when the balance of the purchase money is paid, unless payment in full has been made before the due date, in which case they must be surrendered for registration not later than 16th January 1984.

Tender forms and copies of this prospectus may be obtained at the Bank of England, New Issues, Watling Street, London EC4M 9AA, or at any of the Branches of the Bank of England, or at the Glasgow Agency of the Bank of England, 25 St Vincent Place, Glasgow G1 2EB; at the Bank of Ireland, Moyne Buildings, 1st Floor, 20 Callender Street, Belfast BT1 5BN; at Mullens & Co., 15 Moorgate, London EC2R 6AN; or at any office of The Stock Exchange in the United Kingdom.

BANK OF ENGLAND
LONDON

11th November 1983

THIS NOTICE DOES NOT CONSTITUTE AN OFFER FOR SALE

PARTICULARS OF AN ISSUE OF £400,000,000

VARIABLE RATE TREASURY STOCK, 1981

INTEREST PAYABLE HALF-YEARLY ON 17TH MAY AND 17TH NOVEMBER

1. *An Order in Council has been made and laid before Parliament to amend the Trustee Investments Act 1961. The intention is that this Order shall take effect on 9th June 1977 from which date this Stock would be an investment falling within Part II of the First Schedule to that Act. Application has been made to the Council of The Stock Exchange for the Stock to be admitted to the Official List.*

2. The whole of the Stock will be issued to the Bank of England on 27th May 1977.

3. The principal of and interest on the Stock will be a charge on the National Loans Fund, with recourse to the Consolidated Fund of the United Kingdom.

4. Subject to the provisions of paragraphs 11 to 13 of this notice, the Stock will be repaid at par on 17th November 1981.

5. The Stock will be registered at the Bank of England or at the Bank of Ireland, Belfast, and will be transferable, in multiples of one new penny, by instrument in writing in accordance with the Stock Transfer Act 1963. Transfers will be free of stamp duty.

INTEREST

6. Interest will be payable half-yearly on 17th May and 17th November. Income tax will be deducted from payments of more than £5 per annum. Interest warrants will be transmitted by post.

7. The rate of interest will be variable. Each half-yearly payment will be at a rate per £100 of Stock equal to half of the sum of an indicator rate and a fixed margin of $\frac{1}{2}$. The indicator rate will be the daily average over a reference period of Treasury Bill Rate, the calculation and period of effectiveness of which is described in the Annex.

8. The reference period for the calculation of the indicator rate for each interest payment except the first will be from the ex-dividend date for the preceding interest payment up to the relative ex-dividend date. The ex-dividend date is the last day on which transfers can be lodged at the Bank of England for registration entitling the new holders to receive the next interest payment.

9. The first interest payment will be made on 17th November 1977 at the rate per £100 of Stock of 174/365ths of the sum of the indicator rate and the margin. The reference period for this payment will be the 137 days from 27th May 1977 up to 11th October 1977, the first ex-dividend date.

10. The rate for each interest payment, expressed as a percentage in pounds sterling to two places of decimals rounded, will be announced by the Bank of England on the business day immediately preceding the relative ex-dividend date.

CONVERSION TO FIXED RATE AND OPTIONAL REDEMPTION

11.   If there should be a change in the arrangements for or relating to the issue of Treasury bills which in the opinion of the Bank of England would or could be detrimental to the interests of stockholders, the rate of interest will cease to be variable and will become fixed. Her Majesty's Treasury shall publish, not later than five business days after the change, a notice in the London Gazette specifying the date on which the change is deemed to have taken place. The fixed rate will take effect from the date of the change and will be the sum of the margin and an indicator rate, for the calculation of which the reference period will be from the ex-dividend date for the preceding interest payment up to the date of the change.

12.   In the event of such a change, stockholders will have the right to require Her Majesty's Treasury to redeem their Stock at par and a notice setting out the administrative arrangements will be sent to stockholders by the Bank of England at the appropriate time. Where stockholders exercise this right repayment will be effected within three months from the date of publication of the notice in the London Gazette, and any interest which has accrued will be payable at the same time.

13.   If stockholders together holding 80 per cent or more in nominal value of the Stock out-standing require Her Majesty's Treasury to redeem their Stock, Her Majesty's Treasury will have the right to redeem the remaining Stock at par within six months of the date on which the fixed rate took effect subject to their giving notice of their intention in the London Gazette.

GENERAL

14.   Copies of this notice may be obtained at the Bank of England, New Issues, Watling Street, London EC4M 9AA, or at any of the branches of the Bank of England; at the Bank of Ireland, PO Box 13, Donegall Place, Belfast BT1 5BX; from Messrs Mullens & Co., 15 Moorgate, London EC2R 6AN; or at any office of The Stock Exchange in the United Kingdom.

BANK OF ENGLAND
LONDON

27th May 1977

ANNEX

CALCULATION OF TREASURY BILL RATE

Treasury bills are negotiable obligations of Her Majesty's Treasury, are charged on the National Loans Fund and are issued under the Treasury Bills Act 1877 and the National Loans Act 1968. They are offered for sale by tender by the Bank of England in accordance with the Treasury Bill Regulations 1968.

Under present practice, tenders are received at the Bank of England for 91-day Treasury bills on the last business day of each week, for bills to be issued in the following week. Tenders must be made by or through a London Banker, Discount House or Broker. Tenders are expressed as a price per £100 nominal value of bills and are accepted in descending order of price (i.e. ascend-ing order of discount) until the total of tenders which are to be accepted in whole or in part is equal to or exceeds the amount of bills to be allotted. If the total of tenders at the lowest accepted price exceeds the remaining amount of bills to be allotted, allotments at that price are made *pro rata* to such tenders.

Ninety-one-day Treasury bills are due and payable in full at the Bank of England 91 days after issue, except that, if the due date is not a business day (e.g. a Bank Holiday), they are payable on the first business day thereafter.

Treasury Bill Rate is the average rate of discount on 91-day Treasury bills allotted pursuant to tenders, weighted by the nominal value of bills allotted at each price and expressed as an annual percentage rate of discount calculated to four places of decimals rounded. If allotments are made of bills payable more than 91 days after issue (i.e. because the 91st day after issue will not be a business day), the discount on such bills is converted, for the purpose of calculating Treasury Bill Rate, to a discount for 91 days by dividing it by the number of days to the date on which the bills are payable and multiplying by 91.

Treasury Bill Rate is announced by the Bank of England on the afternoon on which allotments of Treasury bills pursuant to tenders are made. The Rate so announced takes effect on the next business day.

TENDERS MUST BE LODGED AT THE BANK OF ENGLAND, NEW ISSUES (Y), WATLING STREET, LONDON EC4M 9AA, NOT LATER THAN 10.00 A.M. ON THURSDAY, 29TH SEPTEMBER 1983, OR AT ANY OF THE BRANCHES OF THE BANK OF ENGLAND, OR AT THE GLASGOW AGENCY OF THE BANK OF ENGLAND, NOT LATER THAN 3.30 P.M. ON WEDNESDAY, 28TH SEPTEMBER 1983.

ISSUE BY TENDER OF £1,000,000,000

$9\frac{3}{4}$ per cent TREASURY CONVERTIBLE STOCK, 1988

MINIMUM TENDER PRICE £96.50 PER CENT

PAYABLE AS FOLLOWS:

Deposit with tender	£30.00 per cent
On Monday, 31st October 1983	£30.00 per cent
On Monday, 5th December 1983	Balance of purchase money

INTEREST PAYABLE HALF-YEARLY ON 14TH JUNE AND 14TH DECEMBER

This Stock is an investment falling within Part II of the First Schedule to the Trustee Investments Act 1961. Application has been made to the Council of The Stock Exchange for the Stock to be admitted to the Official List.

1.   THE GOVERNOR AND COMPANY OF THE BANK OF ENGLAND are authorised to receive tenders for the above Stock.

2.   The principal of and interest on the Stock will be a charge on the National Loans Fund, with recourse to the Consolidated Fund of the United Kingdom.

3.   The Stock will be registered at the Bank of England or at the Bank of Ireland, Belfast, and will be transferable, in multiples of one penny, by instrument in writing in accordance with the Stock Transfer Act 1963. Transfers will be free of stamp duty.

4.   Interest will be payable half-yearly on 14th June and 14th December. Income tax will be deducted from payments of more than £5 per annum. Interest warrants will be transmitted by post. The first interest payment will be made on 14th June 1984 at the rate of £5.9759 per £100 of the Stock.

5.   Holdings of $9\frac{3}{4}$ per cent Treasury Convertible Stock, 1988 may, at the option of holders, be converted in whole or in part into $9\frac{1}{2}$ per cent Conversion Stock, 2002 (hereinafter referred to as ('Conversion Stock'), as on the following dates and at the indicated rates:

Date of conversion	Nominal amount of Conversion Stock per £100 nominal of $9\frac{3}{4}$ per cent Treasury Convertible Stock, 1988
14th June 1984	£100
14th December 1984	£98
14th June 1985	£96
14th December 1985	£94
14th June 1986	£92

6.   Notices setting out the administrative arrangements for the exercise of the options to convert and forms of acceptance for completion will be issued to holders at the appropriate times. Where a holding is held jointly by more than two holders, options to convert may be exercised by a majority of them. Completed forms of acceptance in respect of each of the options to convert, accompanied by certificates of title for holdings of 9¾ per cent Treasury Convertible Stock, 1988, must be lodged at the Bank of England, New Change, London EC4M 9AA, or at the Bank of Ireland, Moyne Buildings, 1st Floor, 20 Callender Street, Belfast BT1 5BN, not later than 3.00 p.m. on the sixth working day before each date of conversion.

7.   Her Majesty's Treasury have directed that Section 326 of the Income and Corporation Taxes Act 1970 (which relates to the treatment for taxation purposes of financial concerns whose business consists wholly or partly in dealing in securities) shall apply to exchanges of securities made in pursuance of the conversion offer.

8.   Conversion Stock will be an investment falling within Part II of the First Schedule to the Trustee Investments Act 1961, and application will be made to the Council of The Stock Exchange for Conversion Stock to be admitted to the Official List. Paragraphs 2 and 3 of this prospectus will apply equally to Conversion Stock as to 9¾ per cent Treasury Convertible Stock, 1988. Interest on Conversion Stock will be payable half-yearly on 14th June and 14th December. Income tax will be deducted from payments of more than £5 per annum. Interest warrants will be transmitted by post. Conversion Stock will be repaid at par on 14th June 2002.

9.   Holdings of 9¾ per cent Treasury Convertible Stock, 1988, in respect of which options to convert have not been exercised will be repaid at par on 14th June 1988.

10.   **Tenders must be lodged at the Bank of England, New Issues (Y), Watling Street, London EC4M 9AA, not later than 10.00 A.M. on THURSDAY, 29TH SEPTEMBER 1983, or at any of the Branches of the Bank of England or at the Glasgow Agency of the Bank of England, not later than 3.30 P.M. on WEDNESDAY, 28TH SEPTEMBER 1983. Tenders will not be revocable between 10.00 a.m. on Thursday, 29th September 1983, and 10.00 a.m. on Tuesday, 4th October 1983.**

11.   **Each tender must be for one amount and at one price. The minimum price, below which tenders will not be accepted, is £96.50 per cent. Tenders must be made at the minimum price or at higher prices which are multiples of 25p. Tenders lodged without a price being stated will be deemed to have been made at the minimum price.**

12.   **A separate cheque representing a deposit at the rate of £30.00 for every £100 of the *nominal* amount of Stock tendered for must accompany each tender; cheques must be drawn on a bank in, and be payable in, the United Kingdom, the Channel Islands or the Isle of Man.**

13.   **Tenders must be for a minimum of £100 Stock and for multiples of Stock as follows:**

Amount of Stock tendered for	Multiple
£100–£1,000	£100
£1,000–£3,000	£500
£3,000–£10,000	£1,000
£10,000–£50,000	£5,000
£50,000 or greater	£25,000

14.   Her Majesty's Treasury reserve the right to reject any tender or part of any tender and may therefore allot to tenderers less than the full amount of the Stock. Tenders will be ranked in descending order of price and allotments will be made to tenderers whose tenders are at or above the lowest price at which Her Majesty's Treasury decide that any tender should be accepted (the allotment price), which will be not less than the minimum tender price. All allotments will be made at the allotment price: tenders which are accepted and which are made at prices above the allotment price will be allotted in full; tenders made at the allotment price may be allotted in full

or in part only. Any balance of Stock not allotted to tenderers will be allotted at the allotment price to the Governor and Company of the Bank of England, Issue Department.

15. Letters of allotment in respect of Stock allotted, being the only form in which the Stock may be transferred prior to registration, will be despatched by post at the risk of the tenderer, but the despatch of any letter of allotment, and any refund of the balance of the amount paid as deposit, may at the discretion of the Bank of England be withheld until the tenderer's cheque has been paid. In the event of such withholding, the tenderer will be notified by letter by the Bank of England of the acceptance of his tender and of the amount of Stock allocated to him, subject in each case to payment of his cheque, but such notification will confer no right on the tenderer to transfer the Stock so allocated.

16. No allotment will be made for a less amount than £100 Stock. In the event of partial allotment, the balance of the amount paid as deposit will, when refunded, be remitted by cheque despatched by post at the risk of the tenderer; if no allotment is made the amount paid as deposit will be returned likewise. Payment in full may be made at any time after allotment, but no discount will be allowed on such payment. Interest may be charged on a day-to-day basis on any overdue amount which may be accepted at a rate equal to the London Inter-Bank Offered Rate for seven-day deposits in sterling ('LIBOR') plus 1 per cent per annum. Such rate will be determined by the Bank of England by reference to market quotations, on the due date for the relevant payment, for LIBOR obtained from such source or sources as the Bank of England shall consider appropriate. Default in due payment of any amount in respect of the Stock will render the allotment of such Stock liable to cancellation and any amount previously paid liable to forfeiture.

17. Letters of allotment may be split into denominations of multiples of £100 on written request received by the Bank of England, New Issues, Watling Street, London EC4M 9AA, or by any of the Branches of the Bank of England, on any date not later than 1st December 1983. Such requests must be signed and must be accompanied by the letters of allotment (but a letter cannot be split if any payment is overdue).

18. Letters of allotment must be surrendered for registration, accompanied by a completed registration form, when the balance of the purchase money is paid, unless payment in full has been made before the due date, in which case they must be surrendered for registration not later than 5th December 1983.

19. Tender forms and copies of this prospectus may be obtained at the Bank of England, New Issues, Watling Street, London EC4M 9AA, or at any of the Branches of the Bank of England, or at the Glasgow Agency of the Bank of England, 25 St Vincent Place, Glasgow G1 2EB; at the Bank of Ireland, Moyne Buildings, 1st Floor, 20 Callender Street, Belfast BT1 5BN; at Mullens & Co., 15 Moorgate, London EC2R 6AN; or at any office of The Stock Exchange in the United Kingdom.

BANK OF ENGLAND
LONDON
26th September 1983

This is a reprinted version of the prospectus dated 10th March 1981, as amended by the supplement to the prospectus dated 9th March 1982.

TENDERS MUST BE LODGED AT THE BANK OF ENGLAND, NEW ISSUES (X), WATLING STREET, LONDON EC4M 9AA, NOT LATER THAN 10.00 A.M. ON FRIDAY, 27TH MARCH 1981, OR AT ANY OF THE BRANCHES OF THE BANK OF ENGLAND, OR AT THE GLASGOW AGENCY OF THE BANK OF ENGLAND, NOT LATER THAN 3.30 P.M. ON THURSDAY, 26TH MARCH 1981. ENVELOPES CONTAINING TENDERS SHOULD BE MARKED 'INDEX-LINKED TREASURY TENDER'.

ISSUE BY TENDER OF £1,000,000,000

2 per cent INDEX-LINKED TREASURY STOCK, 1996

PAYABLE AS FOLLOWS:

Deposit with tender	£35.00 per cent
On Friday, 1st May 1981	£30.00 per cent
On Tuesday, 26th May 1981	Balance of purchase money

INTEREST PAYABLE HALF-YEARLY ON 16TH MARCH AND 16TH SEPTEMBER

1.   This Stock is an investment falling within Part II of the First Schedule to the Trustee Investments Act 1961. Application has been made to the Council of The Stock Exchange for the Stock to be admitted to the Official List.

2.   THE GOVERNOR AND COMPANY OF THE BANK OF ENGLAND are authorised to receive tenders for the above Stock.

3.   The principal of and interest on the Stock will be a charge on the National Loans Fund, with recourse to the Consolidated Fund of the United Kingdom.

4.   The Stock will be registered at the Bank of England and will be transferable, in multiples of one new penny, by instrument in writing in accordance with the Stock Transfer Act 1963. Transfers will be free of stamp duty.

[In accordance with the right reserved to Her Majesty's Treasury by paragraph 13 of the prospectus, all restrictions contained in the prospectus relating to the eligibility to hold the Stock have been removed, as promulgated by means of a supplement to the prospectus dated 9th March 1982. Accordingly, the provisions of paragraphs 5 to 13 of the prospectus have ceased to have effect.]

14.   If not previously redeemed under the provisions of paragraph 23, the Stock will be repaid on 16th September 1996. The value of the principal on repayment will be related, subject to the terms of this prospectus, to the movement, during the life of the Stock, of the United Kingdom General Index of Retail Prices maintained by the Department of Employment, or any Index replacing that index, such movement being indicated by the Index figure issued monthly and subsequently published in the London, Edinburgh and Belfast Gazettes.

15.   For the purposes of this prospectus, the Index figure applicable to any month will be the Index figure issued seven months prior to the relevant month and relating to the month before that prior month; 'month' means calendar month; and the Index ratio applicable to any month will be equal to the Index figure applicable to that month divided by the Index figure applicable to March 1981.

16.   The amount due on repayment, per £100 nominal of Stock, will be £100 multiplied by the Index ratio applicable to the month in which repayment takes place. This amount, expressed in pounds sterling to two places of decimals rounded to the nearest figure below, will be announced by the Bank of England not later than the business day immediately preceding the date of the penultimate interest payment.

17.   Interest will be payable half-yearly on 16th March and 16th September. Income tax will be deducted from payments of more than £5 per annum. Interest warrants will be transmitted by post.

18.   The first interest payment will be made on 16th September 1981 at the rate of £0.80 per £100 nominal of Stock.

19.   Each subsequent half-yearly interest payment will be at a rate, per £100 nominal of Stock, of £1 multiplied by the index ratio applicable to the month in which the payment falls due.

20.   The rate of interest for each interest payment other than the first, expressed as a percentage in pounds sterling to two places of decimals rounded to the nearest figure below, will be announced by the Bank of England not later than the business day immediately preceding the date of the previous interest payment.

21.   If the Index is revised to a new base after the Stock is issued, it will be necessary, for the purposes of the preceding paragraphs, to calculate and use a notional Index figure in substitution for the Index figure applicable to the month in which repayment takes place and/or an interest payment falls due ('the month of payment'). This notional Index figure will be calculated by multiplying the actual Index figure applicable to the month of payment by the Index figure on the old base for the month on which the revised Index is based and dividing the product by the new base figure for the same month. The procedure will be used for each occasion on which a revision is made during the life of the Stock.

22.   If the Index is not published for a month for which it is relevant for the purposes of this prospectus, the Bank of England, after appropriate consultation with the relevant Government Department, will publish a substitute Index figure which shall be an estimate of the Index figure which would have been applicable to the month of payment, and such substitute Index figure shall be used for all purposes for which the actual Index figure would have been relevant. The calculation by the Bank of England of the amounts of principal and/or interest payable on the basis of a substitute Index figure shall be conclusive and binding upon all stockholders. No subsequent adjustment to such amounts will be made in the event of subsequent publication of the Index figure which would have been applicable to the month of payment.

23.   If any change should be made to the coverage or the basic calculation of the Index which, in the opinion of the Bank of England, constitutes a fundamental change in the Index which would be materially detrimental to the interests of stockholders, Her Majesty's Treasury will publish a notice in the London, Edinburgh and Belfast Gazettes immediately following the announcement by the relevant Government Department of the change, informing stockholders and offering them the right to require Her Majesty's Treasury to redeem their stock in advance of the revised Index becoming effective for the purposes of this prospectus. Repayment to stockholders who exercise this right will be affected, on a date to be chosen by Her Majesty's Treasury, not later than six months from the month of publication of the revised Index. The amount of principal due on repayment and of any interest which has accrued will be calculated on the basis of the Index ratio applicable to the month in which repayment takes place. A notice setting out the administrative arrangements will be sent to stockholders at their registered address by the Bank of England at the appropriate time.

24.   Tenders must be lodged at the Bank of England, New Issues (X), Watling Street, London EC4M 9AA, not later than 10.00 A.M. on FRIDAY, 27TH MARCH 1981, or at any of the Branches of the Bank of England or at the Glasgow Agency of the Bank of England, not later than 3.30 P.M. on THURSDAY, 26TH MARCH 1981. Each tender must be for one amount and at one price which is a multiple of 25p. TENDERS LODGED WITHOUT A PRICE BEING STATED WILL BE REJECTED.

25.   A separate cheque representing a deposit at the rate of £35.00 for every £100 of the *nominal* amount of Stock tendered for must accompany each tender; cheques must be drawn on a bank in, and be payable in, the United Kingdom, the Channel Islands or the Isle of Man. Envelopes containing tenders should be marked 'Index-Linked Treasury Tender'.

26.   Tenders must be for a minimum of £5,000 nominal of Stock and for multiples of Stock as follows:

Amount of Stock tendered for	Multiple
£5,000–£50,000	£5,000
£50,000 or greater	£25,000

27.   Her Majesty's Treasury reserve the right to reject any tender or to allot a less amount of Stock than that tendered for. Valid tenders will be ranked in descending order of price and allotments will be made to tenderers whose tenders are at or above the lowest price at which Her Majesty's Treasury decide that any tender should be accepted (the allotment price). All allotments will be made at the allotment price and tenders which are accepted and which are made at prices above the allotment price will be allotted in full. Any balance of Stock not allotted to tenderers will be allotted at the allotment price to the Governor and Company of the Bank of England, Issue Department.

28.   Letters of allotment in respect of Stock allotted, being the only form in which the Stock may be transferred prior to registration, will be despatched by post at the risk of the tenderer, but the despatch of any letter of allotment, and any refund of the balance of the amount paid as deposit, may at the discretion of the Bank of England be withheld until the tenderer's cheque has been paid. In the event of such withholding, the tenderer will be notified by letter by the Bank of England of the acceptance of his tender and of the amount of Stock allocated to him, subject in each case to payment of his cheque, but such notification will confer no right on the tenderer to transfer the Stock so allocated.

29.   In the event of partial allotment, the balance of the amount paid as deposit will, when refunded, be remitted by cheque despatched by post at the risk of the tenderer; if no allotment is made the amount paid as deposit will be returned likewise. Payment in full may be made at any time after allotment, but no discount will be allowed on such payment. Interest at the rate of 1 per cent per annum over the Bank of England's Minimum Lending Rate on a day-to-day basis may be charged on any overdue amount which may be accepted. Default in due payment of any amount in respect of the Stock will render the allotment of such Stock liable to cancellation and any amount previously paid liable to forfeiture.

30.   Letters of allotment may be split into denominations of multiples of £1,000 on written request received by the Bank of England, New Issues, Watling Street, London EC4M 9AA, or by any of the Branches of the Bank of England, on any date not later than 21st May 1981. Such requests must be signed and must be accompanied by the letters of allotment (but a letter cannot be split if any payment is overdue).

31.   Letters of allotment must be surrendered for registration, accompanied by a completed registration form and, where required, a statutory declaration, when the balance of the purchase money is paid, unless payment in full has been made before the due date, in which case they must be surrendered for registration not later than 26th May 1981.

32.   Tender forms, statutory declaration forms and copies of this prospectus may be obtained at the Bank of England, New Issues, Watling Street, London EC4M 9AA, or at any of the Branches of the Bank of England, or at the Glasgow Agency of the Bank of England; at the Bank of Ireland, PO Box 13, Donegall Place, Belfast BT1 5BX; at Mullens & Co., 15 Moorgate, London EC2R 6AN; or at any office of The Stock Exchange in the United Kingdom.

BANK OF ENGLAND
LONDON

10th March 1981

(Reprinted 9th March 1982,
as amended by the supplement to
the prospectus of the same date.)

Index